THE

OF

JOHN WESLEY

JOHN TELFORD, B.A.

Belfast Northern Ireland **Greenville** South Carolina

First published 1902
This edition 1999

ISBN 1 84030 059 0

Ambassador Publications
a division of
Ambassador Productions Ltd.
Providence House
16 Hillview Avenue,
Belfast, BT5 6JR
Northern Ireland

Emerald House
1 Chick Springs Road, Suite 203
Greenville,
South Carolina 29609, USA
www.emeraldhouse.com

CONTENTS.

CHAPTER IV.

EARLIER YEARS AT OXFORD AND CURACY AT WROOT.

CHAPTER V.

OXFORD METHODISM.

CHAPTER VI.

MISSION TO GEORGIA.

CHAPTER VII.

PREPARATION FOR THE GREAT REVIVAL.

CONTENTS.

CONTENTS.

CHAPTER XI.

EXTENSION OF THE WORK.

CHAPTER XII.

ENCOUNTERS WITH THE MOB.

CHAPTER XIII.

WESLEY AS A TRAVELLER.

CHAPTER XIV.

WESLEY'S PREACHERS.

CHAPTER XVIII.

FROM THE DEATH OF WHITEFIELD TO THE DEATH OF CHARLES WESLEY.

CHAPTER XIX.

WESLEY'S CHURCHMANSHIP.

CHAPTER XX.

PREACHER, WRITER, AND PHILANTHROPIST.

CHAPTER XXI.

INTRODUCTION.

THE greatest historian of the eighteenth century, who has brought to his task clear insight and unlimited resources of learning, has devoted one of his most interesting chapters to "The Religious Revival." He thus expresses his deliberate judgment on the far-reaching results of Methodism :—"Although the career of the elder Pitt and the splendid victories by land and sea that were won during his ministry form unquestionably the most dazzling episodes in the reign of George II., they must yield, I think, in real importance to that religious revolution which shortly before had begun in England by the preaching of the Wesleys and Whitefield." * Mr. Lecky's verdict is substantially approved on all hands. The late lamented J. R. Green † says: "The Methodists themselves were the least result of the Methodist revival. Its action upon the Church broke the lethargy of the clergy. . . . But the noblest result of the religious revival was the steady attempt, which has never ceased from that day to this, to remedy the guilt, the ignorance, the physical suffering, the social degradation of the profligate and the poor."

---

* Lecky, ii., 521.

† "History of the English People," p. 720.

No one can tell what the fate of England would have been but for the Great Revival. Mr. Lecky assigns to Methodism a prominent place among those influences which saved this country from the revolutionary spirit which laid France in ruins, and shows how "peculiarly fortunate" it was that the vast extension of manufacturing industry in the later part of the century had been "preceded by a religious revival which opened a mainspring of moral and religious energy among the poor, and at the same time gave a powerful impulse to the philanthropy of the rich." *

Such considerations appeal to all students of English life. Mr. Lecky has not forgotten another side of Methodism—its work in the house of mourning and the house of death. Wesley's rejoicing, "Our people die well," reminds us that the influence on individual history is even more notable than the influence on society at large. One indeed laid the foundation for the other. Wesley was content to take the old method, the salvation of the world soul by soul.

Three names stand high above the rest of the Methodist company. Whitefield was the orator, Charles Wesley the hymnist and preacher. John Wesley was the central figure, "who embodied in himself not this or that side of the vast movement, but the very movement itself." †
Whitefield died twenty years before Wesley, and a large part of his strength was given to America; Charles Wesley's active itinerancy only lasted about eighteen years; but for half a century John Wesley was the

* Lecky, ii., 637. † Green, p. 719.

best-known man in England. He never ceased to devote himself to the work with the same energy he showed at the beginning of the field-preaching. Wesley is one of the most interesting figures in religious biography. "Few things," Mr. Lecky says, "in ecclesiastical history are more striking than the energy and the success with which he propagated his opinions. He was gifted with a frame of iron, and with spirits that never flagged."*

Wesley's life will therefore never cease to fascinate all readers, as it fascinated Samuel Taylor Coleridge. He belongs to the universal Church. One community bears his name; all Churches have caught his spirit. Erroneous views of his character are gradually losing ground. Southey himself was convinced of his mistake in describing ambition as one of Wesley's ruling motives, and no one would venture to repeat the charge. Other errors still hold their place. Miss Wedgwood speaks of Wesley's "cold self-sufficiency," and says that his brother Charles "was of a richer and softer nature" than he. Others have represented him as harsh and austere. The tribute of his friend Alexander Knox and the testimony of his niece, Miss Wesley, show him, however, in the most attractive light—a man born to love and to be loved. For him there was no happy home, as for his brother; but if he had married Grace Murray, Miss Wedgwood's comparison would not have been possible. As to the charge of self-sufficiency, we must remember that Wesley was left alone at an early stage of the Revival. There is abundant

* Lecky, ii., 627.

evidence that he yearned for congenial fellowship, but that also was largely denied him. What could he do but brace himself for his mission? Must his very fidelity be turned into an occasion of reproach?

In preparing this volume, no available source of information has been neglected. The aim of the biographer has been to set the character and work of one of the greatest benefactors of his country and the world in a light which may attract general readers, and lead others to catch the spirit which moved the great evangelist. On disputed topics the writer has endeavoured to express his own views in such a way as to give no cause of offence to reasonable men of any party.

The call for a new edition of this Life of Wesley has given the opportunity to correct some slight errors and misprints, to add a few details which may make the portrait more complete, and to supply an index and a final chapter showing the progress of Methodism after Wesley's death. It is hoped also that the list of portraits and of Wesley's chief publications, as well as the chronological table and the unique list of Wesley's ordinations, will prove useful to students. Suggestions and criticisms have been carefully weighed, and no pains spared to render the portrait of England's chief evangelist as lifelike as possible. Every day adds to the reputation of John Wesley. The *Spectator* said recently: "In spite of the fact that he had not Whitefield's eloquence, he was a magnetic man. One might apply to him what Dr. Johnson said of Milton: 'He was born for whatever was arduous; difficulties vanished at his touch, and he was not the greatest of wandering evangelists only because he was not the first.' Had he been born in the Middle Ages he would have been the greatest of the friars." *

The *Saturday Review* also pays its tribute: "The extraordinary greatness of Wesley, and the debt which all English Christianity owes to him, are not things which need in our day to be preached to the unbelieving world. The tendency amongst Agnostic men and women of letters, as well as among religious orators, is rather to exaggerate than to underrate Wesley's glory and Wesley's miracles." †

It is not perhaps generally known that Dean Stanley was an enthusiastic admirer of Wesley's Journals. He came into possession of Dr. Kennicott's papers, and read with intense interest the great Hebraist's description of Wesley's last University sermon. The moral heroism of that scene produced such an impression on Stanley's mind that he turned at once to the Journals. "He read them with avidity and wonder, and expressed his admiration of them in the highest terms to another leading member of the University, who made no secret of his Methodist extraction."

Another tribute will appeal strongly to lovers of

* June 6th, 1896. † March 28th, 1891.

English literature. Edward Fitzgerald describes Wesley's Journal as "one of the most interesting books in the language; well worth reading and having, not only as an outline of Wesley's own singular character, but of the conditions of England, Ireland, and Scotland in the last century. . . . Curious to think of this Diary of Wesley's running almost coevally with Walpole's Letter-Diary—the two men born and dying, too, within a few years of one another, and with such different lives to record. . . . If you have not read the little Autobiography of Wesley's Disciple, John Nelson, give a shilling for it. It seems to me something wonderful to read these books, written in a style that cannot alter because natural . . . remarkable to read, pure, unaffected, and undying English, while Addison and Johnson are tainted with a style which all the world imitated."

Mr. Augustine Birrell, Q.C., M.P., has also recently described Wesley's Journal as "the most amazing record of human exertion ever penned by man." In reading it "one was constrained to admire the magnificence of the vigour, the tremendous force of the devotion, and the faith which kept John Wesley in perpetual motion for more than half a century; and one felt glad to be able to place that Journal beside Walpole's Letters and Boswell's Johnson, and to know that in it there were some aspects of the eighteenth century that could not be found elsewhere."

REDHILL,
May 1899.

CHAPTER I.

ANCESTRY AND PARENTAGE.

JOHN WESLEY was born at Epworth Parsonage on June 17th, 1703. A notable ancestry links the founder of Methodism to all the stirring scenes of Nonconformist persecution and controversy during the seventeenth century. Bartholomew Wesley, his great-grandfather, was the son of Sir Herbert Wesley, of Westleigh, Devonshire, and Elizabeth de Wellesley, of Dangan, county Meath, in Ireland. He studied medicine and divinity at Oxford, the university to which his son, grandson, and three great-grandsons afterwards followed him. He married the daughter of Sir Henry Colley, of Kildare, in 1619. Nothing is known about his history till 1640, when he became Rector of Catherston, a little village in the south-west of Dorsetshire. He also held the neighbouring living of Charmouth, but both together only yielded their incumbent an income of £35 10*s*.

The one event of historic interest in his life is connected with the flight of Charles II. after the battle of Worcester, in September, 1651. It was arranged that Charles should cross over to France from Charmouth. The boat in which he was to reach the vessel that lay waiting for him did not come at the appointed time, so that the party had to stay all night at an inn. In the early morning one of their horses was taken to be shod. The blacksmith declared that its shoes had been made in the north of England. When the ostler said that the party of strangers had sat up all night, suspicion was aroused. The ostler ran to consult Mr. Wesley at the church, but as he was reading prayers, there was considerable delay, and Charles was gone before any measures could be taken to prevent his escape. Bartholomew Wesley made no secret of his intention to capture the King. He told a friend in jest that if ever Charles came back, he would be certain to love long prayers, because "he would have surely snapt him" if the prayers had been over earlier.* An account of this scene describes Wesley as the "puny parson." The Rector of Charmouth was apparently a little man, like all the Wesleys.

After the Restoration he was ejected from his living. This trouble fell upon him nearly six months before the general ejection on St. Bartholomew's Day, 1662. His skill in medicine, which had formerly enabled him to render signal service to his poor parishioners, now became his sole means of support. His great-grandson John Wesley inherited his love of medicine, and, as we shall see, found his skill of great service to himself and others. For some time after his ejection, Bartholomew Wesley lived quietly among his old parishioners in Charmouth. He cast in his lot with the persecuted Nonconformists, but no violence seems to have been used against a man who had won general respect by his benevolence and his blameless character. He was probably compelled to leave the district after the Five Mile Act was placed on the statute books; but we only know that he did not long survive his son, who died in 1678.

This son bore the name which afterwards became known in every corner of the kingdom—John Wesley, or Westley,

* *Gentleman's Magazine*, 1785, p 487.

as the name was spelled till Samuel Wesley, the Rector of Epworth, dropped the "t."* His life forms a painful contrast to that of his illustrious grandson, but their spirit and their aims were one. The first John Wesley was born in 1636. As a schoolboy, he was under deep religious conviction. He had a diary, in which he described all the events of his outward life, as well as the workings of his own heart. This diary, which he kept almost to the close of his life, was entrusted by his widow to Dr. Calamy. All trace of it is now lost. It would have been no small privilege to compare it with his grandson's famous journals.

As a student at New Inn Hall, Oxford, his seriousness and diligence remind us much of the Oxford Methodists seventy years later. He applied himself particularly to the study of Oriental languages, in which he made great progress. Dr. Owen, the Vice-Chancellor, had a special regard for the devout and promising young student, who left the University, about the end of 1657 or the beginning of 1658, a warm supporter of Owen's views on questions of Church government. He did not seek episcopal ordination, but joined himself at Weymouth to a small company of Christian people, called a "gathered Church." Among them he first exercised his gifts as a preacher. He found his way among the fishermen, and at Radipole, a village near Weymouth, formed a little Church. His preaching won general favour among "judicious Christians and able ministers," and led to the conversion of many souls.

In 1658, he found a more important sphere. The Vicar of Winterborn-Whitchurch died, and the people chose him as their pastor. He was at once approved by the

* The family has been traced to Welswe, near Wells, in Somerset; hence the name Welswey, Westley, or Wellesley

Triers, Cromwell's Board of Commissioners, who examined every candidate for Holy Orders. The village where he now laboured was five miles from Blandford. It seems to have had a population of four or five hundred people. The income was only thirty pounds. An augmentation of £100 a year was indeed promised, but political changes prevented the fulfilment of this promise.

Shortly after his appointment to this living, in 1659 or 1660, he married Miss White, daughter of the patriarch of Dorchester. This young lady was the niece of Dr. Fuller, the Church historian, who describes her father "as a grave man, who would yet willingly contribute his shot of facetiousness on any just occasion." He had been persecuted by Laud for preaching against Arminianism and the ceremonies. During the civil war, Prince Rupert's soldiers plundered his house and took away his library. He then fled to London, where he was appointed minister of the Savoy. John White was one of the two assessors appointed to assist Dr. Twisse, the first Chairman of the Westminster Assembly. Dr. Burgess, the other assessor, was his wife's brother, and offered a prayer a full hour long from the pulpit of St. Margaret's when the House of Commons and the Assembly met together to sign the "Solemn League and Covenant." Mr. White was sometime Rector of Lambeth, and was offered the wardenship of New College in 1647; but he refused this post to return to his much-loved flock at Dorchester, among whom he died on July 21st, 1648, at the age of seventy-four.

Miss White had therefore lost her father nearly twelve years before her marriage. The Restoration soon wrecked the peace of their home. In the summer of 1661, the young preacher was committed to prison for not using the Book of Common Prayer in his church. Next year his ministry was brought to an end by the Act of Uniformity. He preached his farewell sermon to a congregation of friends in tears, from the text, "And now brethren, I commend you to God and the word of His grace."

Wesley inserted in his journal for 1765* a long conversation between the first John Wesley and Gilbert Ironside, Bishop of Bristol, in which the young pastor defends his position, and shows that his ministry had both a divine call and a divine blessing. "I may be excused," says John Wesley, "if it appears more remarkable to me, than it will do to an unconcerned person." This dialogue was carefully recorded in the Vicar's manuscript diary. The Bishop dismissed him with the words, "Farewell, good Mr. Wesley." His frank, manly spirit had evidently made the happiest impression. The Bishop's approval did not, however, protect the first John Wesley from his enemies.

The young minister lived sixteen years after the ejection of 1662. When compelled to leave Whitchurch, he wished to settle in Melcombe; but the authorities prohibited his residence there under heavy penalties: a fine of twenty pounds on the owner of any house where he might reside and five shillings a week on himself. The Dissenters of Ilminster, Bridgwater, and Taunton, treated him with great kindness. He frequently preached for Joseph Alleine and Mr. Norman, of Bridgwater, as well as to other Nonconformist congregations. Early in May, 1663, a friend at Preston, near Weymouth, offered him a house rent free. Here he remained some time, seizing every opportunity of doing good that presented itself, until he was invited to become the pastor of a congregation at Poole. This position he

* Works, iii., 215, latest edition.

seems to have held until his death. Despite all his caution, he was imprisoned four times under the oppressive laws of his day, and was once obliged to hide himself for a considerable time to escape persecution. Dr. Calamy says he was greatly supported in many troubles, and was often seasonably and wonderfully relieved; but the death of many eminent Christians who were his friends and the increasing rage of the enemies of true religion broke down his spirits. His fight with poverty and trouble closed in 1678, at the age of forty-two years.*

The founder of Methodism was the true successor ot this devoted man. His itinerant ministry, his care for the fisher-folk, his unflinching loyalty to his principles, his success in winning souls, and his simple godly life were all reproduced in his illustrious grandson. The first John Wesley was cautious, moderate, singularly open to conviction. By reading Philip Nye's book on the lawfulness of hearing ministers of the Church of England, his scruples about liturgical service were so far removed that he was able to attend church. He greatly wished to go as a missionary to America, but his purpose was twice foiled by circumstances. That task also was reserved for his more fortunate descendant. They had a numerous family, but only the names of four have been preserved. His widow survived him for thirty-two years. She lived in London during the last years of her life, supported mainly by her sons, Matthew, the London doctor, and Samuel, the Rector of Epworth.

Samuel Wesley was educated at the Free School, Dorchester, until he was fifteen. He was almost fit for the University, but had no means of going there. His Dis-

* Calamy says he was about thirty-three, but see Stevenson' "Wesley Family."

senting friends, however, sent him to London, where he was trained for the Nonconformist ministry. He afterwards saw reason to change his views on the points in controversy with the Church of England. Nonconformity had lost its early devotion. The students at the academy where young Wesley was when he resolved to go to Oxford read the lewdest books. They were encouraged also to write lampoons on the Church. Samuel Wesley was promised a considerable gratuity if he would translate some Unitarian works, but happily he declined the task when he saw what it was. At the time when he was attracted toward the Church of England, he was living with his mother and an old aunt, whom he would have greatly grieved by any intimation of such feeling. He knew no one belonging to the Established Church who could advise him in his sore perplexity. But Samuel Wesley was equal to any emergency. He earnestly sought God's guidance, calmly weighed all the points at issue, then rose early one morning and set out on foot for Oxford, where he entered himself as a "servitor" at Exeter College.

By this step the Wesley family was again united to the Church which had cast them out. Samuel thus enjoyed the advantages of an Oxford training such as both his father and grandfather had received. For many years his life was a sharp struggle. By indomitable industry he supported himself at the University. He entered with two pounds five shillings in his pocket, and left, at the end of five years, with ten pounds, though during his whole term of residence his family and friends had only given him five shillings. He performed his duties as servitor, composed exercises for other students, gave instruction as a private tutor, and collected all his youthful verses, which were published by John Dunton under the title "Maggots;

or, Poems on Several Subjects never before handled." The headings of several pieces may be said to justify this claim to novelty: "The Tame Snake in a Box of Bran," "The Grunting of a Hog," "A Cow's Tail," "A Hat Broke at Cudgels." Such subjects are aptly described as "never before handled" by the muse. It is pleasant to add that the busy student found time to visit the prisoners at the Castle. In later life he often thought of those endeavours to do good with no small satisfaction.

Samuel Wesley took his degree as Bachelor of Arts in June, 1688, and his M.A. degree at Cambridge in 1694. On August 7th, 1688, Dr. Sprat, Bishop of Rochester, ordained him deacon at his palace at Bromley. The following February, Dr. Compton, Bishop of London, admitted him to priest's orders in St. Andrew's, Holborn. After holding a curacy at a stipend of twenty-eight pounds a year, he became chaplain on board a man-of-war. Then he took another London curacy. His salary was thirty pounds; his restless pen added thirty pounds more to his income. Such was the condition of his finances when he married Susanna Annesley.

A special providence seems to have presided over the marriage of the mother of the Wesleys. She was both beautiful and accomplished. More than all else, she was a woman of rare judgment and sterling piety. Her mind was both clear and strong. Her husband's heart safely trusted in her during all the troubles of their long married life, and her gifted sons at Oxford felt that her advice on all subjects both of practical and speculative divinity was of the greatest value. Mrs. Wesley's prudent counsels were also of conspicuous service at several crises of the Evangelical Revival.

Susanna Wesley's father was Dr. Samuel Annesley, "the St. Paul of the Nonconformists." He was Vicar of

St. Giles', Cripplegate, but was ejected in 1662. He afterwards formed a congregation at Little St. Helen's (now St. Helen's), Bishopsgate Street, which was licensed, after the Declaration of Indulgence, in 1672. The Annesley family was settled in Nottinghamshire before the Conquest. The grandfather of the Nonconformist divine was Viscount Valentia, his uncle was the first Earl ot Anglesea. John Wesley's mother was therefore a lady both by birth and breeding,—a fact which must not be lost sight of in studying the character of her children. Mrs. Annesley, like the wife of the first John Wesley, was a Miss White. Her father, John White, was also a member of the Assembly of Divines, in which his namesake, the patriarch of Dorchester, was one of the assessors. He was a barrister, much patronised by the Puritans, and, as member for Southwark, took a leading part in the events which led to the execution of Charles I. Susanna Wesley was the twenty-fourth child of this marriage. She was familiar with the whole controversy between the Nonconformists and the Church of England, and the year before Samuel Wesley went to Oxford had calmly weighed the points at issue and cast in her lot with the Church. She was only thirteen years old at the time when she made this important decision. During the year 1682, in which she made this choice, young Samuel Wesley was present at her sister's marriage to John Dunton, the noted bookseller. It is therefore probable that the young people, who thus left the Nonconformity for which their parents had suffered so much, were already attached to each other, and acted in concert in making this momentous change.

The first eighteen months of their married life seem to have been spent in London, where their first child, Samuel, was born in February, 1690; but in August, 1690, Samuel Wesley became Rector of South Ormsby, whence he removed to Epworth early in 1697. Here he remained as Rector for thirty-nine years, until his death in 1735. His work was embittered by the turbulent Fenmen, then "almost heathens." * A terrible half-century of riot and outrage preceded his appointment. Cornelius Vermuyden, the Dutchman who drained the country, found himself in a nest of hornets. The Fenmen refused to accept compensation for their rights of pasturage, burnt the crops of the foreign settlers, and tried to drown them by laying the whole district under water. Samuel Wesley was not the man to conciliate such unruly people. His first twelve years at Epworth were therefore full of bitter trouble.

This brief notice ot Wesley's ancestry will show that he was descended from a long line of English gentry and clergymen. The highest education and the best breeding had been enjoyed by both sides of the house for many generations.

---

* S. Wesley, jun., "Letters," published by Dr. Priestley, p. 43.

See p. 3. John Wesley speaks of his ordination in the conversation with Bishop Ironside. This ordination, however, was not conferred by "preaching presbyters," nor did it convey the right to administer the Sacraments. He says he was not called to the *office* but to the *work* of the ministry. "When the Church saw the presence of God going along with me, they did, by fasting and prayer, in a day set apart for that end, seek an abundant blessing on my endeavours." It is evident that this was his "ordination": he was simply "sent to preach." The word is used in a wider sense than that which the Bishop gave it: in fact, the conversation cannot be understood unless this difference in the use of the word is borne in mind. He was afterwards approved by the Triers, and preached to one congregation. He did not, however, administer the Sacraments, both because his people were "not fit objects for me to exercise office work among them," and also because he was not qualified to perform it. In Poole, some years later, he became pastor of a congregation to which he is said to have regularly administered the Sacraments.

CHAPTER II.

CHILDHOOD AT EPWORTH.

JOHN BENJAMIN WESLEY, born on June 17th, 1703, was the fifteenth of the Rector's nineteen children. He received the names of two brothers, John and Benjamin, who had died in infancy, but he never used the second name. At the time of his birth there were six children in the Rectory; the rest were dead. Samuel, the only boy, was thirteen years old, and was preparing to enter Westminster School the following year. Charles Wesley was not born for more than four years afterwards.

Epworth, the Lincolnshire town which is honoured as the birthplace of John and Charles Wesley, was then a market-town of about two thousand inhabitants: the population has not increased for two hundred years. It is the principal place in a strip of land once enclosed by five waterways—the Idille and Torne, on the west; the Trent, on the east; the Done, on the north; and the Bykers-dyke, on the south. This was the Isle of Axholme.* The Torne, Done, and Bykers-dyke can still be traced by the willow trees which mark their former channels.† About ten thousand people lived in this strip of country, which is ten miles long and four broad. The fine old church at Epworth, with its massive tower,

* "Ax," is the Celtic word for water. The Anglo-Saxons added *ey*, their name for island, the Danes affixed their *holm* (island). Axeyholme was corrupted to Axelholm, contracted to Axholm, and finally the English *Isle* was prefixed.—*Isaac Taylor's Words and Places.*

† The New Idle flows along the course of the Bykers-dyke. The New Torne runs across the Isle.

has been made familiar by the well-known picture of Wesley preaching on his father's tomb. It stands on rising ground, and when seen from the old Market Place appears to command the town. It is dedicated to St. Andrew. The Parsonage in which John and Charles Wesley were born was destroyed by fire February 9th, 1709. The Rector described his home at South Ormsby as "a mean cot, composed of reeds and clay." The Epworth Parsonage was superior to this. Stonehouse in his "History of the Isle of Axholme"* quotes a description of it in 1607. It was a three-storied building of timber and plaster, thatched with straw, and had seven principal rooms, a kitchen, hall, parlour, buttery, with three large upper rooms and some others for common use. A small garden, a thatched barn, a dovecot, and other outside premises were attached. The whole covered about three acres. In this old house John Wesley was born and taught to read. The present Rectory, a long brick building, "with a high-pitched tiled roof rising from a bold projecting cornice, is an excellent specimen of the sterling unpretentious architecture of the day, a quiet, genuine Queen Anne house, very unlike the crude heaps of incongruities, devoid of repose, which now pass by that name. The garden, with its smooth lawn and long straight walks, bordered with old-fashioned flowers, with hedges of sweet-peas, foxgloves, sweet-williams, and snapdragons, beds of odoriferous pinks, and a wealth of roses, is a delicious pleasure-ground, in the true old English sense of the word, the rival of which one might go far to find." Such is the description of the Rectory given in the *Saturday Review*.† The house remained almost unaltered from Wesley's

* Page 151. † August 1st, 1885. The Lincoln Architectural Society in the Isle of Axholme. The garden seems to have been added about the time of Wesley's death.

boyhood up to 1883, when it was considerably enlarged,* but the air of comfort and quiet prosperity which the Rectory now wears was certainly not its aspect in the days of Samuel Wesley. When John was only two years old his father was committed to Lincoln Castle for debt by his enemies, so that the household was familiar enough with poverty in his childhood. The house was rebuilt within a year at a cost of £400, but the Rector's resources were so straitened that even thirteen years afterwards it was not half furnished.

A good picture of John Wesley's boyhood is gained from Susanna Wesley's account of the training of her children, written at his request on July 24th, 1732.† That training may be said to have begun with the children's birth. Even during the first three months of their life, which were mostly spent in sleep, they were dressed and undressed and their clothes were changed at fixed times. After that period they were, if possible, laid in the cradle awake and rocked to sleep. Until the children were brought into a proper course of sleeping this rocking continued up to the time fixed for them to awake. At first three hours were allowed in the morning, three in the afternoon; then the time was reduced to two hours, until at last they needed no sleep during the day. The children were taught to fear the rod when they were only a year old and to cry softly. By this means the Epworth Parsonage, though full of children, was as quiet as if there had not been one in the house.

As soon as possible, the little table and chairs were set near the family dinner-table, where they could be easily overlooked. The children were taught to ask softly for anything they wanted and to eat whatever was provided

* Some charred timbers of the old Rectory were then found, and pieces distributed as souvenirs.

† Works, i., 387

for the family. As soon as they could handle a knife and fork they sat at the table with their parents. No eating or drinking between meals was allowed. Evening prayers were over at six o'clock. The children then had supper, and at seven o'clock were prepared for bed. First, the youngest was undressed and washed. then the rest in turn. All were in bed by eight.

Mrs. Wesley's first care was to teach her children obedience. She knew that this was not only the way to rule well her large household, but also to secure the happiness of her boys and girls. "I insist," she says in her interesting letter, "upon conquering the will of children betimes, because this is the only strong and rational foundation of a religious education, without which both precept and example will be ineffectual. But when this is thoroughly done, then a child is capable of being governed by the reason and piety of its parents, till its own understanding comes to maturity, and the principles of religion have taken root in the mind." One result of this training was seen in times of illness. There was no difficulty in getting these model children to take even the most unpleasant medicine.

Religious training began as early as possible. Even before they could kneel or speak, they were taught to be quiet at family prayers, and to ask a blessing by signs. As soon as they could speak they repeated the Lord's Prayer morning and evening. A prayer for their parents, some collects, Catechism, and Scripture, were added as soon as they were able to learn them. No profane or rude words were ever heard in the Parsonage. The children were taught to ask quietly for what they wanted. Crying never won anything in this home. No one was allowed to speak to the servants without saying, "Pray give me such a thing." The little people were always expected to say "*Brother* John" or "*Sister* Kezzy." The code of honour observed among them allowed no promise to be broken, no gift reclaimed. No one attempted to take what belonged to his brother or sister. Confession of a fault always averted punishment, so that many temptations to falsehood were removed.

Mrs. Wesley was the schoolmistress of the Parsonage. The glimpse of the local schoolmaster, John Holland, "whose kindness" young Samuel Wesley, who was under him for one year, "wore on his knuckles," and who reduced himself and his family to the verge of starvation by his wickedness, makes us thankful that the mother of the Wesleys was their teacher. Her grandson, Samuel Wesley,* says that she had the happy talent of imbuing a child's mind with every kind of useful knowledge in such a way as to stamp it indelibly on the memory. She began her work as soon as her children were five years old. The day before the little scholar was initiated all household matters were carefully arranged, and every one was strictly charged not to enter the schoolroom from nine to twelve, or from two to five. If we except Kezzy, as to whom her mother's plans were unfortunately overruled, all the children learned their letters the first day save two of the girls, who took a day and a half. For this Mrs. Wesley thought them very dull, but when she knew other children better she altered her opinion. After the alphabet was mastered the children were taught to spell and read first a line, then a verse. No lesson was left till it was perfect. Before the close of morning school each repeated what had been learned; before work was finished in the afternoon the whole day's task was repeated. No loud talking or playing was

* See MS. Reminiscences in British Museum.

allowed in school; every one kept close to work. The progress made was such that Mrs. Wesley herself, who was not easy to please, says, "It is almost incredible what a child may be taught in a quarter of a year by a vigorous application if it have but a tolerable capacity and good health."

The Parsonage was a constant scene of trouble. In 1702 two-thirds of it was burnt down; two years later all the Rector's flax was destroyed. Samuel Wesley made himself many enemies by the prominent share he took in the controversy between the High Church party and the Dissenters. During a contested election he also embroiled himself with his parishioners by his zealous efforts on behalf of the Tory candidate. His lot was cast among a people proverbially turbulent and lawless. The Dutch settlers of the Commonwealth had been roughly treated by the natives of Axholme. All law and order was suspended. Epworth Church was defaced, and the Ten Commandments were torn in pieces by one of the rioters. The house of a Mr. Reading, who collected rents and had shown great enterprise in the cultivation of the soil, was twice burned down by the half-civilised mob, who used the weapons familiar to Irish agrarian outrage. John Wesley ascribed the greatest calamity his father ever suffered to the malice of his unscrupulous parishioners.

On February 9th, 1709, the memorable fire at the Rectory took place. It broke out between eleven and twelve at night, when all the family were in bed. The roof of the corn-chamber was burnt through before any one was aware of the danger. Some of the fire fell upon Hetty Wesley's bed, in a little room adjoining. She at once ran to call her father, who lay in the red chamber. He had heard some one crying "Fire!" in the street a little while before, but did not understand that his own house was in danger. He roused his family and told them to make haste, because the roof was falling fast, and only a thin wall or door kept the flames from the staircase. They had not even time to put on their clothes. Mr. Wesley, with the nurse and two of the children, got downstairs into the garden; the servants and two others escaped through the window. After three fruitless attempts Mrs. Wesley waded through the fire, which scorched her legs and face. At last all were safe save John, then five and a half years old. He had been asleep in the nursery, with three of his sisters, his little brother Charles, and the nurse. When the alarm was given, the nurse snatched up Charles, the youngest child, and bade the rest follow her. John was left in bed fast asleep. In a few minutes he awoke, and, seeing how light the room was, called to the maid to take him up. As no one answered, he put his head out of the curtains and saw streaks of fire on the ceiling. The child jumped out of bed and went to the door, but found that all beyond was in a blaze. He then climbed on the chest which stood near the window. The Rector tried to rush through the flames, which enveloped the staircase, to rescue his boy; but though he made two attempts, holding his breeches above his head as a kind of shield, the fire beat him down. He then went into the garden; and, calling his family around him, all kneeled down whilst he commended the child to God A man below, however, had seen John, and would have run for a ladder; but another spectator said there was no time to lose, and suggested that a light man should be set on his shoulders, so as to lift the little fellow out of the window. The first time the man fell down, but he was helped up again, and was thus able to reach the child. Just as they rescued him the whole roof fell in. Fortunately, it fell inwards, or the boy and his brave deliverers would have been crushed by the weight.

When John was brought to his father by the brave men who had rescued him the Rector cried out, "Come, neighbours, let us kneel down; let us give thanks to God! He has given me all my eight children; let the house go; I am rich enough." Nothing was saved. In about fifteen minutes the building, with all its furniture, books, and papers, was utterly destroyed. John Wesley's wonderful escape always filled him with gratitude. In one of his early prints a house in flames is represented below his own portrait, with the words, "Is not this a brand plucked out of the fire?" * One interesting reference to the event is found in his journals. On Friday, February 9th, 1750, whilst holding a watchnight service in his West Street Chapel, London, "About eleven o'clock," he says, "it came into my mind, that this was the very day and hour in which, forty years ago, I was taken out of the flames. I stopped, and gave a short account of that wonderful providence. The voice of praise and thanksgiving went up on high, and great was our rejoicing before the Lord." Both he and the Methodist people knew by that time for what blessed work he had been spared.

The fire at the Rectory deranged all Mrs. Wesley's plans for nearly a year. Her children were kindly received into several families; and Kezia, their nineteenth child, was born one month after the fire. They were allowed to do as other boys and girls did. They talked with the servants; they ran about and played with other children, both good and bad. John was received into the house of Mr. Hume, a neighbouring clergyman about

* Moore, i., 115.—See a portrait by Virtue in

the misfortunes of whose family he heard a sad account on his return from Georgia.* After the Parsonage was rebuilt Mrs. Wesley began a strict reform. The children had grown careless about the Sabbath, had learned several songs and bad things "which before they had no notion of." They had lost their good manners, and had acquired "a clownish accent and many rude ways." Before the fire no children could be found more obedient to their parents, or better disposed towards religion. Mrs. Wesley felt that she had a difficult task, but she set herself bravely to recover the lost ground. Several new features were now introduced into the training. Psalms were sung both at the opening and close of school. The mother little knew what service her two sons were by-and-bye to render to the cause of sacred song. The habit of general retirement at five o'clock which John and Charles Wesley so carefully observed in later life was then entered upon. The oldest child took the youngest that could speak, the second the next, and thus all the children formed themselves into pairs to read over the Evening Psalms, with a chapter from the New Testament. Before breakfast the Morning Psalms and a chapter of the Old Testament were read in the same way.

John Wesley's escape made his mother the more zealous for her boy's true welfare. Two years after the fire she wrote in the book where she noted down her private meditations,† "I do intend to be more particularly careful of the soul of this child, that Thou hast so mercifully provided for, than ever I have been, that I may do my endeavour to instil into his mind the principles of Thy

* Coke and Moore's "Wesley," 137

† Moore, i., 116.

true religion and virtue. Lord, give me grace to do it sincerely and prudently, and bless my attempts with good success." Such was the effect of her training that his father admitted John to the Communion when he was only eight years old.* He says in his journal,† "I believe till I was about ten years old I had not sinned away that 'washing of the Holy Ghost' which was given me in baptism, having been strictly educated and carefully taught, that I could only be saved 'by universal obedience, by keeping all the commandments of God,' in the meaning of which I was diligently instructed."

The year 1712 was an eventful one in John Wesley's childhood. Whilst his father was in London, attending Convocation, Mrs. Wesley was greatly quickened by an account of the labours of the young Danish missionaries Ziegenbalgh and Plutscho, sent out in November, 1705, under the auspices of Frederick IV., the King of Denmark, to the East Indies for the conversion of the heathen in Malabar. Not long before she had begun to hold services in her kitchen on Sunday evenings for her family and servants. There was no afternoon service during her husband's absence, and his curate was a dry unevangelical preacher, whose religion was summed up in the duty of paying one's debts, which formed the constant theme of his ministry. Mrs. Wesley, therefore, felt it necessary to read with her children and servants. One boy told his parents of the meetings. They begged leave to come, and others joined them, but the number was seldom more than forty. After she read the account of these devoted missionaries, Mrs. Wesley became more zealous. She chose the best and most awakening sermons, and spent more time with the people in religious exercises.

* Benson's "Apology," p. 1. † Works, i., 98.

On the first Sunday in February, 1712, more than two hundred people were present; and many went away because there was no room. John and Charles Wesley were in their mother's congregation. Charles was only four; but John, who was eight and a half, must have followed these services with peculiar interest. The curate appealed to his rector to discourage these novel assemblies, but Mrs. Wesley's defence was so complete that her husband would not interfere. She also resolved to set apart some time every evening to converse privately with each child "in something that relates to its principal concerns." John's turn came on Thursday. How he prized the opportunity may be seen from his letter to his mother, written when he was Fellow of Lincoln. "If you can spare me only that little part of Thursday evening which you formerly bestowed upon me in another manner, I doubt not but it would be as useful now for correcting my heart, as it was then in forming my judgment."

In the April of 1712, John and four more of the Parsonage children had the small-pox. His mother gives a pleasant glimpse of her boy in a letter to her husband in London. "Jack has borne his disease bravely, like a man, and indeed like a Christian, without any complaint, though he seemed angry at the small-pox when they were sore, as we guessed by his looking sourly at them, for he never said anything."* This anecdote is characteristic. Mr. Wesley told Adam Clarke † that when he was a child, and was asked to have fruit or anything else between meals, he would quietly reply, "I thank you. I will think of it." The fact is that Mrs. Wesley did not allow her children to take anything between meals, and John was so well trained that he made this discreet answer.

* Moore, i., 116. † "Wesley Family," ii., 321.

He would never do anything till he considered it well. This habit often gave him some appearance of hesitation. His father once said to Mrs. Wesley, "I profess, sweetheart, I think our Jack would not attend to the most pressing necessities of nature unless he could give a reason for it."* He told John himself, "Child, you think to carry everything by dint of argument; but you will find how very little is ever done in the world by close reason." "Very little indeed," is Mr. Wesley's comment.†

In January, 1714, he was nominated for the Charterhouse. With the exception of some time spent as his father's curate at Wroote, he never lived at Epworth again. He was a frequent visitor, however; and we shall see that he retained his connection with the Lincolnshire town till the close of his long life. It witnessed some of the most blessed scenes of his itinerant ministry. On July 9th, 1779, in connection with a visit, he says, "How true is this trite remark:

> Nescio quâ natale solum dulcedine cunctos
> Ducit, et immemores non sinet esse suâ!
>
> The natal soil to all how strangely sweet!
> The place where first he breathed who can forget!"

That day he preached to a great congregation at his usual stand—the cross—in the market-place. Next day he says, "Taking a solitary walk in the churchyard, I felt the truth of 'One generation goeth, and another cometh.' See how the earth drops its inhabitants, as the tree drops its leaves!"‡

* "Wesley Family," ii., 321.
† Works, xii., 412.
‡ *Ibid.*, iv., 158.

CHAPTER III.

GOWN-BOY AT CHARTERHOUSE.

A MEMORANDUM in Wesley's own writing shows that on January 28th, 1714, he was nominated by the Duke of Buckingham on the foundation of Charterhouse. His Grace, who was at that time Lord Chamberlain, had long been a friend of the Wesleys. Within a week of their disastrous fire the Rector sent an account to him, with a description of his boy's deliverance. The Duke and Duchess had given £26 17*s.* 6*d.* to help Samuel Wesley during his financial troubles in 1703, so that they were old friends. This nomination introduced John Wesley to that famous school for which he cherished a life-long affection. It celebrated its centenary in the year he came up from Epworth. Its founder—Thomas Sutton, the merchant prince—who died at Hackney on December 12th, 1611, at the ripe age of seventy-nine, had resolved to devote his vast wealth to some worthy charity, and after long and anxious thought, determined to found a hospital or home for the poor or aged and also a free school. At first he intended to erect the buildings at Little Hallingbury, in Essex, but he afterwards bought Howard House for £13,000. This mansion, the home of the dukes of Norfolk, had formerly been a Carthusian monastery, in which both Sir Thomas More and Dean Colet "found a temporary retreat from the cares of the world." The house was founded in 1372, and perished at the dissolution of the monasteries in Henry VIII.'s reign. Its prior suffered on the scaffold rather than betray his trust.

The property passed into the hands of the Howards in 1565. The Duke of Norfolk, who was beheaded because of his correspondence with Mary, Queen of Scots was living here at the time he was committed to the Tower. He was released after an imprisonment of some months, and returned to his mansion, under the surveillance of Sir Henry Nevil. He spent much time in beautifying his house, but in 1571 he was again in the Tower. John Wesley's warm sympathy with the unfortunate Queen may have been first stirred by the associations of his school. The property, confiscated for a time by Elizabeth, was afterwards restored to the Howards. In 1603 James I. made this mansion of the family, that had suffered so much for his mother, his first home when he reached London. He kept court there for four days, and knighted more than eighty gentlemen. Such were the historic associations of the Charterhouse. Seven full-length portraits which were entrusted to the care of one of the officers of the hospital by the Duchess of Monmouth, who intended to claim them when happier days dawned, still remain on the walls where they hung in John Wesley's time. The monastery, which was on the system of La Grande Chartreuse, bequeathed its name to the famous foundation of Sutton. Charterhouse is simply a corruption of Chartreuse. In its "Governors' Room," where the managers of the charity used to meet, almost all the illustrious men of England from the time of Henry VIII. to the Restoration have been familiar figures.*

The school was opened on October 3rd, 1614, with forty boys on the foundation, who were educated free of charge,

* Dr. W. Haig Brown's "Charterhouse, Past and Present."

and wore gowns of broad cloth lined with baize. Hence they were called gown-boys. A schoolmaster and an usher had charge of their education. About sixty "town-boys" who were not on the foundation were admitted on payment of school fees. The number of these scholars steadily grew. In 1677 there were forty-four boys on the foundation, but forty was the usual number.

During all the time John Wesley was at the Charterhouse Dr. Thomas Walker was the schoolmaster. He had been appointed in 1679, after four years spent as usher, and held the post till 1728. Andrew Tooke, who succeeded him as schoolmaster, was usher during John Wesley's school-days. Both had been gown-boys. Dr. Walker was sixty-seven years old when John Wesley entered Charterhouse. For forty years he had devoted himself to the school. The inscription on a memorial tablet in the chapel speaks of his exceedingly accurate knowledge of Hebrew, Greek, and Latin, and of his diligence in the discharge of his office. Richard Steele, Joseph Addison, Law, Bishop of Carlisle, Benson, Bishop of Gloucester, and Dr. Davies, the President of Queen's College, Cambridge, who was reputed to be the best Latin scholar of his day in England, were all educated under him. He died on June 12th, 1728, in the eighty-first year of his age. Wesley's quietness, regularity, and application are said to have made him a special favourite with Dr. Walker.*

Andrew Tooke, the usher, was Gresham Professor of Geometry, a Fellow of the Royal Society, and an author of some eminence. His "Pantheon," a school summary of heathen mythology, went through at least twenty-two editions. He was forty-one when John Wesley entered, and had been usher for nineteen years. He died at the

* Southey, i., 25.

age of fifty-eight, having held the headmastership for three years.

Any picture of Wesley's school would be incomplete without some reference to the hospital and its pensioners. No Thackeray had yet arisen to immortalise those eighty decayed gentlemen for whom Thomas Sutton's bounty provided an asylum in their declining years. But the very fact that the school and the hospital were parts of one great institution must always have been impressive. The Master of Charterhouse was both the head of the hospital and a governor of the school. He must be carefully distinguished from the schoolmaster. For one year after Wesley became a scholar the office of Master was held by Thomas Burnet, whose writings enjoyed a great reputation among all the scholars of Europe. Addison wrote a Latin ode in praise of his "Telluris Theoria Sacra," a learned work on terrestrial revolutions. He had successfully resisted James II.'s attempt to intrude a Roman Catholic on the foundation, not quailing even before the brutal Jeffreys. Archbishop Tillotson's recommendation won him the position of secretary and chaplain to William III. He was an intimate friend of Godfrey Kneller's. He died in 1715, at the age of eighty. Dr. King, who had been Preacher of Charterhouse for twenty years, was Burnet's successor. On January 20th, 1726, Dr. Byrom says that he went with Dr. King and two other friends to the Horn Tavern, where they had a pleasant time together. He says that Dr. King always carried in his pocket a copy of the "Imitation of Christ."

The system of fagging seems to have been in full force during Wesley's schooldays. His life there was one of much privation. The elder boys* took the animal food

* Moore, i., 117.

from the juniors,* so that he says, "From ten to fourteen I had little but bread to eat, and not great plenty of that. I believe this was so far from hurting me, that it laid the foundation of lasting health." Isaac Taylor † says, "Wesley learned, as a boy, to suffer wrongfully with a cheerful patience, and to conform himself to cruel despotisms without acquiring either the slave's temper or the despot's." One thing helped much to preserve his strength. His father had given him strict injunctions to run round the garden, which was of considerable extent, three times every morning. Wesley was careful to obey that injunction.‡

One pleasant instance of the influence he exerted at school has been preserved. Mr. Tooke, the usher,§ one day missed all the little boys from the playground. He found, when he began to search, that they were all in the schoolroom around Wesley, who was relating to them instructive stories, which proved more attractive than the playground. Mr. Tooke expressed his pleasure, and wished the boy to repeat this entertainment as often as he could find listeners. A malicious construction has been given to this story. John Wesley is said to have harangued his schoolfellows from the writing desks, and when taken to task by Mr. Tooke for associating with such little boys, to have answered, "Better rule in hell than serve in heaven." Fortunately Charles Wesley's daughter, who had received the true account from her father, was able to confute these statements.

About the time that Wesley entered Charterhouse, his

* Works, iii., 402.
† "Wesley and Methodism," 23.
‡ Moore, i., 117.
§ Stevenson's "Wesley Family," 483.

brother Samuel returned from Oxford to his old school at Westminster as usher. He seems to have married in 1715, and lived close to Dean's Yard. Charles, their youngest brother, came up to Westminster School in 1716, so that the three Wesleys were all in London together for four years, until John went to Oxford in 1720. We catch a glimpse of one pleasant meeting, and see how much Wesley's progress gratified his scholarly brother Samuel. In 1719, when the Rector was in doubt as to the future of Charles, Samuel wrote, "My brother Jack, I can faithfully assure you, gives you no manner of discouragement from breeding your third son a scholar." Two or three months later he tells his father, "Jack is with me, and a brave boy, learning Hebrew as fast as he can."*

Wesley was elected to Christ Church, which he entered on June 24th, 1720.† In 1630 there were twenty-seven exhibitioners at the universities from the foundation of Charterhouse, at a cost of four hundred and thirty-two pounds to the house.‡ The number seems to have varied from twenty-four to twenty-nine. The school thus secured for Wesley the best education he could receive in England. He cherished a life-long feeling of affection for the place, and took a walk through it every year when in London.§ One of these visits forms a singularly interesting link to the thoughts and feelings of the schoolboy: On Monday, August 8th, 1757, he says, "I took a walk in the Charterhouse. I wondered that all the squares and buildings, and especially the schoolboys, looked so little. But this is easily accounted for. I was little myself when I was at

* Whitehead, i., 381.

† Tyerman, i., 19.

‡ The annual pension allowed was afterwards twenty pounds.

§ Moore, i., 117.

school, and measured all about me by myself. Accordingly, the upper boys, being then bigger than myself, seemed to me very big and tall, quite contrary to what they appear now, when I am taller and bigger than them."*

Charterhouse was not a fashionable school like Westminster, so that we do not find many aristocratic names among Wesley's schoolfellows. Charles Wesley's journals refer to not a few of his contemporaries at Westminster, men of title and position. His brother mentions one of his schoolfellows who lived half a mile from Barnard Castle. When he visited that place in May, 1764, this Mr. Fielding invited him to breakfast. "I found we had been schoolfellows at the Charterhouse; and he remembered me, though I had forgot him. I spent a very agreeable hour with a serious as well as sensible man." Four years later he lodged at this gentleman's "lovely house" during his stay in Barnard Castle. Twenty years after his first visit he came again to the neighbourhood, and found that both Mr. Fielding and his wife were dead. His son had let the house to a stranger.†

On June 13th, 1748, the journals record a visit which seems to show that Wesley was at the Charterhouse. "I spent an hour or two with Dr. Pepusch." On April 29th of the same year Charles Wesley writes, "Mrs. Rich carried me to Dr. Pepusch, whose music entertained us much, and his conversation more." Mrs. Rich, who had been converted under Charles Wesley's ministry, was the wife of the proprietor of Covent Garden Theatre, and had free access to all the best musicians of the time. Pepusch

* Works, ii., 421.

† *Ibid.*, iii., 176, 335; iv., 279.

had been organist at the Charterhouse for eleven years, and lived there after his appointment. Wesley was evidently as much interested as his brother by the conversation of the aged musician. He makes a careful note of it in his journal. Dr. Pepusch asserted that the art of music was dead. He maintained that it depended on nature and mathematical principles, which only the ancients understood in their perfection. Tallis and Purcell had made efforts to revive it, but the present masters had no fixed principles at all. Such was the conversation which seems to have taken place within the precincts of the Charterhouse.

One incident of Wesley's schooldays shows that he was a high-spirited youth. "I remember," says Alexander Knox, "Mr. Wesley told us that his father was the person who composed the well-known speech delivered by Dr. Sacheverell at the close of his trial, and that on this ground, when he, Mr. John Wesley, was about to be entered at Oxford, his father, knowing that the Doctor had a strong interest in the college for which his son was devoted, desired him to call on the Doctor in his way to get letters of recommendation. 'When I was introduced,' said Mr. John Wesley, 'I found him alone, as tall as a maypole, and as fine as an archbishop. I was a very little fellow, not taller' (pointing to a very gentlemanlike but very dwarfish clergyman who was in the company) 'than Mr. Kennedy there. He said, "You are too young to go to the University; you cannot know Greek and Latin yet. Go back to school." I looked at him as David looked at Goliath, and despised him in my heart. I thought, "If I do not know Greek and Latin better than you, I ought to go back to school indeed." I left him, and neither entreaties nor commands could have again brought me back to him.'"

One word about Wesley's religious life at Charterhouse

is necessary. At the time of his conversion, in 1738,* after describing his earlier life at home, he proceeds, "The next six or seven years were spent at school, where, outward restraints being removed, I was much more negligent than before, even of outward duties, and almost continually guilty of outward sins, which I knew to be such, though they were not scandalous in the eye of the world. However, I still read the Scriptures, and said my prayers, morning and evening. And what I now hoped to be saved by was, (1) not being so bad as other people, (2) having still a kindness for religion, and (3) reading the Bible, going to church, and saying my prayers." It is evident that the old notions of "universal obedience" in which he had been so carefully trained at home had broken down. He was, he says, as ignorant of the true meaning of the Law as of the Gospel. More evangelical teaching would probably have preserved him from the "outward sins" to which he refers. We must not, however, forget how sensitive his conscience was. A schoolboy who read his Bible morning and evening had not gone far astray.

Whilst he was at Charterhouse Wesley heard of the strange disturbances at Epworth Rectory. The household was kept in a fever of excitement by groans and knockings. The real disturbance began on December 2nd, 1716, though noises had been heard for some time previously, and lasted with intervals of quiet till the middle of February. Sometimes people seemed to be walking noisily about, or running up and down stairs. Wesley's sisters named the disturber "Old Jeffrey," after a former rector. The "ghost" skilfully imitated Mr. Wesley's peculiar knock at the gate, and grew boisterous when he prayed for the king. So serious did matters become, that the Rector urged his

* Works, i., 98.

son Samuel to visit Epworth. He was preparing for the journey when news came that the disturbances had ceased. At the end of March one or two more pranks were played by Jeffrey. Such a story must have made a profound impression on a schoolboy. When John Wesley paid his next visit to Epworth, in 1720, he spent some of his leisure in gathering information, which he published many years later. In August 1726 he copied other details from his father's diary. Professor Salmon thinks that the gay and sprightly Hetty Wesley was the author of the disturbances; and the theory is ingenious and plausible, though it is not convincing. Emilia Wesley speaks of Jeffrey's visits to her in 1750 at West Street, London. It is interesting to find that a rector of Epworth, sixty years ago, was driven to the Continent, with his family, by the strange noises heard in the house.

Wesley was held in honour by his old schoolfellows. On Founder's Day, December 12th, 1727, the stewards for the annual dinner of old Carthusians were Dr. King (Master of the Charterhouse), Mr. John Wesley, Mr. Robert Vincent, and Mr. Edward Doyley. The sum of £34* was paid to Mr. West, the cook for the dinner; wines, etc., cost £30 5*s.* 6*d.*; "paid musick, ten in number, two French horns, £12 12*s.*" Eighty-four persons were at the dinner, of which the total expenses were £92 11*s.* Mr. Vincent paid the bills. At the time of this dinner Wesley had been Fellow of Lincoln College for more than eighteen months.

* These particulars and the bill of fare have been kindly furnished by the Rev. Andrew Clark, of Lincoln College. When we state that roasted pike, fried whitings, flounders, eels, shrimps, tongues, udders, pigeons, venison pasties, chines and turkeys, lamb and ragouts, wild fowls, sweetbreads and asparagus, almond tarts, roasted lobsters, pear tarts creamed, sirloin of roasted beef, fruit, jellies, custards, and florentines, figure on this bill of fare, it will be seen that the stewards made a good bargain.

CHAPTER IV.

EARLIER YEARS AT OXFORD, AND CURACY AT WROOT.

1720—1729.

WESLEY entered Oxford University in June, 1720, a week after his seventeenth birthday. His undergraduate days, like those of his brothers, Samuel and Charles, were spent at Christ Church, Cardinal Wolsey's famous college. He had an allowance of forty pounds a year as a Charterhouse scholar.* Dr. Wigan, an eminent classical scholar of that time, was his first tutor,† but he soon removed to a country living, and Mr. Sherman became his successor. Mr. Badcock describes Wesley at the age of twenty-one as "the very sensible and acute collegian, baffling every man by the subtleties of logic, and laughing at them for being so easily routed; a young fellow of the finest classical taste, of the most liberal and manly sentiments." ‡ He was "gay and sprightly, with a turn for wit and humour." His wit was polished, and all his writing showed the gentleman and the scholar. He had already begun to exercise his poetic gift, and sent one of his compositions to his father, who told him, "I like your verses on the sixty-fifth Psalm, and would not have you bury your talent." To his brother Samuel

---

* Tyerman, i., 26.

† Whitehead, i., 381.

‡ *Westminster Magazine*, 1774, p. 180.

he sent some stanzas after the Latin, composed as a college exercise.* This description of "Chloe's favourite flea" employed him, he says, above an hour on the day before he wrote to his brother. It certainly shows the ease with which he could turn a rhyme. The pleasant vein of his correspondence may be gathered from a letter dated on his twenty-first birthday. Samuel had broken his leg. "I believe," says John, "I need not use many arguments to show I am sorry for your misfortune, though at the same time I am glad you are in a fair way of recovery. If I had heard of it from any one else, I might probably have pleased you with some impertinent consolations; but the way of your relating it is a sufficient proof, that they are what you don't stand in need of. And indeed, if I understand you rightly, you have more reason to thank God that you did not break both, than to repine because you have broke one leg. You have undoubtedly heard the story of the Dutch seaman who, having broke one of his legs by a fall from the mainmast, instead of condoling himself, thanked God that he had not broke his neck. I scarce know whether your first news vexed me, or your last news pleased me more; but I can assure you, that though I did not cry for grief at the former, I did for joy at the latter part of your letter. The two things which I most wished for of almost anything in the world were to see my mother and Westminster once again; and to see them both together was so far above my expectations, that I almost looked upon it as next to an impossibility. I have been so very frequently disappointed when I had set my heart on any pleasure, that I will never again depend on any before it comes. However, I shall be obliged to you if you will tell me,

* Moore, i., 120.

as near as you can, how soon my uncle" (Annesley) "is expected in England, and my mother in London.

"Since you have a mind to see some of my verses, I have sent you some, which employed me above an hour yesterday in the afternoon. There is one, and, I am afraid, but one good thing in them, that is, they are short." *

The young collegian seems to have been disappointed again. Mrs. Wesley came to London to meet her only brother, Mr. Annesley, who was in the service of the East India Company. The newspapers had announced that he was to arrive by a certain vessel, and she came to meet him; but unfortunately he did not sail in that vessel, and was never again heard of.†

Wesley's health during his first years at college was far from vigorous. In a letter to his mother in 1723 he says that whilst walking in the country his nose bled so violently that he was almost choked. He was only able to stop the bleeding by plunging into the river.‡ He was apparently in a chronic state of financial embarrassment. His tutor told him that he would make the fees as low as possible, but he had a constant struggle to make both ends meet. In August, 1724, his mother wrote to ask whether he had any reasonable hopes of being out of debt. She was much concerned for a kind friend that had lent him ten pounds, and encouraged him to hope that they might pick up a few crumbs for him at Epworth before the end of the year. This friend afterwards paid himself out of Wesley's exhibition.§ His father helped him a little; but his own heavy debts, now amounting to three hundred and fifty pounds, left very little either for his home or his children. In one letter he expresses a hope that he will "have no occasion to remember

* Whitehead, i., 382.
† *Ibid.*, i., 383.
‡ Tyerman, i., 25.
§ *Ibid.*, i., 26, 27.

any more some things that are past."* In weighing this sentence, we must not, however, forget Wesley's scanty allowance at Christ Church. It is quite possible that a sprightly young student may not have acted with such rigid economy as the Rector deemed to be necessary. It is not likely that much more than this is meant. On November 1st, 1724, he tells his mother that a great many rogues were about Oxford, so that it was not safe to be out late at night. A gentleman whom he knew was standing at the door of a coffee-house about seven one evening. When he turned round his cap and wig were snatched off his head; and though he followed the thief to a considerable distance, he was unable to recover them. "I am pretty safe from such gentlemen," he adds, "for unless they carried me away, carcase and all, they would have but a poor purchase." These were the days when robbers took special pleasure in stealing the perukes of gentlemen in full dress, who sometimes found it necessary to sit with their back to the horses, lest a piece of the back of the carriage should be cut out, and the head-dress stolen.† The same letter refers to Jack Sheppard's escape from Newgate, which was then exciting great attention in Oxford, and to Dr. Cheyne's "Book of Health and Long Life," a plea for temperance and exercise. The writer condemned salted or highly seasoned food, and recommended a diet of two pints of water, one of wine, with eight ounces of animal and twelve of vegetable food per day. This book led Wesley to eat sparingly and drink water, a change which he considered to be one great means of preserving his health.‡

* Tyerman, i., 30.
† Dr. Doran's "London in the Jacobite Times," i., 395.
‡ Works, iii., 402.

When he went to Oxford, Wesley still "said his prayers," both in public and private, and read the Scriptures, with other devotional books, especially comments on the New Testament. He had not any notion of inward holiness, but went on "habitually, and for the most part very contentedly, in some or other known sin, indeed, with some intermission and short struggles, especially before and after the Holy Communion," which he was obliged to receive three times a year. "I cannot well tell," he says, "what I hoped to be saved by now, when I was continually sinning against that little light I had, unless by those transient fits of what many divines taught me to call repentance." * A conversation which he had late one night with the porter of his college made a lasting impression on his mind, and convinced him that there was something in religion which he had not yet found. At first Wesley indulged in a little pleasantry but when he found that this man had only one coat, and that though nothing had passed his lips that day but a drink of water, his heart was full of gratitude, he said, "You thank God when you have nothing to wear, nothing to eat, and no bed to lie upon. What else do you thank Him for?" "I thank Him," answered the porter, "that He has given me my life and being, and a heart to love Him, and a desire to serve Him." †

The beginning of 1725 seems to have been marked by a great increase of spiritual desire. Wesley was not yet twenty-two. He thought of entering the Church, and consulted his parents. His father wished that he should devote himself to "critical learning," but Mrs. Wesley was greatly pleased by his desire to take orders. His father

* Works, i., 98.

† Rev. John Reynolds, "Anecdotes of Wesley," p. 8.

wrote him on January 26th, 1725, to express his pleasure that his son had such a high conception of the work of a minister, and to point out the motives that should govern his choice of such a life. "The principal spring and motive, to which all the former should be only secondary, must certainly be the glory of God and the service of His Church in the edification of our neighbour. And woe to him who, with any meaner leading view, attempts so sacred a work." His shrewd sense is seen in another paragraph: "You ask me which is the best commentary on the Bible? I answer, The Bible itself. For the several paraphrases and translations of it in the Polyglot, compared with the original, and with one another, are, in my opinion, to an honest, devout, industrious, and humble man, infinitely preferable to any comment I ever saw. But Grotius is the best, for the most part, especially on the Old Testament." * It was in this letter that he told his son he thought it too soon for him to take orders. He changed his opinion, however, before long.† He urged him to give himself to prayer and study, and promised that he would help him with the expenses of ordination.‡ About this time Wesley began to study the "Imitation of Christ," which he had often seen, but never studied carefully. It taught him that true religion was seated in the heart, and that God's law extended to all our thoughts as well as our words and actions. He was very angry with A Kempis for being too strict, though he only read Dean Stanhope's translation; but nevertheless he frequently found much sensible comfort in the reading, such as he had been a stranger to before. Wesley's love of A Kempis never failed. In 1761 he told his friend Byrom that "Thomas a Kempis was next to the Bible." Up to 1725

* Whitehead, i., 385. † *Ibid.*, i., 386. ‡ Tyerman, i., 33.

Wesley had never had any religious friend. Now he was fortunate enough to meet with one, though we do not know his name, who became a true helper. He began to alter the whole form of his conversation, and earnestly sought to lead a new life. He took the Lord's Supper every week, watched against all sin in word or deed, and began to strive and pray for inward holiness. "So that now, doing so much and living so good a life," he says, "I doubted not but I was a good Christian." *

Jeremy Taylor's "Holy Living and Dying," which Wesley met with and studied in 1725, when he was thinking about his ordination, led him to make a more careful use of all his time. He now began to keep those journals which afterwards became such a storehouse of facts about his wonderful itinerancy and his evangelical mission. The difficulties which arose in reading Kempis and Taylor he referred to his father and mother, whose luminous answers did much to form his opinions and save him from asceticism.

Whilst preparing for orders, Wesley won his first convert. Somewhere about the midsummer of 1725,† he and a young gentleman with whom he was intimate quietly left the company in which they were, about eight o'clock one evening, and went to St. Mary's Church to see the funeral of a young lady with whom both of them had been acquainted. As they paced one of the aisles, Wesley asked his companion if he really thought himself his friend, and if so, why he would not do him all the good that lay in his power. When his friend began to protest, Wesley entreated that he might have the pleasure of making him a whole Christian, to which he knew he was halt persuaded already. He

* Works, i., 99. † *Ibid.*, xii., 10.

reminded him that he could not do him a greater kindness, as both of them "would be fully convinced when they came to follow that young woman." Wesley's companion became exceedingly serious, and the good impression was abiding. Eighteen months after this conversation he died of consumption. Wesley saw him three days before his death, and preached his funeral sermon at his special request.

Wesley's financial difficulties were overcome by his father's help, and he was ordained deacon in Christ Church Cathedral on Sunday, September 19th, 1725, by Dr. Potter, then Bishop of Oxford, who also admitted him to priest's orders in the same place on September 22nd, 1728.* Dr. Hayward, who examined him for priest's orders, put one question to him of which Wesley's whole after-history was an illustration, "Do you know what you are about? You are bidding defiance to all mankind. He that would live a Christian priest, ought to know, that whether his hand be against every man or no, he must expect every man's hand should be against him."†

In a sermon, "On Attending the Church Service," Wesley refers to a counsel given him by Dr. Potter, when Archbishop of Canterbury, which also made a lasting impression on his mind: "If you desire to be extensively useful, do not spend your time and strength in contending for or against such things as are of a disputable nature, but in testifying against open, notorious vice, and in promoting real essential holiness."‡

Soon after his ordination, in 1725, Wesley delivered his first sermon. On October 16th, 1771, he says, "I preached at South Lye. Here it was that I preached my first sermon, six-and-forty years ago. One man was in

* Whitehead, i., 397. † Works, xii., 21. ‡ *Ibid.*, vii., 185.

my present audience who heard it. Most of the rest are gone to their long home." * The little village of South Leigh is about three miles from Witney. On January 11th, 1726, he preached a funeral sermon at Epworth for John Griffith, the son of one of Samuel Wesley's parishioners. He dwelt mainly on the folly of indulging grief except for sin from the text 2 Sam. xii. 23. His references to the young man were singularly concise. "It is of no service to the dead to celebrate his actions, since he has the applause of God and His holy angels, and his own conscience. And it is of little use to the living, since he who desires a pattern may find enough proposed as such in the sacred writings." His testimony to Griffith is forcible, though brief. "To his parents he was an affectionate, dutiful son; to his acquaintance an ingenuous, cheerful, good-natured companion; and to me a well-tried, sincere friend." †

After his ordination Wesley quietly pursued his divinity studies. But the matter of pressing interest was his election to a Fellowship at Lincoln College. He devoted himself to the classics and other branches of study, as well as to his "academical exercises." His father had mentioned the Fellowship in his letter on January 26th, 1725. During the following summer Wesley's friends earnestly exerted themselves on his behalf. When Dr. Morley, the Rector of Lincoln, was approached on the subject, he said, "I will inquire into Mr. Wesley's character." He afterwards gave him leave to stand as a candidate, and exerted himself to secure his election. "In July," Wesley's father says, "I waited on Dr. Morley, and found him more civil than ever. I will

* Works, iii., 444.

† *Methodist Magazine*, 1797, p. 425.

write to the Bishop of Lincoln (the visitor of the college) again, and to your brother Samuel the next post. Study hard, lest your opponents beat you." * His opponents at Lincoln College tried to weaken his chance of election by ridiculing his serious behaviour, but timely letters from home helped Wesley to show a firm front against this factious opposition.

On August 2nd, 1725, his father sent him a beautiful little note of encouragement from Wroot :—

"DEAR SON,—If you be what you write I shall be happy. As to the gentlemen candidates you mention, does anybody think the devil is dead, or asleep, or that he has no agents left ? Surely virtue can bear being laughed at. The Captain and Master endured something more for us before He entered into glory, and unless we track His steps, in vain do we hope to share His glory with Him.

"Nought else but blessing from your loving father,

"SAMUEL WESLEY." †

On March 17th, 1726, Wesley was unanimously elected Fellow of Lincoln College. The Fellowship was for natives of Lincoln county, and had been previously held by John Thorold, afterwards Sir John Thorold, who resigned on May 3rd, 1725, but the college had kept the Fellowship vacant. Wesley was admitted on March 28th. The fact that Sir John Thorold was a member of Lincoln College and Wesley's predecessor in this fellowship forms a pleasant link between the itinerant evangelist and the Lincolnshire squire, who preached twice a week, and is

* Whitehead i., 398.
† Tyerman, i., 39.

called "our new star of righteousness" in the correspondence of the day.* Sir John Thorold wrote three theological treatises, which bear witness to the profound interest he felt in all religious questions. He was the great-grandfather of the present Bishops of Rochester and Nottingham (Dr. Thorold and Dr. Trollope).

Wesley's father wrote him a letter, addressed "Dear Mr. Fellow-Elect of Lincoln," enclosing a bill for twelve pounds on Dr. Morley, which he had paid to the Rector's use at Gainsborough, near which town Dr. Morley held the living of Scotton. "You are inexpressibly obliged to that generous man," he says. The expenses connected with the election had greatly taxed Samuel Wesley. He had not much more than five pounds to keep his family from the end of March till after harvest. "What will be my own fate God knows. *Sed passi graviora*" ("But we have suffered heavier troubles"). "Whatever I am, my Jack is Fellow of Lincoln."† John's letter to his brother Samuel shows how timely his father's unexpected help had been. All his debts were paid, the expenses of his "treat" defrayed, and he had still above ten pounds in hand. If he could get leave to stay in the country till his college allowance commenced, he felt that this money would meet all claims upon him.‡

Wesley's first impressions of his new college were very favourable. "I never knew a college besides ours whereof the members were so perfectly well satisfied with one another, and so inoffensive to the other part of the University. All I have yet seen of the fellows are both well-natured and well-bred; men admirably disposed as well to preserve peace and good neighbourhood among

* Mrs. Delaney's Letters, ii., 8.

† "Life and Times of S. Wesley," p. 399. ‡ Works, xii., 17.

themselves, as to promote it wherever else they have any acquaintance." *

How thoroughly economical he was another letter shows.† He wore his hair remarkably long, and flowing loose upon his shoulders.‡ His mother urged him to have it cut for the sake of his health. He thought that it might improve his complexion and appearance to do so, but these were not sufficiently strong reasons to make him incur an expense of two or three pounds a year. In this letter occurs the famous sentence which henceforth became Wesley's motto, "Leisure and I have taken leave of one another. I propose to be busy as long as I live, if my health is so long indulged me."

Charles Wesley came up to Christ Church in 1726, soon after John's removal from that college to Lincoln. His father had been so much pressed by the efforts made for John that he did not expect that he could do anything for Charles when he went up to the University, though he afterwards promised to give him ten pounds a year.§ John and Samuel seem to have carefully considered what Charles could do to lighten his expenses. Mr. Sherman, John's tutor, suggested that his brother might let his room in Christ Church and take a garret in Peckwater, so as to gain about six pounds a year, but John did not approve of this suggestion. Charles, however, was better off than his brother had been. He came up from Westminster, anxious to enjoy himself, and when John spoke to him about religion would answer warmly, "What, would you have me to be a saint all at once?" and would hear no more.

In April, 1726, Wesley obtained leave of absence from

* Works, xii., 17. † Priestley, p. 8. ‡ Whitehead, i., 436.
§ Stevenson, "Wesley Family," p. 127.

the University, and spent the summer in Lincolnshire. He generally read prayers and preached twice every Sunday, besides assisting his father in parish work. He steadily kept up his own studies, and had many opportunities of conversation with his father and mother on religious subjects and matters of general interest, which, with his own reflections, are carefully noted in his diary.* He still cultivated the muse. He had sent two pieces of his poetry to his brother Samuel in March.† Whilst at Epworth he began a paraphrase on Psalm civ., which gives abundant evidence of his vigour of thought and power of versification. His mother gave him some judicious advice about this time, which he carefully followed. "I would not have you leave off making verses; rather make poetry your diversion, though never your business." ‡

On October 21st, 1726, the young Fellow returned to Oxford. His description of Lincoln College shows how congenial were his new surroundings. Dr. Morley was his friend, and the twelve Fellows formed a pleasant little society. "Wesley's room," with a vine creeping round the window, known as "Wesley's vine," is still pointed out to visitors.§ His reputation as a scholar and a man of literary taste was now established in the University. On November 6th he was chosen Greek lecturer and moderator of the classes. Dr. Whitehead says that his skill in logic was universally known and admired.‖ He proceeded Master of Arts on February 14th, 1727, and acquired considerable reputation in his disputation for his degree. He told Henry Moore that he delivered three lectures on the occasion, one on natural philosophy, entitled, "De

* Whitehead, i., 403. † Works, xii., 17.
‡ Whitehead, i., 407. § Tyerman, i., 45. ‖ Vol. i., 403.

Anima Brutorum;" one on moral philosophy, "De Julio Cesare;" a third on religion, "De Amore Dei."*

The Rev. Andrew Clarke, of Lincoln College, has kindly supplied the following particulars of Wesley's connection with that college.† On May 6th, 1726, he was nominated by the Sub-rector to preach the sermon at St. Michael's Church on St. Michael's Day, which was always delivered by one of the Fellows. Wesley was nominated again in 1732. He was appointed Claviger (or keeper of one of the three keys of the treasury) on November 6th, 1726, and again in 1731, each time for a twelvemonth. From 1726 to 1730 he was lecturer in logic; from 1726 to 1728, and again from 1729 to 1734, lecturer in Greek; from 1730 to 1735, lecturer in philosophy. All these appointments date from November 6th. On May 6th in three different years,—1737, 1743, and 1749,—Wesley was nominated by the Sub-rector to preach the sermon by a Fellow in All Saints' Church, on the dedication festival of that church. In 1731, 1737, and 1743, he was chosen, with another Fellow, to preach the Lent Sermons at Combe Lingu, Oxon. In 1737 Wesley was in Georgia, but the sermons might be preached by a substitute. The Pocket Guide for Oxford in 1747 says that Lincoln College had its Rector, twelve Fellows, nine scholars, twenty exhibitioners, and about seventy other students.

* Moore, i., 144.

† When Wesley entered Lincoln College, Dr. Morley was Rector, John Brereton, afterwards Rector of Great Leighs, Essex, Senior Fellow and Sub-rector for the year. The other Fellows were Dr. W. Lupton (Prebendary of Durham; died December 13th, 1726), Knightly Adams (afterwards Rector of Great Leighs), William Vesey (Chaplain of St. Michael's, Oxford), Thomas Vaughan, John Tottenham, Euseby Isham (Rector 1731—

After taking his Master's degree Wesley felt that his time was more at his own disposal. Hitherto the University curriculum had been the guide of his studies. Now he was able to follow the plan of work which he had marked out for himself. He had fully come over to his mother's opinion that there were many truths that it was not worth while to know. He even laid aside a controversy between Bishop Hoadly and Bishop Atterbury when he had reached the middle of it. "I thought the labour of twenty or thirty hours, if I was sure of succeeding, which I was not, would be but ill rewarded by that important

---

1755), Richard Hutchins (Rector 1755—1781. "The college never had a better Rector in its history, and few of its benefactors have been more munificent"), Michael Robinson (Chaplain of All Saints', Oxford, Rector of Great Leighs), Benjamin Mangey (died 1730), Charles Dymoke, John Wesley.

The Fellows of Lincoln were required to take orders within a year, and to secure their B.D. degree within seven years after they became M.A. Wesley escaped the obligation to proceed as Bachelor of Divinity. John Crosby, treasurer of Lincoln Cathedral in 1476, founded a fellowship which required its holder to study canon law and take a degree in that faculty. After the Reformation the degree in civil law took its place. When a Fellow found it inconvenient to take his B.D. he was elected to this canonist fellowship, which he held till he had taken his B.D. After Dr. Morley vacated this, in 1703, eight other Fellows had held it from three to five years each. On July 13th, 1736, when in Georgia, Wesley was elected to it. He would not give it up, as he did not wish to take his B.D., and held it till 1751. The result was that he was the junior in college standing of all Fellows who took the degree. These facts explain Wesley's inquiry on June 18th, 1741, about "the exercises previous to the degree of Bachelor in Divinity."

Though admitted Fellow on March 28th, 1726, Wesley, according to custom, received nothing for half a year. On September 28th, his first "commons" was paid. This was 1*s.* 4*d.* per week when in residence. In 1731 and 1732 he received

piece of knowledge whether Bishop Hoadly had understood Bishop Atterbury or no."*

A letter from one of the Fellows of Lincoln College at the close of 1727 may show in what high esteem Wesley was held in his college. Mr. Fenton had a perpetual curacy, which kept him from Oxford, so that he had not seen Wesley.

"LINCOLN COLLEGE, *December 28th*, 1727.

"SIR,—Yesterday I had the satisfaction of receiving your kind and obliging letter, whereby you have given me a singular instance of that goodness and civility which is essential to your character, and strongly confirmed to me the many encomiums which are given you in this respect by all who have the happiness to know you. This makes me infinitely desirous of your acquaintance. And when I consider those shining qualities which I hear daily mentioned in your praise, I cannot but lament the great misfortune we all suffer in the absence of so agreeable a person from the college. But I please myself with the thoughts of seeing you here on Chapter-day, and of the happiness we shall have in your company in the summer. In the

£2 15*s*. 4*d*. from this source; in 1735, £1 9*s*. 4*d*.; in 1739, 8*s*.; in 1740, 4*s*. 8*d*. From obits, allowances of 1*s*., 8*d*., or 6*d*. given to all Fellows in residence on the anniversary of the death of eleven college benefactors, Wesley received an average of 7*s*. 8*d*. in the years before he went to Georgia, the maximum attainable being 9*s*. 4*d*. a year. In 1740 he had 6*d*.

The "buttery" books, in which charges for beer, bread, butter, and cheese appear, show that Wesley's expenses for such articles were much the same as those of the other resident Fellows, and rather smaller than those of many of the undergraduates. The charges against him vary from 2*s*. 3*d*. to 13*s*. 3*d*. a week in items from a farthing upwards.

* Works, xii., 9.

meantime, I return you my most sincere thanks for this favour, and assure you, that if it should ever lie in my power to serve you, no one will be more ready to do it than, sir,

"Your most obliged and most humble servant,

"LEW. FENTON." *

Wesley had fixed hours ot work in the morning and afternoon, and never suffered himself to deviate from the plan he had laid down. Monday and Tuesday were thus devoted to the Greek and Latin classics; Wednesday to logic and ethics; Thursday to Hebrew and Arabic; Friday to metaphysics and natural philosophy; Saturday to oratory and poetry, chiefly composing; Sunday to divinity. At intervals he studied French, which he had begun to learn two or three years before, and read a great number of modern books on all subjects. He first read an author regularly through; then, on a second perusal of the book, he transcribed the important or striking passages. Euclid, Keil, Gravesande, Sir Isaac Newton, and other mathematical writers, whose works he weighed with great care, are mentioned in his diary. He also sometimes amused himself with experiments in optics.†

Wesley's removal from Christ Church to Lincoln had one happy result. As soon as he determined to become a real Christian, not merely a nominal one, he found that his acquaintance were as ignorant of God as himself; but whilst he was aware of his ignorance, they were not aware of theirs. He tried to help them, but without success. "Meantime," he says, "I found, by sad experience, that even their harmless conversation, so called, damped all my good resolutions. I saw no possible way of getting rid of them, unless it should please God to remove me to

* Whitehead, i., 414. † *Ibid.*, i., 411.

another college. He did so, in a manner contrary to all human expectation. I was elected Fellow of a college where I knew not one person." He was aware that many would call upon him for various reasons, but he had made up his mind to have no chance acquaintance. He narrowly observed the temper and behaviour of all who came, and determined that he would only cultivate the friendship of those who were likely to lead him on the way to heaven. He did not return the visits of those who were not of this spirit. Such people, therefore, gradually left him to himself. When he wrote this account he said that this had been his invariable rule for about threescore years.*

Wesley behaved as courteously as he could, but he was determined both to redeem the time and save his own soul. On March 19th, 1727, he tells his mother that the conversation of one or two friends, of whom he should always speak with gratitude, had first taken away his relish for most other pleasures. He had now begun to lose his love for company—"the most elegant entertainment next to books,"—so that, unless the persons had a religious turn of thought, he felt much better pleased without them. He was inclined to prefer some more retired position than he had at Oxford, where he might fix his habits of mind "before the flexibility of youth was over." A school in Yorkshire had lately been offered him, with a good salary. What charmed him most, however, was the description of the place which some gentlemen had given him the previous day. It lay in a little valley, so hemmed in by hills that it was scarcely accessible. There was no company in the school, and scarcely any outside. This account, which his visitors thought would

* Works, vi., 473.

put such a post out of the question, strongly attracted Wesley. He adds, "I am full of business, but have found a way to write without taking any time from that. It is but rising an hour sooner in the morning, and going into company an hour later in the evening, both which may be done without any inconvenience." *

About this time, probably in 1728, he began that system of early rising which he continued till the end of his life. He used to awake every night about twelve or one, and remain awake some time. He felt convinced that he lay longer in bed than nature required, and procured an alarum which awoke him at seven next morning, nearly an hour earlier than the previous day. He still lay awake as usual. Next morning he rose at six, with the same result. The following night he set his alarum for five, but he awoke as before. The fourth day he rose at four, and slept all through the night. He could say, after sixty years, that he still rose at four o'clock, and that, taking the year round, he did not lie awake a quarter of an hour together in a month.† It must be remembered that in later years, after a long, wearisome ride on a hot day, Wesley would lie down and sleep for ten or fifteen minutes. He would then rise refreshed for his work. He never could bear to sleep on a soft bed.‡

On August 4th, 1727, he left Oxford to assist his father, who held the small living of Wroot in addition to that of Epworth, and found it difficult to pay a curate or to get one to his mind. He had been anxious for some time to have his son with him. Wesley's principal work lay at Wroot, whilst his father stayed at Epworth, but they seem to have made occasional changes. Wesley went to Westminster to visit his brother Samuel on August 4th;

* Works, xii., 11. † *Ibid.*, vii., 69. ‡ Whitehead, ii., 471.

then he set out for Lincolnshire, where he acted as his father's curate until November, 1729.

Wroot was a little village surrounded by bogs, about five miles from Epworth. The Wesleys seem to have lived there from 1725 until John Wesley came over to help his father. The road between Epworth and Wroot was so rough that Samuel Wesley felt that his son could not get from one place to the other without hazarding his health or life.* The journey had to be made by boat. It was impossible to go afoot or on horseback, because the waters were out in the Fen Country. The boat took them as far as Scawsit Bridge; then they walked across the Common to Epworth. It was by no means a pleasant passage. The water washing over the side of the boat laid up the Rector in June, 1727, just before John Wesley came home to help him. During one of these journeys, in 1728, he also had a narrow escape from drowning. The boat was driven by the fierce stream and wind against another craft, and filled with water.† The church at Wroot was a small brick building; the parishioners were unpolished and heavy.‡ They appear in singularly unattractive colours in some lines written by Wesley's clever sister Hetty:—

> High births and virtue equally they scorn,
> As asses dull, on dunghills born;
> Impervious as the stones their heads are found,
> Their rage and hatred steadfast as the ground.§

From its inaccessible position through bogs and floods the place had been called "Wroot-out-of-England." The rude country folk still treasured up the strange stories about William of Lindholme, the hermit, known as a wizard in league with the evil one.

* Stevenson's "Wesley Family," 127. † *Ibid.*, i., 129.
‡ Tyerman, i., 58. § "Oxford Methodists," 378.

Wesley's work at Wroot had not much immediate fruit. It is included in his description, "From the year 1725 to 1729 I preached much, but saw no fruit of my labour. Indeed, it could not be that I should; for I neither laid the foundation of repentance, nor of believing the Gospel; taking it for granted that all to whom I preached were believers, and that many of them needed no repentance."*

He made several visits to Oxford during these two years of parish life. In October, 1727, though suffering from the ague, which was endemic in that part of Lincolnshire, he went up to the University. This journey seems to have been made on election business, at the request of the Rector of Lincoln College, of whose kindness he entertained such a lively sense that he used to say, "I can refuse Dr. Morley nothing." We find one other reference to this friend. At the end of January, 1751, at the pressing request of Dr. Isham, then Rector of Lincoln College, Wesley went to Oxford to vote for a member of Parliament. The candidate for whom he voted was not elected, but he did not regret his journey. "I owe much more than this to that generous, friendly man, who now rests from his labour."† He travelled on horseback, and spent ten days at his college. The journey was painful, as his ague often made him feel very ill on the road. On July 27th, 1728, he went up to the University by way of London, and was ordained priest by Dr. Potter, who had himself been a Fellow of Lincoln. Next year, on June 16th, he spent about two months at Oxford, where he found the little Society of Methodists already meeting together under the leadership of his brother Charles.

John Wesley's life at Wroot was the only experience

* Works, viii., 468. † Whitehead, i., 413; Works, viii., 226.

he had as an English parish clergyman.* On April 13th, 1759, he called on Mr. Romley, of Burton, near Epworth, one of his former parishioners, a lively, sensible man, eighty-three years old, by whom, he says, "I was much comforted."† In September, 1767, after Wesley had preached in the riding-school at Northampton, to a large and deeply serious congregation, he mentions that a lady, who had been one of his parishioners at Epworth nearly forty years before, waited on him. He took tea at her house next day.

The quiet life at Wroot was broken in upon by a letter from Dr. Morley, dated October 21st, 1729. He told Wesley that it was felt necessary, in order to discipline and good government, that the junior Fellows who were chosen Moderators should personally attend to the duties of their office unless they could get some other Fellow to preside for them. Mr. Hutchins had been kind enough to promise to take Mr. Fenton's place, so that he might not be compelled to give up his perpetual curacy; Mr. Robinson would have supplied Wesley's, but he had to serve two cures fourteen miles distant from Oxford, and the roads for ten miles at least were as bad as those around Epworth. "We hope," says the Rector, "it may be as much for your advantage to reside at college as where you are, if you take pupils, or can get a curacy in the neighbourhood of Oxon. Your father may certainly have another curate, though not so much to his satisfaction; yet we are persuaded that this will not move him to hinder your return to college, since the interest of college and obligation to statute requires it." This letter brought Wesley back to Oxford, to become the head of the Methodist movement in the University.

* His curacy near Oxford was scarcely parish work.

† Works, ii., 473.

CHAPTER V.

OXFORD METHODISM.

WESLEY returned to Oxford on November 22nd, 1729. Dr. Morley's letter had suggested that he might take pupils or a curacy. He himself put eleven pupils under Wesley's care immediately after his return, and in this work he continued until his mission to Georgia. Dr. Morley died on June 12th, 1731, and was succeeded by Dr. Isham on July 9th. The journal for 1776 * shows what a zealous tutor Wesley was. "In the English colleges," he says, "every one may reside all the year, as all my pupils did; and I should have thought myself little better than a highwayman if I had not lectured them every day in the year but Sundays." In later years he sometimes read lectures to his preachers on theology, logic, and rhetoric, in much the same manner as with his pupils at the University. As a tutor he was singularly diligent and careful, and laboured earnestly to make those under his charge both scholars and Christians.†

It will have been observed that Wesley was called to Oxford to preside at Moderations. Public disputation formed a large part in the University training of those days. The Moderator was the chairman and arbitrator at such discussions. At Lincoln College these exercises were held every day, so that the junior Fellow gained a

---

* Works, iv., 77.

† *Ibid.*, i., 417.

thorough grasp of all the niceties of formal logic, which proved invaluable to him amid the heated and often captious controversies of later days. He gratefully refers to this training in a well-known passage of his works. "For several years I was Moderator in the disputations which were held six times a week at Lincoln College in Oxford. I could not avoid acquiring hereby some degree of expertness in arguing, and especially in discerning and pointing out well-covered and plausible fallacies. I have since found abundant reason to praise God for giving me this honest art. By this, when men have hedged me in by what they call demonstrations, I have been many times able to dash them in pieces, in spite of all its covers, to touch the very point where the fallacy lay; and it flew open in a moment."*

Such was Wesley's life during the last six years he spent at Oxford. But the surpassing interest of these years is found in the rise of Methodism in the University. We have seen that Charles Wesley, who had come up from Westminster School in 1726, spent his first year in diversion, and rebuffed his brother when he spoke to him about religion. Whilst John was at Wroot, however, Charles became more serious. He had devoted himself to study, and soon found that diligence led him to seriousness. In the beginning of the year 1729 he wrote to consult John about keeping a diary, and expressed his conviction that, though at present he was deprived of his brother's company and assistance, yet he was persuaded that it was through his means that God would establish the work He had begun. In May, 1729, on the eve of John's visit to Oxford, Charles tells him of a modest, humble, well-disposed youth who had fallen into vile hands. Charles had been able to rescue

* Works, x., 353.

him, and the friends now took the Sacrament together every week. He felt the need of help himself. "I earnestly long for and desire the blessing God is about to send me in you. I am sensible *this* is my day of grace, and that upon my employing the time before our next meeting and next parting will in great measure depend my condition for eternity." *

John Wesley came in June and spent two months with his brother. During his stay he passed almost every evening with the little Society which had gathered round Charles. The call from Dr. Morley must have given no small pleasure to these friends. Charles Wesley, who was nearly twenty-two, had taken his degree, and become a college tutor. He was now fairly launched, as his father reminded him in an affectionate letter written in January, 1730. Beside the Wesleys, William Morgan, a commoner of Christ Church, and Robert Kirkham, of Merton, seem to have been the principal members of this little Society. When Wesley came to Oxford he was at once recognised as their head. Gambold, who was introduced to him a few months after his return, and who joined the Methodists, says, "Mr. John Wesley was always the chief manager, for which he was very fit; for he not only had more learning and experience than the rest, but he was blest with such activity as to be always gaining ground, and such steadiness that he lost none. What proposals he made to any were sure to charm them, because they saw him always the same. What supported this uniform vigour was the care he took to consider well of every affair before he engaged in it, making all his decisions in the fear of God, without passion, humour, or self-confidence; for though he had naturally a

* Jackson, "Charles Wesley," i., 15.

very clear apprehension, yet his exact prudence depended more on humanity and singleness of heart. To this I may add that he had, I think, something of authority in his countenance, though, as he did not want address, he could soften his manner, and point it as occasion required. Yet he never assumed anything to himself above his companions. Any of them might speak their mind, and their words were as strictly regarded by him as his were by them."

The name of "Methodists" was given to the friends before John Wesley came into residence.* A young gentleman of Christ Church, struck with the exact regularity of their lives and studies, said, "Here is a new sect of Methodists sprung up." In December, 1730, Wesley tells his parents, that he expected the following night to be in company "with the gentleman who did us the honour to take the first notice of our Society. I have terrible reasons to think he is as slenderly provided with humanity as with sense and learning. However, I must not let slip this opportunity, because he is at present in some distress, occasioned by his being about to dispute in the schools on Monday, though he is not furnished with such arguments as he wants. I intend, if he has not procured them before, to help him to some arguments that I may at least remove that prejudice from him, 'that we are friends to none but those who are as queer as ourselves.'" † The name "Methodist" was quaint, and not inappropriate. The members of the little Society were soon known by it throughout the University. The title was not new. It was used to describe an ancient school of physicians who thought that all diseases

* Whitehead, i., 420.

† Miss Wedgwood, "John Wesley," p. 57.

might be cured by a specific method of diet and exercise. In 1639, there is a reference in a sermon preached at Lambeth to "plain packstaff Methodists," who despised all rhetoric.* About forty years before it found its most famous application it was given to Dr. Williams and other Nonconformist divines to describe their views on the method of man's justification before God.† "Methodist" was not the only name given to the Society. The Reforming Club, the Godly Club, the Holy Club, Sacramentarians, Bible Moths, Supererogation men, and Enthusiasts were all in use.‡ John Wesley was called the Curator, or Father of the Holy Club.§

At first the four friends met every Sunday evening, then two evenings a week were passed together, and at last every evening from six to nine. They began their meetings with prayer, studied the Greek Testament and the classics, reviewed the work of the past day, and talked over their plans for the morrow. They met either in John Wesley's room, or in that of some other member of the Society. After prayers, the chief subject of which was charity,‖ they had supper together, and John Wesley read some book. On Sunday evening they read divinity. They fasted on Wednesday and Friday, and received the Lord's Supper every week, coming to Christ Church when the Sacrament was not given in their own colleges A system of self-examination brought all their conduct under searching review. On Sunday they examined themselves as to the "Love of God and simplicity," on Monday on "Love of Man." A glance at the entire

---

* Crowther.

† Other instances of the use of the word in 1706 and 1741 will be found in Thomas Jackson's Life of Charles Wesley, i., 18.

‡ Jackson, i., 29. § Works, i., 12, 13. ‖ Gambold's letter.

scheme will show how carefully the Oxford Methodists sought to order their lives. They studied to do the will of God in all things, to pray with fervour, to use ejaculations or hourly prayers for humility, faith, hope, love, and the particular virtue they set themselves to seek each day. The members repeated a collect at nine, twelve, and three, and had their stated times for meditation and private prayer. The "Love of Man" led them to inquire whether they had been zealous in doing good, had persuaded all they could to attend the means of grace and to observe the laws of the Church and the University, or had shown all kindness and used all prayer for those around them.

The 24th of August, 1730, was a memorable day for the little Society. Up to this time they had quietly pursued their studies and their devotional exercises, doing all the good that lay in their power. Now they entered upon that work of charity which was to bear such blessed fruit. Mr. Morgan, the son of a gentleman in Dublin, led the way. He had visited a man lying at the jail under sentence of death for the murder of his wife, and had spoken to one of the debtors there. What he saw convinced him that much good might be done by any one who would take pains to teach the prisoners. He spoke so often of this that John and Charles Wesley went with him to the Castle. They now agreed to visit there once or twice a week. Morgan also led the way in the visiting of the sick. The friends were soon busy enough. They resolved to spend an hour or two a week in looking after the sick, provided that the minister of the parish in which any of these lived should not be opposed to it.

John Wesley wrote his father an account of their work, asking his counsel, that nothing might be done rashly. On September 21st, 1730, he replied, "And now, as to your own designs and employments, what can I say less of them than *valde probo;* and that I have the highest reason to bless God that He has given me two sons together at Oxford, to whom He has given grace and courage to turn the war against the world and the devil, which is the best way to conquer them?" He expresses his satisfaction that they had such a friend as Mr. Morgan to break the ice for them, and says that he must adopt him as his own son. "Go on then," he adds, "in God's name, in the path to which your Saviour hath directed you, and that track wherein your father has gone before you! For when I was an undergraduate at Oxford I visited those in the Castle there, and reflect on it with great satisfaction to this day. Walk as prudently as you can, though not fearfully, and my heart and prayers are with you."

His father advised them to lay their plans before any clergyman who had the oversight of the prisoners. In obedience to this advice, Wesley waited upon Mr. Gerrard, the Bishop of Oxford's chaplain, who had the spiritual care of any condemned prisoners. He heartily approved of their visits and of John Wesley's intention of preaching at the prison once a month. Soon afterwards he also communicated to them the Bishop's satisfaction with their work. Thus encouraged, they laboured with fresh zeal. Their numbers did not grow fast. A year after John Wesley's return to Oxford there were only five members in the Holy Club. Some, no doubt, had joined them and withdrawn. Mr. Kirkham, of Merton, reported to his friends that he was much rallied for his connection with them, and that the Club had become a common subject of mirth at his college. So far were the young Methodists from any desire to offend the prejudices of the University that Wesley at once wrote to his father for further advice.

Never does the father of the Wesleys appear to greater advantage than in the counsels which he gave. "I question," he says on December 1st, 1730, "whether a mortal can arrive to a greater degree of perfection than steadily to do good, and for that very reason patiently and meekly to suffer evil. Bear no more sail than is necessary, but steer steady." The outcry still continued. The young Methodists quietly asked both friends and opponents whether it did not concern all men to imitate Him who went about doing good. If so, had they not a clear call to visit the poor, the sick, and the prisoners that they might do them all the good that lay in their power? Mr. Gerrard, the Bishop's chaplain, formed a high estimate of Wesley. He told George Lascelles, who was an opponent of the Methodists, that Wesley "would one day be a standard-bearer of the Cross, either in his own country or beyond the seas." * A Miss Potter, probably the daughter of the Bishop of Oxford, read with Wesley, and was under the influence of Oxford Methodism for a time.†

To their deep sorrow, Morgan went home to Ireland in consumption. This devoted young man, who had "broken the ice" for the Wesleys, and led them to engage in those works of charity which they delighted to fulfil for nearly sixty years, died in peace on August 26th, 1732. "He kept several children at school, and when he found beggars in the street he would bring them into his chambers and talk to them." Mr. Gambold, who gives these particulars, joined the little Society about six months before his death, and was greatly impressed by "his calm and resigned behaviour, hardly curbing in a confident joy in God." Samuel Wesley, jun.,‡ wrote

* *Methodist Magazine*, 1832, p. 793.

† *Wesleyan Times*, October 1st, 1866.

‡ Moore, i., 192.

some "In Memoriam" verses, which beautifully describe his zeal and devotion :—

> No fair occasion glides unheeded by;
> Snatching the golden moments as they fly,
> He, by few fleeting hours, ensures eternity.*

Morgan died early, but his care for the poor and for the prisoner was the legacy which he left to his friends the Oxford Methodists. His impress is thus stamped on every page of Methodism. Robert Kirkham, son of a Gloucestershire clergyman, left Oxford to become his uncle's curate in 1731. The Wesleys were now the only members of the first group. But others were added to the circle. John Gambold, afterwards a Moravian bishop, had come up to Oxford from the country determined to find some religious friend. One day an old acquaintance entertained him with some sketch of the whimsical Mr. Charles Wesley. This account had a different effect from that which was intended. Gambold began to think that Charles Wesley might be a good Christian. He at once went to his room, and became his fast friend. He was afterwards introduced to John Wesley, and cast in his lot with the despised Methodists. Benjamin Ingham, their companion in the mission to Georgia, joined them in the year Morgan died. Thomas Broughton, afterwards secretary of the Society for Promoting Christian Knowledge, became a member of the Society the same year. John Clayton was added to their number in the spring of 1732. Mr. Rivington, the bookseller, had mentioned him to the two Wesleys when they called at his shop in London, seven or eight months before, but they did not make his acquaintance till Clayton met John Wesley in the street, and introduced himself, giving Mr. Rivington's

* John Wesley's Works, i., 15.

"service." Clayton first suggested that the friends should observe the fasts of the Church, a suggestion they at once adopted. James Hervey, whose works once enjoyed such popularity, joined the brotherhood somewhat later than Clayton. Two or three pupils of Wesley and Clayton and one of Charles Wesley's also became members of the Society.

The most important addition was made on the eve of the mission to Georgia. George Whitefield had come up to Oxford strongly prepossessed in favour of the Methodists. He greatly admired their devotion, and wished to join them, but no opportunity offered. At last, hearing that a poor woman in one of the workhouses had attempted to cut her throat, he sent the news to Charles Wesley. The messenger, an old apple-woman, was strictly charged not to mention his name, but happily she did not observe her instructions. Charles Wesley at once invited Whitefield to breakfast with him next morning. In this remarkable way that life-long friendship commenced which contributed so greatly to the Evangelical Revival. Whitefield joined the Society, and soon won a convert of his own. He gives * an interesting sketch of the circumstances which kept down the numbers of the Oxford Methodists. Some fell away in time of temptation; others were turned aside by the displeasure of a tutor or the head of a college; whilst the "change of gown" consequent on a higher degree, and the fear of reproach, led many more to forsake the little company

No sketch of the Oxford Methodists would be complete without some reference to Wesley's self-denying charity. The members of the Holy Club were accustomed to give away each year whatever remained after they had made

* Jackson's "C. Wesley," i., 25.

provision for their own necessities. Many friends also contributed every quarter to their relief fund. This was employed to release those confined for small debts, or to purchase books, medicine, and other things needed for their work. When they found any poor family that deserved help, they saw them at least once a week, sometimes gave them money, read to them, and examined their children.

Wesley was foremost in all this good work. "I abridged myself," he says, "of all superfluities, and many that are called necessaries of life." * This self-denial was practised at a time when he was far from robust. His brother Samuel, who visited Oxford in the spring of 1732, afterwards wrote a poetical epistle, in which he asks :—

> Does John seem bent beyond his strength to go,
> To his frail carcase literally foe,
> Lavish of health, as if in haste to die,
> And shorten time, t' ensure eternity ? †

When he had an income of thirty pounds a year he lived on twenty-eight, and gave away two. Next year he received sixty pounds, and gave thirty-two in charity. By limiting his expenses to the same sum, he was able to give away sixty-two pounds the third year, and ninety-two the fourth. One cold winter's day a young girl, one of those whom the Methodists maintained at school, came to his room. He noticed her thin linen gown and her half-starved look, and inquired if she had no clothes more suitable for winter wear. When he learned that she had not, he put his hand in his pocket, but found that he had scarcely any money. Immediately he thought, "Will thy Master say, 'Well done, good and faithful

* Works, i., 99. † *Ibid.*, viii., 228. ‡ *Ibid.*, vii., 36.

steward? Thou hast adorned thy walls with the money which might have screened this poor creature from the cold! Oh, justice! Oh, mercy! Are not these pictures the blood of this poor creature'?"* By denying himself, Wesley was able to pay the mistress and clothe some, if not all, of the children.† There were about twenty scholars. Wesley's journal for October, 1739, shows how deeply he regretted that this useful work had afterwards been given up because there was no one to support it.

The fidelity and care with which the friends carried on their prison work is shown by a letter from Mr. Clayton to Wesley, who was then in London. It is dated August 1st, 1732. The prisoners in "Bocardo," a debtors jail above the north gate of the city, had done nothing but quarrel since Wesley left Oxford. Those in the Castle were more hopeful. The Methodists set those prisoners who were more advanced to teach the rest. All could now read tolerably well save two, one of whom read moderately; the other, a horse-stealer, knew his letters, and could spell most of the monosyllables. Two boys could say the Catechism to the end of the Commandments, and could repeat the morning and evening prayer in "Ken's Manual." Clayton had watched over the school, as well as the prison, and had obtained leave to visit St. Thomas' Workhouse twice a week. The letter mentions the prisoners by name, and shows how intimately the particulars of each case were understood by these practical philanthropists. They spared no pains to awaken better feeling and to save the prisoners from any relapse into their old habits.

Wesley's life during the last six years at Oxford was

* Works, vii., 21.

† Gambold. See Whitehead's "Wesley."

devoted to his work as a tutor and to his labours of love in connection with the Oxford Methodists. For a few months in the early part of 1730 he held a curacy eight miles from Oxford, for which he received a salary at the rate of thirty pounds a year. He was the more willing to accept this duty because it enabled him to keep his horse, which he began to fear that he must part with.* In 1731 he and Charles began to converse in Latin. They afterwards found the facility thus acquired of great advantage in their intercourse with the Moravians. The habit was kept up to the end of their lives. During the spring of this year the brothers walked over to Epworth, where they stayed three weeks, and then returned on foot to Oxford. This visit taught them that four or five-and-twenty miles was an easy and safe day's journey in hot weather as well as cold, and that it was easy to read as they walked for ten or twelve miles without feeling faint or weary.† Mr. Kirkham assured them, on the word of a priest and a physician, that if they would take the same medicine once or twice a year, they would never need any other to save them from their family gout. They felt in every way stronger for their journey. "The motion and sun together, in our last hundred and fifty miles' walk, so thoroughly carried off all our superfluous humours, that we continue perfectly in health, though it has been a very sickly season."

Wesley was in London in 1731, and again in the summer of 1732, when he was chosen a member of the Society for the Propagation of Christian Knowledge. During the latter visit he went over to Putney to see William Law, then tutor to young Mr. Gibbon, the

* *Wesleyan Times*, May 12th, 1866.
† Works, xii., 6, 11.

father of the historian. Law's books, which Wesley met with after he became Fellow of Lincoln, had produced a profound impression on his mind. By Law's advice, he now began to read the "Theologia Germanica," and other Mystic books. He admired these writings, but escaped the snare of Mysticism, and gave up reading such works even before he went to Georgia. He soon saw, in fact, that practical religion was impossible for those who lived in the dreamland of Mysticism. The Mystic writers made good works appear mean and insipid to him. He never resigned himself entirely to this quietism, nor felt able to omit what God enjoined; but yet, he wrote, as he was returning from Georgia, "I know not how, I fluctuated between obedience and disobedience. I had no heart, no vigour, no zeal in obeying, continually doubting whether I was right or wrong, and never out of perplexities and entanglements. Nor can I at this hour give a distinct account how I came back a little toward the right way; only my present sense is this—all the other enemies of Christianity are triflers; the Mystics are the most dangerous; they stab it in the vitals, and its serious professors are most likely to fall by them."* In 1733 he was at Epworth twice. In the January visit his horse fell over a bridge not far from Daventry, and Wesley had a narrow escape of his life. In May he spent a Sunday with his friend Clayton, in Manchester, and then went on to see his father.

The way in which Wesley laid himself out to help his pupils may be seen in the excellent counsels on reading which he gave to one of them. "You, who have not the assurance of a day to live, are not wise if you waste a moment. The shortest way to knowledge seems

* On January 25th, 1738 (Whitehead, ii., 57).

to be this: 1. To ascertain what knowledge you desire to attain. 2. To read no book which does not in some way tend to the attainment of that knowledge. 3. To read no book which does tend to the attainment of it, unless it be the best in its kind. 4. To finish one before you begin another. 5. To read them all in such order that every subsequent book may illustrate and confirm the preceding." * He also wrote a sermon for his pupils on the duty of receiving the Lord's Supper as frequently as possible.†

The sermons which he preached before the University in 1733 and 1734 deserve notice. Of the first, on "The Circumcision of the Heart," he said in 1765‡ that it contained all that he then thought concerning salvation from all sin, and loving God with an undivided heart. The sermon in 1734 Charles Wesley describes as his brother's "Jacobite sermon," for which he was "much mauled and threatened more." § Wesley had, however, shown it to the Vice-Chancellor before he preached it, so that he was able to answer all objectors. Nothing further is known about this discourse. But Law and Clayton were both non-jurers, and Wesley may have used some expression which was misconstrued. He had already become an itinerant preacher. During the year 1734 he travelled more than a thousand miles. He had before learned to read as he walked. He now began the practice of reading on horseback, which made him a well-read man even amid the unceasing toils of later life. So incessant were his labours, and so abstemious his diet, that his health was much affected. His strength was greatly reduced, and he had frequent returns of blood-

* *Methodist Magazine*, 1850, p. 1064. † *Ibid.*, 1787, p. 229.
‡ Works, iii., 213. § Priestley's Letters, p. 15.

spitting. One night in July the hæmorrhage was so serious that it awoke him out of his sleep. The violence of this attack, and the sudden way in which it came on in the darkness, made him cry, "Oh, prepare me for Thy coming, and come when Thou wilt." His friends were greatly alarmed. But by the advice of a physician, joined with proper care and daily exercise, Wesley gradually regained his strength.*

His father's health was fast breaking up. It was evident that he could not long be spared. Anxious discussions were held as to the future of the family. The Rector wished his eldest son to take some steps to secure the next presentation to the living, but Samuel would not listen to the proposal. It was then suggested that John Wesley should become Rector of Epworth. This arrangement would preserve their old home, endeared by nearly forty years of family life.† The Rector had spent much money on rebuilding the Parsonage and improving his glebe. He was, therefore, anxious that it should not pass out of the family. He was solicitous for his parishioners also. He mentions some "mighty Nimrod," the prospect of whose succession was almost enough to bring down his grey hairs with sorrow to the grave. The people had a "great love and longing for John." Considerable pressure was put upon him by his father, and especially by his eldest brother, to persuade him to take the living. But Wesley was clearly convinced that this was not his vocation. He puts the whole matter very forcibly in one letter,‡ "Another can supply my place at Epworth better than at Oxford, and the good done here is of a far more diffusive nature. It is a more extensive benefit to sweeten the fountain than to do the

* Moore, i., 208. † Priestley, p. 50. ‡ Works, xii., 24.

same to particular streams." This was a sufficient answer to all appeals. His work as the head of the Oxford Methodists had been rightly estimated by his father: "I hear my son *John* has the honour of being styled the *Father of the Holy Club;* if it be so, I am sure I must be the grandfather of it; and I need not say that I had rather any of my sons should be so dignified and distinguished, than to have the title of 'His Holiness.'" * In considering the advantages of his position at Oxford, Wesley gives a prominent place to the benefits which he derived from association with friends of kindred spirit. He had no trifling visitors, except about an hour in a month, when he invited some of the Fellows to breakfast. There were the workhouses and prisons to visit, the scholars to watch over; there was neither care nor uncertainty as to his income, and he had a fund of about eighty pounds, which he could use in charitable work. Such arguments for continuing at Oxford are intelligible enough. It is somewhat strange, however, to find the man on whom unbounded responsibility afterwards sat so lightly stating that the care of two thousand souls at Epworth would crush him, and that he would not be able to stand his ground for a single month against intemperance in sleeping, eating, and drinking, or against irregularity in study and general softness and self-indulgence.† Such fears serve to show John Wesley's high ideal of duty. They also prove that the man whose restless itinerancy is the marvel of all readers of the journals sacrificed his own inclinations to devote himself, body and soul, to his evangelistic work. A short time before his father's death, John Wesley seems to

* Whitehead, i., 426. † Works, i., 179.
‡ Priestley, "Letters," 21.

have yielded to the wish of his family about the living at Epworth, but he was not successful in any application he made for it.* Mr. Oglethorpe interested himself in the matter, but without result.

On April 25th, 1735, Samuel Wesley, died at the age of seventy-two. He had exhausted his strength in his efforts to finish his learned treatise on the Book of Job, which was almost through the press at the time of his death. John Wesley had spent some time in London overlooking the printing in 1734, and was able to present a copy to Queen Caroline, to whom it was dedicated, before he sailed for Georgia. John and Charles were by their father's side during his last hours. His mind and heart were at rest. He said to John, "The inward witness, son, the inward witness; this is the proof, the strongest proof, of Christianity."† The day before his death he told Charles, "The weaker I am in body the stronger and more sensible support I feel from God." His family gathered round his bed, and showed forth the Lord's death together. The dying man received the Sacrament with difficulty, but soon seemed to revive. John Wesley asked him, "Sir, are you in much pain?" He answered with a smile, "God does chasten me with pain; yea, all my bones with strong pain. But I thank Him for all; I bless Him for all; I love Him for all." He spoke many words of comfort to his family, and often laid his hands upon the head of his son Charles with the exhortation: "Be steady. The Christian faith will surely revive in this kingdom; you shall see it, though I shall not." To his daughter Emily he said, "Do not be concerned at my death; God will then begin to manifest Himself to my family." John Wesley read the Commendatory Prayer by his father's

* Priestley, "Letters," 53. † Works, xii., 100.

bed. "Now," said the dying man, "you have done all." Just before sunset he entered into rest. Three days later he was buried "very frugally, yet decently, in the church-yard, according to his own desire." A few months more, and the happy circle at the University was broken up. The devotion which had made the Oxford Methodists instant in all good works was now to pass through a sharp trial in America before it found its highest field in the labours of the Great Revival.

CHAPTER VI.

THE MISSION TO GEORGIA.

ON October 21st, 1735, John and Charles Wesley sailed for Georgia. A charter had been obtained from George II. in June, 1732, creating the narrow strip of country between South Carolina and Florida into a British colony. It lay between the river Savannah on the north and the Alabama on the south, with a coast line of rather more than sixty miles. This territory was vested in twenty-one trustees, of whom Colonel (afterwards General) Oglethorpe was the chief. As a member of Parliament, he had interested himself greatly in the sufferings of small debtors, and had obtained a committee to inquire into the state of the prisons. Many unfortunate debtors were thus released. Oglethorpe's practical sympathy led him to devise some means of support for his new constituency. The colony was thus founded for the benefit of the poor, and he became its governor. Parliament voted £10,000, the Bank of England £10,000, and before long £36,000 was raised to carry out the work.

In February, 1733, one hundred and twenty emigrants, under the care of Oglethorpe, reached the spot where Savannah now stands. A year later, a party of Protestants, driven out from Salzburg, in Germany, because they had renounced popery, settled in the colony where England had offered them an asylum. Some Scotch

Highlanders and Moravians followed. The emigrants with whom the Wesleys sailed were the fifth company that went to find a home in Georgia. Oglethorpe had returned to England after spending a year in the colony, bringing with him some of the Indians of the district, whose visit helped largely to increase public interest in the whole scheme.

Dr. Burton, of Corpus Christi College, Oxford, was one of the trustees for the colony. He was no stranger to the Oxford Methodists, and urged them to undertake a mission to Georgia. Oglethorpe, who had been a friend and correspondent of Samuel Wesley, was also anxious to secure the co-operation of his sons. John Wesley sought advice from his brother Samuel and from William Law. He also went to Manchester to consult his friend Clayton. Thence he travelled to Epworth, to lay his plan before his mother. Her answer was, "Had I twenty sons, I should rejoice if they were all so employed." Wesley therefore expressed his willingness to undertake the mission on September 18th. He was sent out by the Society for the Propagation of the Gospel in Foreign Parts, who allowed him fifty pounds a year. His motives in accepting this mission were a sincere desire to work out his own salvation and a longing to preach Christ to the Indians. He imagined that the pomp and show of the world could have no place in the wilds of America.

Charles Wesley, much against the will of his brother Samuel, accepted the position of secretary to the Governor. He was ordained just on the eve of the voyage. Benjamin Ingham, at John Wesley's express request, accompanied the brothers. Charles Delamotte, the son of a Middlesex magistrate, could not bear to be separated from Wesley. His family were greatly opposed to his going out, but at last granted a reluctant consent. These were the four friends who sailed in the *Simmonds.** At Westminster, on Tuesday afternoon, October 14th, they took boat for Gravesend, where their vessel lay. Dr. Burton, Mr. Morgan, and Mr. James Hutton accompanied them. Charles Morgan was the brother of their early friend who had broken the ice for the Wesleys at Oxford, and induced them to visit the prisoners and the sick. It is pleasant to find him filling his brother's place in this farewell scene. Mr. Tyerman says that he and Kirkham, after the Oxford days, "drift away into the great ocean of existence and leave no track behind them." Wesley's journals show, however, that he visited Morgan near Dublin in July, 1769. James Hutton had been introduced to the Wesleys at Oxford, whilst there on a visit. He invited the brothers to stay at his father's house in Westminster when they came to town. The Huttons lived in College Street, next door to the house in which Samuel Wesley resided whilst usher of Westminster School. When John Wesley came to London, a sermon he preached led to the conversion of young Hutton and his sister. James Hutton greatly wished to go to Georgia, but his parents were not willing for him to take a step which would interfere so much with his business prospects. Morgan and Hutton remained at Gravesend on Wednesday and Thursday. Each day the friends received the Lord's Supper together.

The *Simmonds* lay for a week at Gravesend after the party went on board. Mr. Oglethorpe thoughtfully assigned them two cabins in the forecastle, in order that they might have more privacy. That which the Wesleys occupied was of good size, so that the four friends could comfortably meet together in it to read and pray. They

* Or *Symond* (F. Moore's "Georgia").

found twenty-six Moravians on board, going out to the colony under the care of David Nitschman, their bishop. As soon as his friends returned to London, John Wesley began to learn German in order to converse with them. The Methodists were now busily employed. They rose at four and went to bed between nine and ten. Every moment of the day was mapped out. The first hour after they rose was given to private prayer; then they read the Scriptures, and compared them with the writings of the primitive Church. Breakfast was ready at seven. Public prayers were at eight. The friends then separated to various studies until noon. John Wesley learnt German. Charles wrote sermons. At twelve they met to pray and devise plans for the good of themselves or their fellow-passengers. Dinner was at one. John Wesley then talked with the passengers about religion until four o'clock, the hour for public prayers. From five to six was spent in retirement. At six, supper was served. John Wesley then read in his cabin to a few of the passengers, and at seven attended the Moravian service. The friends spent another hour together, and then lay down to rest on their mats and blankets. Neither the roaring of the sea nor the motion of the ship could disturb their well-earned rest.* It is evident that the little company of Methodists were as devoted to their work on board ship as at the University.

Besides the crew and the Germans, there were about eighty English passengers on board. The *Simmonds* was a vessel of two hundred and twenty tons, under the command of Captain Joseph Cornish; the other vessel, the *London Merchant*, also chartered by the trustees, was about the same size. Her captain was called John

* Works, i., 18, and "Oxford Methodists," 68.

Thomas. One of his Majesty's sloops, the *Hawk*, Captain Joseph Gascoigne, which had been ordered to proceed to Georgia for the defence of the colony from the Spaniards, sailed with them, but soon parted company under stress of weather. Mr. Oglethorpe was to have sailed in the *Hawk*, but he preferred to stay with the emigrants. He spared no pains to secure the comfort of his company. When the weather was fine he visited the *London Merchant* to see that all on board were properly cared for. The Methodist party dined at Oglethorpe's table. There were two hundred and twenty-seven passengers in the two ships.*

The vessels were detained at Cowes till December 10th. Charles Wesley, who was known to the clergyman, preached three or four times in the church during the five weeks spent here. At last they were able to set sail with forty vessels that had been becalmed like themselves. Their voyage was a succession of storms. John Wesley, ashamed of his unwillingness to die, asked himself, "How is it thou hast no faith?" The good impression already made on his mind by the humility and devotion of the Moravians was increased by their fearlessness in the tempest. He found that they were delivered from the spirit of fear, as well as from pride, anger, and revenge. Whilst they were singing a psalm the sea broke over the vessel, split the main sail in pieces, and poured in between the decks as if the great deep had already swallowed them up. The Germans calmly sang on. Even the women and children were not afraid to die. Their spirit made the deeper impression on Wesley because the English passengers were trembling and screaming with terror. It was too good an opportunity to be lost. He went about

* F. Moore's "Voyage to Georgia."

among his own countrymen trying to show them the difference between him that feareth God and him that feareth Him not.

On the 5th of February, 1736, the *Simmonds* sailed into the Savannah river. Next morning, at eight, the emigrants set foot on American soil. Wesley and his friends knelt down with the Governor to thank God for their safety amid all the perils of the sea. Mr. Oglethorpe then took boat for Savannah, leaving the emigrants to assemble on shore and await his return. Next day he was with them again. Mr. Spangenberg, a Moravian minister from Savannah, came with him. Wesley sought his advice about his own work. Spangenberg asked him a few questions. His first inquiry, "Does the Spirit of God bear witness with your spirit that you are a child of God?" surprised Wesley so that he did not know what to answer. The German observing this, asked, "Do you know Jesus Christ?" He paused, and said, "I know He is the Saviour of the world." "True," was the reply; "but do you know He has saved you?" Wesley answered, "I hope He has died to save me." Spangenberg only added, "Do you know yourself?" Wesley replied, "I do." "But I fear they were vain words," is his comment. Wesley's heart clave to this faithful friend. He made many inquiries about the Moravian Church at Hernhuth, and spent much time in the company of the German settlers.

The scene of Wesley's ministry was the town of Savannah, which lay on an eminence forty or fifty feet above a bend of the fine river, which at that point was about a thousand feet across. The settlement was a mile and a quarter in circumference. It had forty houses, all of the same size, belonging to the first settlers, and a hundred to a hundred and fifty built more recently, some of which were two or even three stories high. Their planed boards and a coat of paint gave an air of comfort to these homes.* The Court House served as a church. Wesley found Mr. Quincy, the minister whom he was to succeed, still in Savannah, so that he did not get possession of his wooden parsonage until the middle of March. He lived on board the *Simmonds* for three weeks; then he and Mr. Delamotte lodged with the Germans. During these first weeks Wesley had some pleasant intercourse with the Indians, who gave him a very hearty reception. He hoped that God had a great work for him to do amongst them.

On Sunday, March 7th, Wesley began his ministry at Savannah by preaching on the Epistle for the day, the thirteenth chapter of the First Epistle to the Corinthians. He described the death-bed of his father at Epworth, and another death-bed which he had seen in Savannah. The people crowded into the church, and listened with deep seriousness and attention to their new pastor. Such was the general interest awakened by his ministry that ten days later a ball arranged by a gentleman had to be given up. The church was full for prayers, whilst the ball-room was almost empty. The influence which he exerted may also be seen from another incident. A lady assured him when he landed that he would see as well-dressed a congregation as most he had seen in London. Wesley found that she was right. He soon began to expound the Scriptures which relate to dress with a forcible application. From that time he saw neither gold nor costly apparel in the church. The ladies of his congregation were generally dressed in plain linen or woollen.† About seven hundred people were

* F. Moore's "Georgia," p. 24.

† Works, xi., 474.

under his pastoral care.* Savannah itself had about 518 inhabitants.† The Parsonage, which comfortably accommodated Wesley and his friends, had many conveniences, with a good garden. Charles Wesley and Ingham went on to Frederica, a hundred miles south of Savannah; John Wesley and Delamotte remained in Savannah. Before the end of the month Wesley had arranged weekly Communion and morning and evening prayers. Delamotte had begun to teach a few orphan children. Their work was interrupted by the arrival of Ingham from Frederica with news of Charles Wesley's painful situation. Neither the form nor the power of godliness existed among the settlers there. They had slandered Charles Wesley to the Governor, and Mr. Oglethorpe had weakly allowed himself to deal most harshly with his secretary. Charles Wesley was denied even the commonest comforts, and his life was in peril through the malice of his unscrupulous enemies. John Wesley and Delamotte started in haste to Frederica, whilst Ingham remained in charge of the church and school at Savannah. The troubles at Frederica were greatly relieved by this visit, but little could be done in such a soil. By the middle of May business brought Charles Wesley to Savannah, and John took his place for five weeks in Frederica. He laboured with great zeal, but with small success. After Charles Wesley sailed for England in August, 1736, John Wesley spent some days in Frederica. He found less prospect than ever of doing good. Many of the people were "extremely zealous and indefatigably diligent" to hinder the work, and few of those who were of a better mind durst show their feeling for fear of the displeasure of the opponents. He says, "After having beaten the air in this unhappy place for

* Tyerman, i., 142

† Works, xii., 16

twenty days, on January 26th, 1737, I took my final leave of Frederica. It was not any apprehension of my own danger, though my life had been threatened many times, but an utter despair of doing good there, which made me content with the thought of seeing it no more."

Wesley's labours were now confined to Savannah. He had less prospect than ever of preaching to the Indians, for which purpose alone he had gone to America. The trustees for the colony had appointed him minister of Savannah without his knowledge, but he only consented to hold that post until the way opened for his mission to the heathen. The serious parishioners had importunately urged him to watch over them a little longer till some one could supply his place, and he was the more willing to accede to this request because the Indians were engaged in wars, which left them no time, they said, to listen to the Gospel. At the end of February, 1737, Mr. Ingham started for England to enlist fresh workers for the mission. By his hands Wesley forwarded a letter of thanks for the parochial library sent out by Dr. Bray and his associates to Savannah. In it he gives an account of the school which Mr. Delamotte conducted. There were thirty or forty children, who learned to read, write, and cast accounts. Before morning school, and also after the work of the day was over, Delamotte catechised the younger children; in the evening the older scholars were instructed. Mr. Wesley catechised all on Saturday afternoon, and on Sunday before evening service. Immediately after the Second Lesson a select number of the scholars repeated their Catechism in the church. Wesley afterwards explained and applied what had been repeated both to the children and the congregation. Some of the boys in Delamotte's school were inclined to despise those who came without shoes or stockings. Wesley, therefore, took his friend's post, and went to his work barefoot. The boys were amazed, but Wesley kept them to their books, and before the end of the week had cured them of their vanity. The pains taken with the children bore good fruit. On Whit-Sunday, 1737, four of them, who had been carefully trained every day for several weeks, were admitted to the Communion at their own earnest and repeated desire. Their zeal stirred up many of their companions. The children began to attend more carefully to the teaching, and a remarkable seriousness appeared in their whole behaviour and conversation.

Wesley's later Sundays in America were full of work. He read prayers in English from five to half-past six, at nine in Italian to a few Vaudois. From half-past ten to half-past twelve he had an English service, with sermon and Communion. At one he held a French service, at two instructed the children, at three read evening prayers. After this Wesley joined with as many as his largest room would hold in reading, prayer, and praise, and at six attended the Moravian service, "not as a teacher, but a learner." On Saturdays he read prayers in French and German in two neighbouring settlements. In cases of serious illness he visited the sick every day. His work in Savannah won him general respect. He says that he had ease, honour, and abundance—what he neither desired nor expected in America.

A fortnight later the storm began to burst. On Sunday, August 7th, he says, "I repelled Mrs. Williamson from the Holy Communion." This lady was the niece of Mr. Causton, the storekeeper and chief magistrate of Savannah. During the voyage to America, Mr. Oglethorpe had been much struck with Wesley's ability, and felt that, if it were not for what he regarded as his religious enthusiasm, he might greatly help him in the colony. He tried, therefore, to get Wesley married. Miss Sophia Hopkey, Mr. Causton's niece, was the lady whom he thought most eligible. She was beautiful, elegant in her manners, and intelligent. Wesley was introduced to her a month after his arrival in Georgia. Miss Hopkey afterwards went to Frederica. John Wesley wrote about her to his brother on March 22nd. "I conjure you," he says, "spare no time, no address or pains, to learn the true cause of the former distress of my friend. I much doubt you are in the right. God forbid that she should again, in like manner, miss the mark. Watch over her; help her as much as possible. Write to me how I ought to write to her." *

When Wesley visited Frederica in October he found that her religious life had suffered much in that uncongenial place. "Even poor Miss Sophy was scarce the shadow of what she was when I left her. I endeavoured to convince her of it, but in vain; and to put it effectually out of my power so to do, she was resolved to return to England immediately. I was at first a little surprised, but I soon recollected my spirits and remembered my calling." After speaking of his efforts for the people he adds: "My next step was to divert Miss Sophy from the fatal resolution of going to England. After several fruitless attempts I at length prevailed; nor was it long before she recovered the ground she had lost." The young lady became his comforter when the Governor returned from an expedition and took no notice of Wesley. When he mentioned this to her she said, "Sir, you encouraged me in my greatest trials; be not discouraged yourself. Fear nothing; if Mr. Oglethorpe will not, God will help you." Two days later they took

* Whitehead, ii., 15.

boat together for Savannah. They were six days on the way. Mr. Wesley significantly describes it as "a slow and dangerous, but not a tedious passage."

Miss Sophy took every opportunity of being in Wesley's company. She begged him to assist her in her French, and when he was laid by with a fever, brought on by his yielding to Oglethorpe's wish that he should show the people that he did not consider it wrong to eat animal food, she waited on him day and night during his five days' illness. She consulted Oglethorpe as to the dress which would be most pleasing to the young clergyman, who disliked all gaudy attire. Henceforth she always dressed in white. In December, 1736, Wesley advised her to sup earlier, and not immediately before she went to bed. He says, "She did so, and on this little circumstance what an inconceivable train of circumstances depend!—not only 'all the colour of my remaining life' for her, but perhaps all my happiness too, in time and in eternity." So far all seemed to favour a marriage between Wesley and this young lady. On February 5th, however, difficulties arose. It was not till another month had passed that Wesley became convinced that he ought not to marry Miss Hopkey. His friend, Mr. Delamotte, asked him if he intended to marry her, and plainly showed him the lady's art and his own simplicity. Delamotte's suspicions led Wesley to consult the Moravian bishop who had come over in the *Simmonds*. Bishop Nitschman said that the matter needed to be carefully weighed, but expressed no opinion at the moment. Some time after Wesley resolved to lay the case before the Elders of the Moravian Church. When he entered the house where they were assembled he found Delamotte with them. He explained the purpose for which he had come. The Bishop answered that they had considered his case, and asked whether he would abide by their decision. Wesley, after some hesitation, replied that he would. "Then," said Nitschman, "we advise you to proceed no further in this business." Wesley meekly said, "The will of the Lord be done." He behaved with great caution, though he clearly saw what pain the change in his conduct gave to Miss Hopkey. He determined, by God's grace, to pull out his "right eye." But he could not yet find courage for the painful task. The lady, however, helped him. She became engaged to Mr. Williamson, one of the settlers, a young "man of substance," * on March 8th, and married him four days later. The husband, to quote Wesley's description, was "not remarkable for handsomeness, neither for greatness, neither for wit, or knowledge, or sense, and least of all for religion." Wesley made the following entry in his journal: "On Saturday, March 12th, God being very merciful to me, my friend performed what I could not."

Wesley's trouble threw fresh light on Ezekiel's bereavement. He had often thought the command not to mourn or weep at such a loss was one of the most difficult ever given, but he never really understood the difficulty till now, when, "considering the character I bore, I could not but perceive that the word of the Lord was come to me likewise." Forty-nine years afterwards the sorrow was still fresh in his mind. "I remember when I read these words in the church at Savannah, 'Son of man, behold, I take from thee the desire of thine eyes with a stroke,' † I was pierced through as with a sword, and could not utter a word more. But our comfort is, 'He that made the heart can heal the heart.'" It was a severe trial. Wesley had walked with Mr. Causton to his country lot on March 7th, and plainly felt that if God had given him such

* Coke and Moore's "Wesley," 119. † Ezek. xxiv. 16.

a retirement with the companion he desired, he might have forgotten the work for which he was born, and have set up his rest in this world.

Before long he saw that it was well he had not followed his own inclination. Mrs. Williamson was not so pious as he had supposed. On July 3rd he told her of some points in her behaviour which he thought reprehensible. She was extremely angry, said that she did not expect such treatment from him, and at the turn of the street through which they were walking home from the Communion service abruptly left him. Next day Mrs. Causton expressed regret for her niece's behaviour, and wished to have Wesley's objections in writing. He furnished these, and also wrote kindly to Mr. Causton. Five weeks later Wesley repelled Mrs. Williamson from the Communion. She had not expressed her regret for the faults which he had pointed out, nor made any promise of amendment. The storm now burst. Up to this time Wesley had worked in Savannah with great success. The people loved him; his services were well attended, and everything prospered. It is not correct to speak of his mission in Georgia as a failure. But all was changed by this faithful exercise of discipline. Mr. Causton was determined to revenge what he regarded as the insult offered to his niece. Wesley refused to answer for his conduct in a purely ecclesiastical matter before a civil court. Nevertheless he was summoned to appear. A grand jury, carefully chosen from those likely to condemn Wesley, found ten bills against him. He was charged with speaking and writing to Mrs. Williamson without her husband's consent, with repelling her from the Communion, with not declaring his adherence to the Church of England, with dividing the service on Sundays, and with other matters. The first count alone was of a civil nature, and Wesley had a complete answer to that. He had only written once to Mrs. Williamson since her marriage, and that at Mr. Causton's request, in reference to those things in her conduct which he disapproved. Wesley attended six or seven courts to answer this charge, but his enemies were careful to allow him no opportunity to clear himself. Twelve of the grand jurors who dissented from the finding of the majority sent a statement to the trustees of the colony, in which they clearly answered all the charges. As to repelling Mrs. Williamson, Wesley had often declared in full congregation that, according to the rubric, he required previous notice from any one desiring to communicate. He had actually repelled several persons for non-compliance. The other matters were either misstatements or concerned points entirely outside the province of the grand jury. The protesting minority was composed of three constables, six tithing-men, and three others. If the jury had been constituted, as it ought to have been, of the four constables and eleven tithing-men, no bill could therefore have been found against Wesley. An account of the colony, published in 1741,* shows Causton's tyranny and insolence in a very clear light. He threatened juries, contradicted his colleagues on the bench, and was perfectly intoxicated with power. He was, in fact, a man of no position or character, who had left England because of some charge in connection with the revenue.

When it became clear that he would not be allowed to justify himself, Wesley consulted his friends whether he should not return at once to England. He was not able to preach to the Indians, and felt that he could do Georgia greater service by representing the true state of things to the trustees than by remaining at Savannah. His friends

* Jackson, "C. Wesley," i., 94.

all agreed that he ought to go, but not yet. This was on October 7th. Meanwhile his enemies continued to plot against him. On November 22nd, Mr. Causton went so far as to read some affidavits to Wesley, in which it was stated that he had abused Mr. Causton in his own house, calling him a liar and a villain. All Wesley's friends now felt that the time for his departure had come. He at once told Mr. Causton that he intended to leave Savannah immediately, and put an advertisement in the Great Square stating that he would shortly sail for England, and asking that those who had borrowed books from him would return them as soon as convenient. On December 2nd, two hours before he was to set out for Carolina, the magistrates sent for him, and told him he must not leave the colony, because he had not answered the allegations. Wesley easily disposed of this frivolous attempt to put him in the wrong, and refused to give bail for his appearance at their court. They then issued an order requiring all officers of the colony to prevent his departure. This step was simply taken to save appearances; the magistrates were only too glad to be relieved of the presence of a faithful reprover whom they could neither silence nor intimidate. As soon as evening prayers were over, about eight o'clock on Friday, December 2nd, 1737, Wesley took boat, with three friends, for Carolina, on his way to England.

Mr. and Mrs. Williamson and their son, who was intended for the Church, are mentioned by a correspondent of the *Gentleman's Magazine*,* who seems to have met them some years before at their house in Smith Street, Westminster. This writer had gone out to Georgia as a boy in the same ship as Mr. Williamson.

* 1792, p. 24.

He lodged at Mr. Causton's, attended Wesley's early morning prayers, and tells us that he himself was not insensible to the beauty and virtues of Miss Hopkey. Wesley had gone out as a missionary, with an allowance of £50 from the Society for the Propagation of the Gospel. He did not wish to accept even this small amount. He sent the trustees an account of a year's expenses for Mr. Delamotte and himself, which, deducting extraordinary charges, such as the repairs of the Parsonage and journeys to Frederica, amounted only to £44 4*s.* 4*d.* He wished to take nothing more than this, but yielded to the advice of his brother Samuel, who pointed out it might be unjust to his successor to refuse, and that he might give his stipend away as he thought good. During the troubles of his last weeks in Savannah ten pounds arrived from the Vice-Provost of Eton. Wesley says he had been for several months without a shilling in the house, but not without peace, health, and contentment. He had given up animal food and wine before the *Simmonds* left Gravesend, and had confined himself chiefly to rice and biscuit. This course he followed in Georgia. Oglethorpe, as we have seen, once invited him to dinner, and begged that he would show those who reported that he held it wrong to eat animal food and drink wine that they were mistaken. Wesley complied, and was in consequence seized by a fever, which laid him aside for five days. With this exception he enjoyed splendid health in Georgia. The warm climate entirely cured him of the spitting of blood, which had lasted several years.* He continued to eat little, and carefully limited his hours of sleep. He was incessantly at work, visiting, preaching, and teaching the children. He took part of the three hundred acres of

* Works, iii., 402.

glebe land at Savannah to form a good garden, and frequently worked in it with his own hands. During his journeys in the colony he often slept all night in the open air, exposed to all the dews that fell; sometimes he was wet through with dew and rain, but he never took any harm from the exposure. He wore Indian shoes, and slept rolled up in a blanket.* Though he travelled through places infested with wild beasts, he would never carry a weapon. He said that he had a cane to try the depth of the rivers through which he had to wade, but would not have a ferrule at the end of it lest it should look like a weapon.†

After a trying journey of ten days, Wesley reached Charlestown. The party lost their way in the woods, and suffered greatly from cold and hunger. Mr. Delamotte, who had joined Wesley on the way, stayed with him some days. He then returned to Savannah. On the 22nd December Wesley went on board the *Samuel*, Captain Percy, bound for England. One of his parishioners from Savannah, a young gentleman who had been a few months in Carolina, and a Frenchman, sailed with him. At first he suffered much from the motion of the vessel, but a return to his old diet soon relieved him. There were about twenty souls on board. All received Wesley's counsels kindly. He felt strangely reluctant to speak to them at first, and even went among the sailors for several days intending to do so without being able. At last he took courage, and spoke to every one on board. To the Frenchman, who had no one else with whom he could converse, Wesley read and explained a chapter in the New Testament every morning. He also taught two negroes and instructed the

* *Westminster Magazine*, 1792, p. 24.
† Reynolds' "Anecdotes," p. 37.

cabin-boy. His leisure was spent in abridging M. de Renty's life, which he finished on 6th January. The vessel met a hurricane in the middle of the month, but made a good passage. On Wednesday morning, February 1st, 1738, Wesley landed safely at Deal, at half-past four.

This voyage was a time of great heart-searching. On Sunday, January 8th,* Wesley was clearly convinced of unbelief. He had not the faith in Christ that preserves from fear. St. Cyprian's Works, which he read during his voyage, delivered him from the vain desire of solitude, by which he had long hoped to make himself a Christian. He was still troubled by the fear of death. He had shown his faith by his works, giving all his goods to the poor, and following after charity. But if a storm arose, he began to doubt. What if the Gospel were not true, if all his zeal and suffering had been in vain? "I went to America to convert the Indians, but oh! who shall convert me?" This was the burden of his soul in the hour when fear of death terrified him. He closes his Georgian journal with that painful summary of the lessons of his mission:—"It is now two years and almost four months since I left my native country in order to teach the Georgian Indians the nature of Christianity. But what have I learned myself in the meantime? Why (what I the least of all suspected), that I, who went to America to convert others, was never myself converted to God." He speaks, as St. Paul spoke to the Corinthians, of his labours and sufferings, but confesses that these did not entitle him to be called a Christian. He had learned in the ends of the earth that he was fallen short of the glory of God. He now desired with all his heart to find that faith which would deliver him from fear and doubt, and bring the sensible assurance of acceptance with God.

* Works, xii., 33.

The blessing for which Wesley longed was near at hand. We cannot altogether accept his statements in this review of the past. He himself saw things in their true light some years later, when, in republishing his journals, he added four brief notes. "I, who went to America to convert others, was never myself converted to God," is his statement. His note, "I am not sure of this," expresses the feeling with which we read his words. "I am a child of wrath," is his groan on the ocean. "I believe not," is the later verdict. "I had," he says, in another note, "even then the faith of a *servant*, though not that of a *son*." The blessing of confidence in God, which he craves, is truly described as "the faith of a son." Wesley was only able to read his own history aright when all things had become new. He was still in darkness, but yet a few more steps, and he knew the joyful sound, and walked in the light of God's countenance.

Whitefield, who landed in Georgia on May 7th, 1738, bears emphatic testimony to the results of his friend's mission. "The good Mr. John Wesley has done in America is inexpressible. His name is very precious among the people, and he has laid a foundation that I hope neither men nor devils will ever be able to shake. Oh that I may follow him as he has followed Christ!" *

* Whitefield's "Journals."

CHAPTER VII.

PREPARATION FOR THE GREAT REVIVAL.

WESLEY read prayers and expounded a portion of Scripture to a large company at Deal before he set out for London. He reached "Feversham" on the same evening. He now caught his first glimpse of English life after his absence in America, and of the need for a great revival of true religion in his native land. "I here read prayers, and explained the Second Lesson, to a few of those who were called Christians, but were, indeed, more savage in their behaviour than the wildest Indians I have yet met with." He expected a cold reception from Mr. Delamotte's family at Blendon, but he no sooner mentioned his name than their welcome constrained him to say, "Surely God is in this place, and I knew it not!" His brother Charles, who had been in England for fourteen months, had prepared the way for him here. Mrs. Delamotte and her whole family had been won over. She had been indignant with the Wesleys because her son Charles had gone with them to Georgia, but some weeks before Wesley's visit she had acknowledged that she loved her son too well. From that time her behaviour to Charles Wesley was entirely changed.

In the evening of Friday, February 3rd, 1738, Wesley was again in London. None of his friends knew of his return. When his brother Charles was told, on the

Friday afternoon, that John had come back, he could not believe it till he saw him. They met that night, when Charles learned the deplorable state of the colony. Mr. Oglethorpe, who was in England, was evidently annoyed by the unvarnished account which Wesley gave to the Board of Management. The trustees themselves were surprised to hear such news, and to learn how scanty the population was. Wesley said that he had reason to believe that some of them had not forgiven him for his statements. Mr. Oglethorpe told Charles that his brother must take care, as there was a strong spirit raised against him, and people said he had come over to do mischief to the colony. Wesley's sole purpose, of course, was to help the settlers, and he was not the man to hide any of the facts. In October the trustees removed Causton from all his offices, and refused to accept his accounts as correct.

More important events now claim attention. Among the reasons to bless God which Wesley mentions in connection with his mission to Georgia was his introduction to many members of the Moravian Church at Hernhuth, and the fact that he had learned German, Spanish, and Italian, so that his "passage was opened to the writings of holy men" in those languages. The day before he gave the trustees of Georgia an account of the colony, he met, at the house of a Dutch merchant, Mr. Weinant, Peter Böhler and two friends who had just landed from Germany. When Wesley found that they had no friends in London, he secured them lodgings near Mr. Hutton's, in Westminster, where he generally stayed whilst in London. From that time he lost no opportunity of conversing with them. Böhler was twenty-five years old. He had studied theology at the University of Jena, and had just been ordained by Zinzendorf for work in Carolina. On February 17th the Wesleys travelled to Oxford with their new friend. Wesley talked much with him, but did not understand his views, and was greatly puzzled when Böhler said, "My brother, my brother, that philosophy of yours must be purged away." Böhler, in a letter to Count Zinzendorf, gives his impressions of his new friends: "I travelled with the two brothers, John and Charles Wesley, from London to Oxford. The elder, John, is a good-natured man; he knew he did not properly believe on the Saviour, and was willing to be taught. His brother, with whom you often conversed a year ago, is at present very much distressed in his mind but does not know how he shall begin to be acquainted with the Saviour. Our mode of believing in the Saviour is so easy to Englishmen that they cannot reconcile themselves to it; if it were a little more artful, they would much sooner find their way into it." *

Wesley spent a couple of days at Oxford, where he preached at the Castle on Sunday to a numerous and serious congregation. Then he returned to London. Ten days later he saw his mother once more at Salisbury. He was just ready to start for Tiverton to visit his eldest brother, when he received a message that Charles was dying at Oxford. He set out without delay, but found, to his great relief, that the danger was past. By this means he renewed his intercourse with Böhler, who was still at Oxford, and had been at Charles Wesley's side in his illness. "By him," he says, "(in the hand of the great God), I was, on Sunday, the 5th" (March, 1738), "clearly convinced of unbelief, of the want of that faith whereby alone we are saved." Wesley immediately concluded that he was unfit to preach. He consulted Böhler, who urged him to go on. "But what can I preach?" said

* *Wesleyan Magazine*, 1854, p. 687.

Wesley. "Preach faith *till* you have it," said his friend; "and then, *because* you have it, you *will* preach faith." This sound advice Wesley followed. It is interesting to know that the first person to whom he offered salvation by faith was a prisoner who lay under sentence of death at the Castle. Here, in the place to which his friend Morgan had introduced him more than seven years before, he began his work as a preacher of the righteousness of faith. The incident is the more remarkable because Böhler had many times asked Wesley to speak to this man, but he had refused because he was a zealous assertor of the impossibility of a death-bed repentance. Wesley's prejudices were yielding at last.

A short journey to Manchester, which he took in the middle of March with his friend Mr. Kinchin, Dean and Fellow of Corpus Christi College, another Oxford Methodist, shows how carefully he embraced every opportunity of doing good. All hearts seemed to open to him and his friend. They had prayer at the inns, and spoke to the servants as well as to those whom they met on their journey, with the happiest effect. Peter Böhler had returned from London when they again reached Oxford. He amazed Wesley more and more by his description of the holiness and happiness which are the fruits of living faith. Wesley began to read the Greek Testament again that he might judge whether this teaching was of God. He and Mr. Kinchin visited the condemned prisoner. They prayed with him, first using several forms of prayer, and "then in such words as were given" them at the moment. The man, who had knelt down in great heaviness, rose up after a time, saying eagerly, "I am now ready to die. I know Christ has taken away my sins; and there is no more condemnation for me.' Soon afterwards he died in perfect peace

Up to this time, in every religious Society he visited, Wesley had been accustomed to use a collect or two, then the Lord's Prayer. Afterwards he expounded a chapter in the New Testament, and concluded with three or four collects and a psalm. On the Saturday after the scene in the Castle, his heart was so full in a meeting of Mr. Fox's Society that he could not confine himself to the forms of prayer generally used. "Neither do I purpose," he adds, "to be confined to them any more, but to pray indifferently, with a form or without, as I may find suitable to different occasions." This marks a notable step in Wesley's preparation for his evangelistic work.

Before the end of April he was convinced that Böhler's views on the nature and fruits of faith were truly Scriptural. As yet he could not understand how it could be instantaneous, but, to his astonishment, the Acts of the Apostles showed that nearly all the conversions there described were instantaneous. He was ready to conclude that such wonders were only wrought in the first ages of Christianity, but the testimony of several living witnesses taught him that God still wrought thus in many hearts. "Here ended my disputing," he says; "I could now only cry out, 'Lord, help Thou my unbelief!'" Wesley found his friends as much prejudiced against instantaneous conversions as he himself had been. When he spoke on the subject at Blendon, Charles Wesley was very angry, and told him he did not know what mischief he had done by talking thus. Both of the brothers refer to the conversation in their journals. Charles says, "We sang, and fell into a dispute whether conversion was gradual or instantaneous. My brother was very positive for the latter, and very shocking: mentioned some late instances of gross sinners believing in a moment. I was much offended at his worse than unedifying discourse. Mrs. Delamotte left us abruptly. I stayed, and insisted, a man need not know when first he had faith. His obstinacy in favouring the contrary opinion drove me at last out of the room. Mr. Broughton was only not so much scandalised as myself." Wesley had struggled too long with his own doubts to be impatient with those who had not yet reached the same position as himself. He adds to his own account of his brother's indignation at this discussion the significant words, "And, indeed, it did please God then to kindle a fire, which, I trust, shall never be extinguished."

Wesley was recalled from Oxford on the 1st of May by the return of his brother's illness. He found Charles at the house of James Hutton, near Temple Bar. Here, on the same evening, a little Society, formed by the advice of Böhler, met for the first time. It was afterwards transferred to Fetter Lane. The Wesleys were closely associated with it until the excesses of the Moravian teachers compelled them to withdraw. The friends agreed to meet every week, to form themselves into bands of five to ten members, and to speak freely to each other about their religious life. The bands were to have a general meeting every Wednesday evening, and a lovefeast once a month on a Sunday evening from seven to ten. All who wished to join the Society were to remain on trial for two months. Two days after the Society was formed Charles Wesley was convinced by a long and particular conversation with Böhler of the true nature of evangelical faith. Next day this friend, who had been so greatly blessed to the brothers, embarked for Carolina. Wesley says, "Oh, what a work hath God begun since his coming into England, such an one as shall never come to an end till heaven and earth pass away!"

The brothers were now resolutely seeking after this living faith. Their friend Mr. Stonehouse, the Vicar of Islington, was also convinced of the truth. On Whit-Sunday, rather more than a fortnight after Böhler left London, Charles Wesley found the joy and peace he sought. He was suffering from another attack of his pleurisy. Just as he was about to remove from James Hutton's to his father's, Mr. Bray, "a poor, ignorant mechanic," who knew nothing but Christ, came to see him. Charles felt that he was sent to supply Böhler's place, and removed to his house in Little Britain instead of going to Westminster. Here he found peace. John Wesley and some friends had visited him on the morning of Whit-Sunday, and had sung a hymn to the Holy Ghost. Afterwards John went to hear Dr. Heylyn, the popular Rector of St. Mary-le-Strand. He was well known to the Doctor, in concert with whom it had been arranged that he should prepare an edition of A Kempis. His friend and counsellor, William Law, had also been Heylyn's curate in the days when he was such "a gay parson that Dr. Heylyn said his book" ("The Serious Call") "would have been better if he had travelled that way himself." * Wesley assisted the Doctor with the Communion, as his curate was taken ill in the church. After this service he heard the surprising news that his brother had found rest to his soul.

Wesley remained in much heaviness until the following Wednesday, May 24th, 1738. At five that morning he opened his Testament on the words, "There are given unto us exceeding great and precious promises." In the afternoon some one asked him to go to St. Paul's. The anthem was, "Out of the deep have I called unto Thee, O Lord. . . . O Israel, trust in the Lord, for with the Lord there is mercy, and with Him is plenteous redemption. And He shall redeem Israel from all his sins."

* Byrom's "Journals," i., 523.

That evening he went very unwillingly to a Society in Aldersgate Street where some one was reading Luther's preface to the Epistle to the Romans. "About a quarter before nine, while he was describing the change which God works in the heart through faith in Christ, I felt my heart strangely warmed. I felt I did trust in Christ, Christ alone, for salvation; and an assurance was given me, that He had taken away *my* sins, even *mine*, and saved *me* from the law of sin and death." Wesley at once began to pray earnestly for his enemies, and publicly testified to all present what he now felt. He was much tempted when he returned home, but when he prayed the temptations fled. He soon found how different they were from his former struggles. Then he was sometimes, if not often, conquered; now he was always conqueror.

Charles Wesley's journal gives us a happy description of this memorable night: "Towards ten, my brother was brought in triumph by a troop of our friends, and declared, 'I believe.' We sang the hymn with great joy, and parted with prayer." "The hymn" was one Charles Wesley had composed the previous day on his own conversion. He had laid it aside for fear of pride, but resumed it when Mr. Bray encouraged him "to proceed, in spite of Satan." Now the brothers were able to sing it together.

> Oh, how shall I the goodness tell,
> Father, which Thou to me hast showed?
> That I, a child of wrath and hell,
> I should be called a child of God,
> Should know, should feel, my sins forgiven,
> Blest with this antepast of heaven! *

The position which Wesley now took up gave no small scandal to some of his old friends. The Huttons, of

* Hymn 30, Wesleyan Hymn Book.

Westminster, and his brother Samuel were especially troubled. Mrs. Hutton wrote to Samuel Wesley at Tiverton within a fortnight after the memorable scene at Aldersgate Street. Whilst her husband was reading a sermon of Bishop Blackall's to one of the religious Societies of the time assembled in his study, Wesley stood up and startled them by the statement that five days before he was not a Christian. Mr. Hutton answered, "Have a care, Mr. Wesley, how you despise the benefits received by the two Sacraments." Mrs. Hutton was not in the study at the time. Wesley, however, repeated his statement in the parlour, where they met for supper. Mrs. Hutton then said, "If you have not been a Christian ever since I knew you, you have been a great hypocrite, for you made us all believe that you were one." Wesley explained his meaning. "When we renounce everything but faith and get into Christ, then, and not till then, have we any reason to believe that we are Christians." The Huttons were in the parlour, with their son and daughter, their niece, two or three ladies who boarded at the house, two or three of Wesley's "deluded followers," and two or three gentlemen who knew Wesley, but did not yet share "his notions." Mrs. Hutton dreaded the effect on her own children, who reverenced Wesley so greatly. She calls him "my son's pope."

Though Wesley had now attained to the righteousness of faith, his mind was not fully at rest. He was often in heaviness through manifold temptation, and was not a little perplexed by the conflicting counsels of his friends. At last he made up his mind to visit the Moravian settlement at Hernhuth. He had fully resolved on this journey before he left Georgia, and had written to Count Zinzendorf. He now saw that the time for his visit was come. "My weak mind could not bear to be thus sawn asunder. And

I hoped the conversing with those holy men, who were themselves living witnesses of the full power of faith, and yet able to bear with those that are weak, would be a means, under God, of so establishing my soul, that I might go on from faith to faith, and 'from strength to strength.'" Three weeks after his "conversion" he sailed from Gravesend to Rotterdam.

Before describing this interesting visit it is necessary to speak of Wesley's correspondence with his friend and adviser William Law. He met with Law's "Christian Perfection" soon after he became Fellow of Lincoln College, and when the "Serious Call" was published it exercised a powerful influence on his mind. He had already determined to live a religious life. He was much offended by several things in Law's books, and "had objections to almost every page,"* but they convinced him more than ever of the exceeding height, breadth, and depth of the law of God. The light flowed in upon his soul so mightily that everything appeared in a new aspect, and he determined to keep all the commandments of God.† He paid several visits to Mr. Law at Putney, and in 1734 consulted him about one of his pupils, who had lost all relish for religious duties.

After Peter Böhler left London Wesley wrote to Mr. Law. He had been trying for twelve years to order his life according to the "Serious Call;" for two years he had regularly preached after the model of Law's books. Now that the light had come, he naturally remembered his master. On May 14th, 1738, he wrote a letter in which he explained to Mr. Law how his teaching had broken down in practice. Both he and his hearers acknowledged that the Law was wonderful, but all were

* Works, viii., 366. † *Ibid.*, i., 99.

convinced that it was impossible to make it the rule of life. Wesley adds, "Under this heavy yoke I might have groaned till death had not a holy man, to whom God lately directed me, upon my complaining thereof, answered at once, 'Believe, and thou shalt be saved.'" He inquires why Mr. Law did not give him this advice, and beseeches him to consider whether the true reason was not that he did not possess this faith himself.

The last paragraph of the letter might have been softened with advantage, but Wesley would not have felt justified without speaking plainly. "Once more, sir, let me beg you to consider whether your extreme roughness and morose and sour behaviour, at least on many occasions, can possibly be the fruit of a living faith in Christ? If not, may the God of peace and love fill up what is yet wanting in you." Mr. Overton, Law's biographer,* says that "there was an asperity of manner, a curtness of expression, an impatience of everything that appeared to him absurd and unreasonable, . . . which made most men with whom he came into contact rather afraid of him." So much for the truth and meaning of the charge. There is nothing in this letter that is inconsistent with Wesley's high esteem for the man who had so greatly influenced his religious life and character. The utmost that can be said is that it is very plain speaking. But that was characteristic of Wesley, and surely twelve years of bondage to form may justify such freedom, quite apart from the more important fact that Wesley had learned the way of faith, to which he feared that his friend was still a stranger.

Law replied on May 19th. He reminds Wesley that he himself had prepared a translation of A Kempis, and asks

---

* "William Law," p. 59.

that the fault of not leading him to faith may be divided between them. He satisfactorily explains his conversation with Böhler, to which Wesley had referred. He reminds Wesley that he had put the "Theologia Germanica" into his hands, and if that book did not plainly lead to Christ, he "was content to know as little of Christianity" as Wesley was pleased to believe. This letter has been described as a triumphant answer, which clearly proves that Wesley was no match for his distinguished correspondent. But whatever Law may have felt about Christianity, he had not guided the Wesleys into the way of faith. They were groaning under the yoke till Böhler was sent to lead them into peace. That fact remains, and Law's letter did not shake Wesley's position. Wesley was far too able a reasoner to lose sight of the essential point. Hence his answer to Mr. Law, which must be acknowledged to be a complete reply. He carefully separates all extraneous questions, and quietly holds Mr. Law to the main issue, that he had not done anything to lead him to grasp that great truth "He is our propitiation, through faith in His blood." This letter is so important that a facsimile is given of the draft copy which afterwards came into the hands of the Rev. Henry Moore. The corrections show with what care Wesley prepared his reply.

Mr. Law wrote another letter,* but it calls for no special comment. Law protested against any attempt to make him responsible for defects in Wesley's knowledge. His impression of Wesley is interesting. "You seemed to me to be of a very inquisitive nature, and much inclined to meditation." For this reason he had put the "Theologia

* C. Walton's "Notes and Materials for a Biography of Law." Printed for private circulation. 1854.

Germanica" into his hands. Charles Wesley's journal for 1739 describes an interesting visit which he paid to Law, with his friend John Bray.* Law was sorry that the Methodists had not been dispersed into livings where they might have leavened the Church. Charles Wesley told him his experience. "'Then am I,' said he, 'far below you (if you are right), not worthy to bear your shoes.' He agreed to our notion of faith, but would have it that all men held it; was fully against the laymen's expounding, as the very worst thing, both for themselves and others. I told him he was my schoolmaster to bring me to Christ; but the reason why I did not come sooner to Him was my seeking to be sanctified before I was justified. . . . Joy in the Holy Ghost, he told us, was the most dangerous thing God could give. I replied, 'But cannot God guard His own gifts?' He often disclaimed advising, 'seeing we had the Spirit of God,' but mended upon our hands, and at last came almost quite over." This is a pleasant sequel to the correspondence.

In 1756 Wesley published "An Extract of a Letter to the Rev. Mr. Law." This was occasioned by some of Law's later writings, which Wesley thought erroneous and likely to lead many astray. This has been described as an "angry pamphlet," as his first letter to Law has been called an "angry letter."† Anger is far enough from both. They are calm and dispassionate throughout. Law describes it as "a juvenile composition of emptiness and pertness, below the character of any man who had been serious in religion but half a month." The pamphlet can be found in Wesley's Works,‡ and every one may judge

* Vol. i., 159.

† Overton's "English Church," ii., 72.

‡ Vol. ix., 466—509.

how far these strictures are deserved. Wesley quietly comments on various passages from Law's writings. "I have now, sir, delivered my own soul; and I have used great plainness of speech, such as I could not have prevailed on myself to use to one whom I so much respect on any other occasion." This is a fair description of a calm, well-reasoned treatise, which, notwithstanding Law's strictures on its emptiness and pertness, clearly shows what a blow that eminent writer had struck at the roots of all vital Christianity by his perilous Mysticism. Dr. Byrom, Law's devout disciple, who was also the friend of Wesley, notes in his journal,* that he urged Wesley "to repent of that wicked letter." Wesley stayed with his old friend a considerable time, and talked very freely with him, but Byrom was only able to prevail upon him to say that if he published a second edition of the letter, "he would soften some expressions in it." Two years later, in April, 1761, when Wesley was again in Manchester, Byrom returned to the subject, but could not bring Wesley to say anything more about this tract than he did on his previous visit. He added, "I do not treat him" (Law) "with contempt, as he does me." Mr. Overton † does ample justice to Wesley's position in this publication. He says, "The letter was not 'wicked,' nor 'unchristian,' nor 'ungentlemanly,' nor did it deserve the entire obliteration which Byrom suggested. The question with him would be, Is such teaching likely to do my people practical harm? And remembering that he had seen what had been the practical effect of the sort of diluted Mysticism of the London Moravians upon his people, we can hardly wonder that he concluded that

* Part ii., pp. 593, 629. † Life of Law, p. 383.

harm would be done. Hence this well-meant, if not very judicious attempt to counteract the evil."

Wesley had taught his people to read Law's "Serious Call" and his "Christian Perfection." He often referred to Law in the highest terms, as "that strong and elegant writer," "that great man," etc. In his sermon "On a Single Eye," he spoke of the "Serious Call" as "a treatise which will hardly be excelled, if it be equalled, in the English tongue, either for beauty of expression or for justness and depth of thought." These words were spoken only eighteen months before Wesley's death. His brother Charles used to call Law "our John the Baptist." He shut the brothers up under "the law of commandments contained in ordinances" till they groaned for deliverance. Many painful years might have been spared them had he acted the part of Peter Böhler, and led them to rest on the atonement of Christ for salvation. The Wesleys had a strong case against him in this respect, and John Wesley stated it fairly, with a sincere desire for the best interests of a man whom he never ceased to love and honour. His pamphlet supplied the people whom Wesley had taught to read his earlier books with a much-needed antidote to Law's later views.

Wesley's visit to the Moravian settlement of Hernhuth, on the borders of Bohemia, in 1738 gave him confidence in the teaching by which he had gained peace of mind and heart. Continental travelling was not very pleasant in those days. At Goudart several inns refused to entertain the party. With much difficulty they "at last found one, where they did us the favour to take our money for some meat and drink and the use of two or three bad beds." Ingham, Wesley's companion in Georgia, was with him. There were three other English travellers and three Germans. At Frankfort Wesley had a pleasant interview with Peter Böhler's father. At Marienborn he found Count Zinzendorf, who had hired a large house, where about ninety people of different nationalities lived together. Wesley lodged with one of the members of this community a mile from Marienborn. He had come to seek living proofs of the power of faith; people saved from inward and outward sin by "the love of God shed abroad in their hearts," and from all doubt and fear by the abiding witness of "the Holy Ghost given unto them." These witnesses he now constantly met with. He usually spent the day in talking with those who could either speak Latin or English, as he could not converse easily in German. He stayed a fortnight, heard Zinzendorf preach, and attended a conference where the Count spoke largely on justification and its fruits.

On August 1st, after a journey which illustrates the annoyances to which travellers on the Continent were exposed in those days, Wesley reached the Moravian settlement. Hernhuth lay about thirty miles from Dresden, on the border of Bohemia. About a hundred houses stood on some rising ground, with high hills at a distance. There were evergreen woods on two sides, gardens and cornfields on the others. The settlement was on the highway from Zittau to Löbau. The Orphan House stood in the middle of the one long street, an apothecary's shop below, a chapel, which would seat about six hundred people, above. At a small distance from either end of the Orphan House ran a row of houses, forming two squares. The Count's house was a small plain building, like the rest, with a large garden, in which vegetables and fruit were grown for the common use.

Wesley and his friends had a convenient lodging assigned them in the house for strangers. He found a Mr. Hermsdorf, whom he had often talked with in

Georgia; and this friend did everything in his power to make the visit useful and agreeable. Wesley zealously attended public services, lovefeasts, and conferences. Christian David, the founder of the Church at Hernhuth, came two days after Wesley reached the place. He had been converted from Popery, and had preached far and wide throughout Moravia, till his name was a household word. When persecution arose his converts found a retreat at Hernhuth. David was only a carpenter, but he was a man of great devotion and spiritual insight. Wesley heard him preach four times. Each time he chose just the topic that the English visitor would have desired him to choose. The abstract of these discourses in the journals shows with what care Wesley weighed his teaching. Christian David gave him a clear and full account of his own life and of the founding of the settlement at Hernhuth. These particulars, with the experience of other members of the community and a description of its discipline and constitution, will be found at length in Wesley's second journal. He was greatly refreshed in spirit by his sojourn at Marienborn and Hernhuth. So many living witnesses to the reality of saving faith inspired him with confidence. He could doubt no more. "I would gladly have spent my life here," he says; "but my Master calling me to labour in another part of His vineyard, on Monday, 14th, I was constrained to take my leave of this happy place; Martin Döber, and a few others of the brethren, walking with us about an hour. Oh, when shall THIS Christianity cover the earth, as the 'waters cover the sea'?"

Wesley reached London on Saturday night, September 16th, 1738, a month after he left Hernhuth. He had been absent from England three months. On Sunday he says, "I began to declare in my own country the glad tidings of salvation, preaching three times, and afterwards expounding the Scripture to a large company in the Minories." This was at the house of Mr. Sims, where Charles Wesley had preached the two previous Sunday evenings, the first time to two hundred, and the next to three hundred hearers. The brothers met each other on the night of John's arrival. "We took sweet counsel together," Charles says, "comparing our experiences." Next night also he writes, "My brother entertained us with his Moravian experiences." Charles also had much to tell. Mrs. Delamotte and her son William, who had been greatly prejudiced against the new teaching, had now received it to their own salvation. He was able to speak of Jack Delamotte, the first convert of the hymnology of the revival. In singing "Who for me, for me, hast died," he had found the words sink into his soul, and could have sung for ever, being full of delight and joy. Charles returned from Blendon in June, rejoicing that seven souls had been led to Christ by his ministry. His visits to Newgate and the hour spent under the gallows at Tyburn, which he describes as the most blessed hour of his life, all showed John what a work God had already begun. Nor was he without a share in the harvest. At Blendon, whilst Charles was reading his brother's sermon on faith, the gardener found that blessing. Next evening, when he read it again at the house of Mr. Piers, the Vicar of Bexley, "God set His seal to the truth of it, by sending His Spirit upon Mr. Searl and a maidservant, purifying their hearts by faith." Such facts show how the brothers must have rejoiced together. John had come from Germany, laden with testimonies to the power of grace. Charles had been reaping in English homes and in English prisons the success which showed that the fields were white already to harvest.

The next six months were spent between London and Oxford, with one visit to Bristol. Wesley preached in all churches that were open to him, and in various "Societies." He visited Newgate and the Castle and city prisons at Oxford. He lost no opportunity of doing good. The journals show that Wesley's mind was not yet fully established in the faith. Charles Delamotte, his old companion in Georgia, troubled him not a little. He stayed with Wesley at Oxford four or five days, and told his friend that he was still trusting in his own works, and did not believe in Christ. Wesley begged of God an answer of peace, and opened on those words, "As many as walk according to this rule, peace be on them, and mercy, and upon the Israel of God."

On the threshold of the Great Revival, a few words may be devoted to its special teaching. Throughout life Wesley was faithful to all the doctrines of the Reformation and the English Church. Repentance for sin, justification by faith, and holiness of heart and life were the constant themes of his ministry and his writings. His long bondage to doubt made him careful to show the way of acceptance. The doctrine of assurance, on which he laid such stress, appears in an alluring light in his brother's hymns and in his own sermons. Wesley rendered inestimable service by bringing out into clear light the blessed truth that no Christian need walk in darkness, but may rejoice in the assurance of acceptance with God. Entire sanctification was set in its proper light as the goal towards which every Christian should press. Wesley fixed no time and prescribed no methods for this work. He was content to urge his people to grow in grace, and to strive to gain all the mind that was in Christ.

The opening paragraphs of his "Earnest Appeal to Men of Reason and Religion" are perhaps the finest epitome of the ruling purpose of the Great Revival. The lifeless, formal religion of the time was a sad contrast to that religion of love which they had found. The love of God and all mankind "we believe to be the medicine of life, the never-failing remedy for all the evils of a disordered world, for all the miseries and vices of men. Wherever this is, there are virtue and happiness going hand in hand. There is humbleness of mind, gentleness, long-suffering, the whole image of God, and at the same time a peace that passeth all understanding, and joy unspeakable and full of glory. . . . This religion we long to see established in the world, a religion of love, and joy, and peace, having its seat in the inmost soul, but ever showing itself by its fruits, continually springing forth, not only in all innocence (for love worketh no ill to his neighbour), but likewise in every kind of beneficence, spreading virtue and happiness all around it." Wesley then shows how he and his friends had long wandered in darkness, having no man to guide them into "the straight way to the religion of love, even by faith." The blessed change it had wrought in their own souls gave them confidence in urging all to seek the same joy. "By this faith we are saved from all uneasiness of mind, from the anguish of a wounded spirit, from discontent, from fear and sorrow of heart, and from that inexpressible listlessness and weariness, both of the world and ourselves, which we had so helplessly laboured under for many years, especially when we were out of the hurry of the world and sunk into calm reflection. In this we find that love of God and of all mankind which we had elsewhere sought in vain. This, we know and feel, and therefore cannot but declare, saves every one that partakes of it both from sin and misery, from every unhappy and every unholy temper."

CHAPTER VIII.

THE BEGINNING OF THE GREAT AWAKENING.

THE condition of England when Methodism appeared has been described by all writers in the most sombre colours. Southey says, "There never was less religious feeling, either within the Establishment or without, than when Wesley blew his trumpet, and awakened those who slept." In 1732 the *Weekly Miscellany* * states that zeal for godliness looked as odd upon a man as the dress of his great-grandfather. Freethinkers' clubs flourished. In August, 1736, Dr. Byrom drank tea with Mr. Rivington, the bookseller, Wesley's friend and publisher. Rivington said that many of the young men of his parish had left off all public service and professed Deism, and that there was a visible decline in the sale of good books.† Bishop Burnet found the Ember Weeks the burden of his life. Candidates for ordination were scandalously ignorant of the Bible. Dr. Watts ‡ called upon every one to use all efforts "for the recovery of dying religion in the world." Archbishop Secker, then Bishop of Oxford, asserts "that an open and professed disregard to religion is become, through a variety of unhappy causes, the distinguishing character of the present age; that this evil is grown to a great height

---

* Tyerman, i., 217.

† Byrom's "Journals," ii., 63.

‡ Preface to his "Humble Attempt."

in the metropolis of the nation, and is daily spreading through every part of it." It had already brought in, he says, "such dissoluteness and contempt of principle in the higher part of the world, and such profligate intemperance and fearlessness of committing crimes in the lower, as must, if this torrent of iniquity stop not, become absolutely fatal." This charge was delivered in the very year the Wesleys were led into the light. In 1741 the Bishop mourns again over "this unhappy age of irreligion and libertinism." Isaac Taylor says that Methodism preserved from extinction and reanimated the languishing Nonconformity of the eighteenth century, "which, just at the time of the Methodistic revival, was rapidly in course to be found nowhere but in books." * Besides the moral and religious reformation wrought among the colliers of Kingswood and the north, as well as among the Cornish miners, the Evangelical Revival leavened the Church of England with its own spirit. The Church had grown corrupt. Its best friends mourned that the clergy laboured under more contempt than those of any other Church in Europe because they were so remiss in their labours.† They would never regain their influence, Burnet said, till they lived better and laboured more. Their preaching seemed as if its sole aim was to fit men for this world.‡ The population had doubled since the settlement of the Church under Elizabeth, towns and cities had far outgrown their old proportions, yet no endeavour had been made for any adequate increase of religious instruction. The old religion, Lecky says,§ seemed everywhere loosening around the minds of men ; and it had often no great influence even on its defenders. Montesquieu

* "Wesley and Methodism," p. 54.
† Southey's "Wesley," i., 279.
‡ Lecky, ii., 544.
§ *Ibid.*, ii., 530.

affirmed that not more than four or five of the members of Parliament were regular attendants at church.*

In 1736 every sixth house in London was a grogshop,† and the ginsellers hung out boards announcing that they would make a man drunk for a penny, dead-drunk for twopence, and find him straw to lie on till he recovered from his carouse. Cellars strewn with straw were actually provided for this purpose. Lecky gives some painful pictures of the time.‡ In 1735 the quantity of British spirits distilled was 5,394,000 gallons; twenty-one years before it was only two million, and in 1684 little more than half a million gallons. In 1742 it was more than seven millions. The London medical men stated in 1750, when more than eleven million gallons were consumed, that there were fourteen thousand cases of illness, most of them beyond the reach of medicine, that were directly attributable to the mania for gin-drinking. Parliament found this gigantic evil tax its resources to the utmost. The Mohocks—a club of young gentlemen, formed in 1712—committed the most horrible outrages in the streets of the metropolis. Neither men nor women were safe from these drunken fiends. It was a favourite amusement with them to squeeze their victim's nose flat on his face and bore out his eyes with their fingers. Their prisoners were pricked with swords or made to caper by swords thrust into their legs. Women were rolled down Snow Hill in barrels. Watchmen and constables were utterly inefficient. Robbers often defied all attempts to seize them, and kept the city in terror by day as well as by night.

* "Notes sur l'Angleterre."
† Tyerman's "Wesley," i., 62.
‡ "England in the Eighteenth Century," i., 479—491.

The great awakening was now to begin. Isaac Taylor* says, "No such harvest of souls is recorded to have been gathered by any body of contemporary men since the first century;" and on the ground of "expansive and adventurous Christian philanthropy," he holds that the founders of Methodism have no rivals. On December 11th, 1738, Wesley, who was then at Oxford, heard that Whitefield had returned from Georgia. He at once hastened to meet him. Next day he says, "God gave us once more to take sweet counsel together." When Wesley returned from Hernhuth he found that the little Society in Fetter Lane had increased from ten to thirty-two members. Here, on New Year's Day, 1739, the Wesleys, Whitefield, Ingham, Hall, Kinchin, Hutchins, and some sixty others held a lovefeast. "About three in the morning, as we were continuing instant in prayer, the power of God came mightily upon us, insomuch that many cried out for exceeding joy, and many fell to the ground. As soon as we recovered a little from that awe and amazement at the presence of His majesty, we broke out with one voice, 'We praise Thee, O God; we acknowledge Thee to be the Lord.'"

In this way the year which saw the dawn of the Revival was ushered in. Oxford Methodism gave its name to the new movement, but it knew little about the righteousness of faith which the friends had at last attained. The preachers of the Evangelical Revival were able to proclaim the acceptable year of the Lord. Oxford Methodism had no such message to deliver, and without such a message there could have been no revival. Whitefield was the pioneer in field-preaching. His popularity from the beginning of his ministry was unbounded. The whole city

* "Wesley and Methodism," pp. 130, 135.

of Bristol was stirred by his early sermons, and when he came to London the people flocked to hear him with the same eagerness. He sailed for Georgia in January, 1738, with the view of assisting Wesley. On his return to England his popularity was undiminished. He soon found, however, that he would not be allowed to preach in churches. He had come to England to collect money for his orphan-house in Georgia, but all doors were closed. When he visited Bristol he was shut out of the pulpits, and was not even allowed to preach to the inmates of the prison. Two clergymen were bold enough to offer him their churches, but the Chancellor of the diocese threatened that Whitefield should be suspended and expelled if he continued to preach in the diocese.

Whitefield felt that he had a message to deliver; thousands were eager to hear it. He remembered that his Master taught by the lake or on the mountain; and moved by this example, on February 17th, 1739, he ventured to preach to the colliers at Kingswood in the open air. There were two hundred people in his first congregation, but the second time he preached there were two thousand. Soon ten or twenty thousand gathered to hear him. A gentleman lent him a large bowling-green in the heart of Bristol, where he preached to a vast congregation. For six weeks he had glorious success. Then he wrote to Wesley, urging him to come and take charge of the work in Bristol and Kingswood, whilst he visited other places. Wesley was fully employed in London, where he was invited to expound the Scriptures in many of the religious Societies of the time as well as in the Society at Fetter Lane. He describes one week's work in a letter to Whitefield. On Sunday, February 25th, he preached first at St. Katharine's, then at Islington, where the church was crowded and very hot. "The fields, after service, were white with people praising God." At a later hour three hundred were present at a Society in the Minories; thence he went to Mr. Bray's house, and after the Society meeting at Fetter Lane, to another house, where also they "wanted room." On Tuesday evening he had meetings at four, six, and eight; on Wednesday a women's meeting; on Thursday two or three hundred met at the Savoy; on Friday a friend's parlour was more than filled, and another room was twice filled by eager listeners.*

Wesley was reluctant to leave such promising work, but Whitefield and his friend Seward urged him in the most pressing manner to come to Bristol without delay. At this time both the Wesleys were accustomed to seek for direction, as a last resort, in any emergency by opening the Bible and looking at the first text that met their eye. This strange custom they and their friends had learned from the Moravians. All the verses which Wesley thus found seemed to threaten some great disaster. Charles Wesley would scarcely suffer the journey to be mentioned, but when he opened his Bible on those words, "Son of man, behold, I take from thee the desire of thine eyes with a stroke; yet shalt thou not mourn or weep, neither shall thy tears run down," his opposition was silenced. The Society at Fetter Lane was consulted about the journey, but could reach no conclusion. At last it was decided by lot that Wesley should go to Bristol.

On Saturday, March 31st, he met Whitefield in that city. He stood in his friend's congregation next day with conflicting feelings. "I could scarce reconcile myself at first to this strange way of preaching in the fields, of which he

* Whitefield's "Journal."

set me an example on Sunday; having been all my life (till very lately) so tenacious of every point relating to decency and order, that I should have thought the saving of souls almost a sin if it had not been done in a church." The same day Whitefield left the city. Wesley spent the evening with a little Society in Nicholas Street, where he expounded the Sermon on the Mount—a pretty remarkable precedent of field-preaching, as he calls it. In this way he got ready for his first out-of-doors sermon. It was four o'clock on Monday afternoon when he "submitted to be more vile." From a little eminence in a ground adjoining the city he spoke to three thousand people from Luke iv. 18, 19: "The Spirit of the Lord is upon me, because He hath anointed me to preach the Gospel to the poor." "Is it possible," he asks, "that any one should be ignorant that it is fulfilled in every true minister of Christ?" Wesley and his hearers little thought how gloriously it would be fulfilled in himself for more than half a century.

He remained in Bristol till June 11th, 1739. He had reason to say, "Oh, how has God renewed my strength, who used ten years ago to be so faint and weary with preaching twice in one day!" He read prayers every morning at Newgate, and expounded the Scripture in one or more of the religious Societies every evening. On Monday afternoon he preached out of doors near Bristol, on Tuesday at Bath and Two Mile Hill alternately, on Wednesday at Baptist Mills, every other Thursday near Pensford, every other Friday in another part of Kingswood, on Saturday afternoon and Sunday morning at the Bowling Green. On Sunday he also preached at eleven near Hannam Mount, at two at Clifton, at five on Rose Green. After this he sometimes visited one of the Societies, and then held a lovefeast. His congregation at seven in the morning often consisted of five or six thousand people. Services like these taxed his strength to the utmost.

A few days after he reached Bristol three women agreed to meet together weekly in a little Society; four young men also met in the same way. On the 9th of May a piece of ground was taken in the Horse Fair, near St. James' Church yard, where a room was to be built large enough to contain the Societies at Nicholas Street and Baldwin Street, with their friends. Three days later the foundation stone of this first Methodist preaching-place was laid, with great thanksgiving. Wesley had appointed eleven feoffees, on whom he relied to provide funds and take charge of the work. He soon found his mistake. The trustees did nothing to raise money. The whole work was ready to stand still. Wesley took upon himself the payment of the workmen. Before he knew where he was he thus incurred a liability of more than a hundred and fifty pounds. The subscriptions did not reach forty pounds. Whitefield urged Wesley to take the building entirely into his own hands, as the feoffees would have power under the deed to turn him out if he did not preach as they wished. This was excellent advice. Wesley therefore cancelled the deed, and took the whole responsibility upon himself. Money he had not, nor any human prospect or probability of procuring it. "But I knew," he says, "'the earth is the Lord's, and the fulness thereof,' and in His name set out, nothing doubting."

Bristol witnessed many strange scenes under Wesley's ministry. These scenes did not, however, begin in that city. On January 21st, 1739, whilst he was expounding at Mr. Sims', in the Minories, all were surprised to hear a well-dressed, middle-aged woman suddenly cry out as in the agonies of death. Her cries continued some time, and she seemed in the sharpest anguish. Next day she called on Wesley, at his special request. He learned that she had been under strong conviction of sin three years before, and had suffered such distress of mind that she had no comfort or rest day or night. She consulted the clergyman of the parish, who told her husband that she was stark mad, and advised him to send for a physician. The doctor blistered and bled his patient, but could discover no remedy. Under Wesley's word she found a faint hope that He who had wounded would undertake her cause, and heal the soul which had sinned against Him. Such scenes became frequent in Bristol, both in the Society rooms and in the open air. Men and women cried out aloud under Wesley's word, as in the agonies of death. Prayer was then offered for them, and before long they were generally able to rejoice in God their Saviour. Sometimes a violent trembling seized the hearers, and they sank to the ground. At one meeting in the Baldwin Street room Wesley's voice could scarcely be heard for the groans and cries of the people. A Quaker, who was greatly displeased at what he regarded as dissimulation, was biting his lips and knitting his brows, when he dropped down in a moment. His agony was terrible to witness. Prayer was made; and he soon cried out, "Now I know thou art a prophet of the Lord."

One of the most remarkable cases was that of John Haydon, a weaver. He was a stout Churchman, regular in all his life and habits. He heard that people fell into strange fits at the meetings, and came to see for himself. At Baldwin Street, on the night when the indignant Quaker was struck down, Haydon had his wish. After the meeting he went about among his friends till one o'clock in the morning, labouring to persuade them that it was all a delusion of the wicked one. He sat down to dinner on the day after this meeting, but wished to finish "a sermon which he had borrowed on 'Salvation by Faith.'" As he read the last page he changed colour, fell from his chair, and began screaming terribly and beating himself against the ground. The neighbours flocked about the house. Between one and two Wesley, who was often called to visit people in such circumstances, was told in the street of this occurrence, and came into the house. The room was full of people. Haydon's wife would have kept them outside, but he said, "No; let them all come; let all the world see the just judgment of God." He was lying on the floor, held by two or three men, when Wesley entered, but at once fixed his eye on him. Stretching out his hand, he cried, "Ay, this is he who, I said, was a deceiver of the people. But God has overtaken me. I said it was all a delusion; but this is no delusion." He then roared out, "O thou devil! Thou cursed devil! Yea, thou legion of devils! Thou canst not stay. Christ will cast thee out. I know His work is begun. Tear me to pieces, if thou wilt; but thou canst not hurt me." No sooner had he spoken than he began to beat himself on the ground. His breast heaved, and great drops of sweat rolled down his face. Wesley and his friends prayed earnestly till the sufferer's pangs ceased; both body and soul were then set at liberty. In the evening Wesley visited him again. The man's voice was gone, and he was as weak as a child, but he was full of peace and joy.

Similar convulsions seized some of Wesley's hearers in London and in Newcastle. It is a striking fact that they occurred chiefly under John Wesley's ministry. Charles Wesley was more impassioned as a preacher, Whitefield was more vehement and exciting, but Wesley's calm and measured argument, in which every word went home to the hearts and consciences of his hearers, was most frequently attended by these convulsions of body and mind. There is no doubt that some cases were impostures. In August, 1740, Charles Wesley had to talk sharply to a girl of twelve, who now confessed that she had cried out or pretended to be seized with fits about thirty times, in order that Wesley might take notice of her. In June, 1743, at Newcastle, Charles Wesley ordered one girl to be carried out. She was violent enough in her cries till she got outside, but when she was laid outside the door she found her legs and walked off. Another night he gave notice that whoever cried so as to drown his voice should be quietly carried to the end of the room. This timely warning produced such a good effect that his "porters" had no employment the whole service.

Charles Wesley gives a judicious account of these convulsions. "Many, no doubt, were, at our first preaching, struck down, both soul and body, into the depth of distress. Their *outward affections* were easy to be imitated." At Newcastle, where he declared that he thought no better of any one for crying out or interrupting his work, all listened quietly. There is no doubt that he acted wisely. He regarded "the fits" as a device of Satan to stop the work, and found that "many more of the gentry" came when quiet was restored. People who hoped to attract attention by their convulsions soon found that it was not worth while to distress themselves. But when all deductions have been made, many of the earlier cases are still unaccounted for. No explanation meets these cases save that which ascribes them to intense conviction of sin. This has often been known to throw body and mind into an agony of distress. When the Bechuanas began to embrace Christianity, after Robert Moffat had laboured for nine years without success, the chapel at Kuruman was filled with a storm of sobs and cries which made it almost impossible to continue the service. Before the rise of Methodism similar scenes had been witnessed in New England, and even in Scotland. A physician who suspected that fraud had much to do with these manifestations was present at a meeting in Bristol. One woman whom he had known many years broke out "into strong cries and tears." He could hardly believe his own eyes. He stood close to her, observing every symptom, till great drops of perspiration ran down her face, and all her bones shook. He was puzzled, because he saw at once that this was neither fraud nor any natural disorder. When both body and soul were healed in a moment the doctor acknowledged the finger of God.

One of Wesley's visits to Bath, in June, 1739, is memorable for his encounter with Beau Nash. There was great excitement in the city when it was known that Nash would come to interrupt the service. Wesley was entreated not to preach, but he would not yield to such an unworthy suggestion. The event showed that he was right. Bath was at that time the most fashionable watering-place in England. More than eight thousand families are said to have visited it every year.* James Hervey, who stayed there four years after his friend Wesley's encounter with Nash,† says, "Every one seems studious of making a gay and grand appearance. It is, I think, one of the most glittering places I ever beheld. 'Anointed with oil, crowned with rose-buds, and decked with purple and fine linen,' they sport away their days, chanting to the sound of the viol, drinking wine in bowls, and stretching themselves on

* Lecky, i., 554.
† "Oxford Methodists," p. 231.

couches of ivory." Nash was king of the revels. He was an adventurer and a gamester, but all Bath acknowledged his rule and carefully observed the regulations which he posted in the pump-room. Ball-dresses and dances were all fixed by the Beau. His equipage was sumptuous. He usually travelled from Bath to Tunbridge in a post chariot and six greys, with outriders, footmen, French horns, and every other appendage of expensive parade. He always wore a white hat, and, to apologise for this singularity, said he did it purely to secure it from being stolen; his whole dress was tawdry.*

Wesley had a much larger audience than usual. The rich and great came with the crowd to witness the expected discomfiture of the Methodist preacher. They were "sinking apace into seriousness," whilst Wesley showed that the Scripture had concluded all under sin, when Nash appeared, and coming close to the preacher, asked by what authority he did these things. All the people waited for the answer. The King of Bath must have presented a strange contrast to the Methodist clergyman. Wesley quietly replied that he preached "by the authority of Jesus Christ, conveyed to me by the (now) Archbishop of Canterbury, when he laid hands upon me, and said, 'Take thou authority to preach the Gospel.'" Nash then said that the meeting was a conventicle; but Wesley quietly told him that it was not a seditious meeting, and was, therefore, not a conventicle, nor contrary to the Act of Parliament. Foiled here, Nash simply repeated his assertion, and turned to a more promising accusation. "I say it is. And, besides, your preaching frightens people out of their wits." "Sir," said

* Life of R. Nash. London, 1772. P. 49.

Wesley, "did you ever hear me preach?" "No," was the answer. "How then can you judge of what you never heard?" "Sir, by common report," said Nash. "Common report is not enough. Give me leave, sir, to ask, Is your name Nash?" The Beau answered, "My name is Nash." Wesley replied, "Sir, I dare not judge of you by common report: I think it is not enough to judge by." Nash had had enough on that head. He paused a while to recover himself, then said, "I desire to know what this people comes here for." Wesley had no need to speak. A woman in the company broke out, "Sir, leave him to me; let an old woman answer him. You, Mr. Nash, take care of your body; we take care of our souls; and for the food of our souls we come here." Nash slunk away without uttering another word. Wesley had come off with flying colours. His quiet answers may have shown the fashionable gamester his folly in meddling with a man who was such a thorough master of fence, and the poor woman's happy sally completely turned the tables on him. James Hervey, during his visit in 1743, also wrote Nash a faithful letter, in which he called on him to repent before the books should be opened at last, so that the King of Bath was not left without reprovers.

As Wesley returned to his friend's house the street was full of people who hurried to and fro, "speaking great words." When, however, Wesley answered their inquiries by saying, "I am he," they were silent at once. Several ladies followed him to Mr. Merchant's. He went into the room where he was told that they were waiting to speak to him. "I believe, ladies, the maid mistook; you only wanted to look at me. I do not expect that the rich and great should want either to speak with me, or hear me, for I speak the plain truth—a thing you hear little of, and do not desire to hear." A few words passed between them; then Wesley retired.

He was recalled to London in the middle of June, 1739, by letters which reported that great confusion had arisen in the Society at Fetter Lane for want of his presence and counsel. He reached the metropolis on June 13th. After receiving the Sacrament at Islington Church, Wesley met his mother, whom he had not seen for a year. He had then read her an account of the work of grace in his own heart, which she greatly approved. She heartily blessed God, who had brought her son to so just a way of thinking. Whilst Wesley was in Germany some one forwarded a copy of that paper to one of his relations, who sent an account of it to Mrs. Wesley. Wesley found her under strange fears that he had erred from the faith. The true facts had been so utterly disguised that his mother did not recognise the paper which she had heard from end to end. This matter was happily cleared up; and the mother of the Wesleys spent her last years at the Foundery, rejoicing in the spread of Methodism, and rendering no small service to her son by her wise counsels.

The evening of his arrival Wesley met the Society at Fetter Lane. A French prophetess had strangely imposed on the simple-minded people. She professed to be immediately inspired, and roared outrageously when Charles Wesley prayed. He had wrung a confession from one man that clearly showed she was a woman of immoral life, but Bray was vehement in her defence. When John Wesley met the Society her champions were much humbled, and all agreed to disown her. He was able to report that it pleased God to remove many misunderstandings and offences that had crept in, and to restore in good measure "the spirit of love and of a sound mind." Two members of the Society who had renounced all connection with the Church of England were left off the roll.* On the Saturday all met together to humble themselves before God for their unfaithfulness. A great blessing rested upon them. No such time had been known since the memorable New Year's outpouring.

Wesley stayed five days in London. He had not only succeeded in restoring peace at Fetter Lane, but had taken his place as a field-preacher in London. The day after his arrival he went with Whitefield to Blackheath. Twelve or fourteen thousand people had assembled. Whitefield surprised him by asking him to preach in his stead, "which I did," he says, "though nature recoiled, on my favourite subject, 'Jesus Christ, who of God is made unto us wisdom, righteousness, sanctification, and redemption.' I was greatly moved with compassion for the rich that were there, to whom I made a particular application. Some of them seemed to attend, while others drove away their coaches from so uncouth a preacher." He preached on Sunday morning at seven, in Upper Moorfields, to six or seven thousand people (Charles Wesley says, "above ten thousand people, as was supposed"), and at five in the evening on Kennington Common to about fifteen thousand. The following Sunday Charles Wesley ventured to follow his brother's example. He had been driven from his curacy at Islington by the action of the churchwardens, and had gone with Whitefield to his open-air services, but as yet he had not ventured to preach out of doors in London. The three friends were now enlisted in this work.

Wesley made four journeys from London to Bristol in

* See Chapter X. The Methodist Society had not yet been formed.

1739. He visited Oxford four times, made a short stay in Wales, and went to Tiverton with Charles Wesley, when they heard of their eldest brother's death. The first three months of the year were mainly spent in London; then Wesley was in Bristol for five months, so that he was only able to devote about two months more that year to London.

Samuel Wesley, the eldest son of the Rector of Epworth, died at Tiverton on November 6th, 1739, in his fiftieth year. He had anxiously followed the later course of his brothers, and was greatly opposed to their field-preaching. Only seventeen days before his death he remonstrated with his mother for countenancing "a spreading delusion, so far as to be one of Jack's congregation." "For my own part," he says, "I had much rather have them picking straws within the walls than preaching in the area of Moorfields." * Samuel Wesley was a good Christian, though his Church principles were so stiff. In the seclusion of his school life, he was quite unable to understand the constraint which led his younger brothers to go into the highways to declare the Gospel to the perishing. They were quite as loyal Churchmen as he, and had been as ardent in their support of order, but necessity was laid upon them to preach the Gospel. Samuel Wesley died in faith. "My poor sister," says John Wesley, "was sorrowing almost as one without hope. Yet we could not but rejoice at hearing, from one who had attended my brother in all his weakness, that, several days before he went hence, God had given him a calm and full assurance of his interest in Christ. Oh, may every one who opposes it be thus convinced that this doctrine is of God!"

* Priestley, p. 109. The reference is to Bedlam, which had not yet been moved from Moorfields to its present site.

CHAPTER IX.

THE MORAVIAN AND CALVINIST CONTROVERSIES.

UP to this time the Wesleys, who had been shut out of the churches, had preached in the open air, or "expounded" at the Society in Fetter Lane and other similar Societies. Some better arrangements were now essential. Wesley says, "On Sunday, November 11th, 1739, I preached at eight o'clock to five or six thousand, on the spirit of bondage and the Spirit of adoption, and at five in the evening to seven or eight thousand, in the place which had been the King's foundery for cannon.* Oh, hasten Thou the time when nation shall not rise up against nation, neither shall they learn war any more." This foundery became the head-quarters of Methodism until City Road Chapel was built in 1778. In 1716, when the damaged cannon taken by Marlborough from the French were being recast there, a tremendous explosion tore off part of the roof, and broke down the galleries, killing several of the workmen, and injuring others. A young Swiss called Schalch had foreseen the danger and warned the Surveyor-General of the Ordnance. All who would take warning left the place and thus escaped. Schalch was appointed Master Founder, and directed to choose another locality for casting the King's cannon. He chose

* Whitehead, ii., 125.

the rabbit-warren at Woolwich. The old building was thus left in ruins. It stood, about fifty feet from Providence Row, on the east side of Windmill Hill, now Tabernacle Street, parallel with City Road, and a few yards to the east of it, just above Finsbury Square. The building had a frontage of forty yards, with a depth of about thirty-three.

It was in November, 1739, that two gentlemen, who up to that time were entire strangers to Wesley, asked him to preach here. Wesley consented. He was afterwards pressed to buy it. The purchase money was a hundred and fifteen pounds, but heavy repairs and necessary alterations raised the expense to about eight hundred pounds. Galleries had to be erected for men and women, the Society-room had to be enlarged, and the whole structure thoroughly repaired. Some friends, including Mr. Ball and Mr. Watkins, lent Wesley the purchase money; and subscriptions were raised. The first year two hundred pounds was contributed, the next a hundred and forty pounds, but the people were so poor that five years after the opening there was still a debt of three hundred pounds. There were two entrances, one leading to the chapel, the other to the preachers' house, the school, and the band-room. The chapel would seat about fifteen hundred people on its plain benches. Men and women sat apart, and no one was allowed to claim any place as his own: those who came first sat down first. The women sat in the front gallery and under it, the men in the side galleries and in the seats below them. About a dozen benches, with rails at the back, were provided for women in front of the pulpit. In the band-room, behind the chapel, classes and prayer-meetings were held. One end of it was fitted up as a schoolroom; the other became Wesley's "Book

Room," where Methodist literature was sold. Above the band-room were Wesley's apartments; at the end of the chapel stood the house for the preachers. A coach-house and stable completed the accommodation.

The Foundery was closed for repairs in the early part of 1740. Silas Told, who afterwards became Wesley's schoolmaster there, attended the five o'clock service one morning in June, 1740. He found it a ruinous place, with an old pantile covering, decayed timbers, and a pulpit made of a few rough boards. Exactly at five o'clock a whisper ran through the congregation, "Here he comes! here he comes!" Wesley stepped forward in his robes, and gave out a hymn. The singing enraptured the stranger, but he did not like the extempore prayer, because he thought it savoured too much of Dissent. His prejudice quickly abated when Wesley began to preach from the words, "I write unto you, little children, because your sins are forgiven you." The friend who had brought Told to the Foundery asked him how he liked Mr. Wesley. He replied, "As long as I live I will never part from him."

The time had now come when the importance of having a Methodist centre became clear. A month after Silas Told's visit to the Foundery the final breach at Fetter Lane occurred. We have seen that Wesley was recalled from Bristol in June, 1739, by the grave disorders which had sprung up. He was able to restore peace; but the mischief was not at an end. At Oxford in December he received disquieting accounts from London. Scarcely one in ten retained his first love; most of the rest were in the utmost confusion, biting and devouring one another. Wesley had a long and particular conversation with Mr. Molther, a Moravian minister, who had come to England on October 18th, on his way to Pennsylvania. He became very popular, and remained in London till September, 1740, when he was summoned to Germany. Molther soon caused trouble by teaching that no man had any degree of faith unless he enjoyed the full assurance of faith and the abiding witness of the Spirit. He maintained that the gift of God which many had received through Peter Böhler's labours was not justifying faith. Wesley could not accept doctrines which were opposed to all his own experience and to the plain teaching of the New Testament. Molther also held that the way to find faith was to be "still." Those who desired the blessing were to give up the public means of grace. They were not even to pray or to read the Scriptures, nor to attempt to do any good works.

On New Year's Day, 1740, Wesley tried to teach the Society the true Scriptural doctrine of stillness from the words, "Be still, and know that I am God." Two days later such a spirit of love and peace as they had not known for months rested upon the Society. Before February closed he found, however, that some of the members, not content with neglecting the means of grace, were constantly disputing with those who were of a better spirit. At the end of April the trouble became more serious. Wesley at once returned to London when he heard of the confusion. His brother Charles had suffered much during the previous weeks. Mr. Stonehouse and Charles Delamotte had both been led astray. Charles Wesley foresaw that a separation was now inevitable. He was not the man to make any truce with those who dishonoured the ordinances of God, but he was exposed to no small annoyance in consequence of his firmness. One of the fanatics declared that there were only two ministers in London—Molther and Bell—who were true believers. John Bray asserted that it was impossible for any one to be a true Christian out of the Moravian Church.

When Wesley came to London he and his brother had an interview with Molther, who still defended his erroneous views. Wesley was utterly at a loss what to do. More than fifty persons, who had been greatly troubled by this new gospel, spoke to him. "Vain janglings" sounded in his ears wherever he went. At Fetter Lane one evening the question of ordinances was broached. Wesley begged, however, that they might not be always disputing, but might rather give themselves to prayer. During his ten days' stay Wesley laboured, both by his public addresses and his visits, to undo the mischief and save the erring; but the difficulty was only postponed. When he returned to London in the beginning of June he began to expound the Epistle of St. James as an antidote to the temptation to leave off good works. Poor Stonehouse said that he was going to sell his living, because "no honest man could officiate as a minister in the Church of England." At one meeting in Fetter Lane Mr. Ingham bore noble testimony for the ordinances of God and the reality of weak faith. But they would neither receive his saying nor Wesley's.

On Sunday, June 22nd, Wesley says, "Finding there was no time to delay without utterly destroying the cause of God, I began to execute what I had long designed,—to strike at the root of the grand delusion." From the words, "Stand ye in the way; ask for the old paths," he gave an account of the manner in which God had worked two years before, and showed how tares had recently been sown among the wheat. During the following week he laboured every day to guard the members at the Foundery against the errors that were rife. On July 16th the Fetter Lane Society resolved that Wesley should not be allowed to preach there. "This place," they said, "is taken for the Germans." When some asked if the Germans had converted any soul in England, whether they had not done more harm than good by raising a spirit of division, and whether God had not many times used Mr. Wesley to heal their divisions when all were in confusion, some of the agitators even ventured to assert that they were never in any confusion at all. At eleven o'clock Wesley withdrew from this useless debate.

Two days later he received the Sacrament, with his mother and a few of his friends. They afterwards consulted as to the course they should adopt. All saw that matters had reached a crisis, and were of one mind as to the course to be pursued. The following Sunday evening, July 20th, Wesley went, with Mr. Seward, afterwards one of the leading Calvinists, to the lovefeast in Fetter Lane. He said nothing till the conclusion of the meeting; then he read a paper which in a few sentences summed up the controversy, and gave expression to his conviction that their teaching about weak faith and the ordinances was flatly contrary to the Word of God. "I have warned you hereof again and again, and besought you to turn back to the law and the testimony. I have borne with you long, hoping you would turn. But as I find you more and more confirmed in the error of your ways, nothing now remains but that I should give you up to God. You that are of the same judgment, follow me." Without another word he withdrew, eighteen or nineteen others accompanying him.

The Methodist company, thus separated from the rest, now met at the Foundery. Twenty-five men joined it. All but two or three of the fifty women in band at Fetter Lane desired to cast in their lot with the Wesleys. Some weeks before—on June 11th—the Wesleys and Ingham had succeeded in remodelling the bands at Fetter Lane, so that those who still observed "the ordinances" might not be scattered one or two in a band of disputers and be harassed and sawn asunder, as they had so long been. Charles Wesley summed up the result in his journal: "We gathered up our wreck,—'raros * nantes in gurgite vasto,' for nine out of ten are swallowed up in the dead sea of stillness. Oh, why was this not done six months ago? How fatal was our delay and false moderation!" † The step then taken did something to preserve the faithful remnant who now met at the Foundery. This breach at Fetter Lane is a painful subject. But every one must share Charles Wesley's regret that the separation was not made earlier. His brother hoped against hope. His patience and longsuffering were characteristic. At last he was forced to take some step. The Fetter Lane Society had virtually expelled him on the Wednesday before he read his paper. He had no other course but to enter his protest and withdraw, with any whom he could save from the perilous snare of these teachers.

The Evangelical Revival now began to bear precious fruit in London. Up to this time the controversies and errors of Fetter Lane had been fatal to growth. In a letter to Zinzendorf on March 14th, 1740, James Hutton says that "John Wesley, being resolved to *do* all things himself, and having told many souls that they were justified who have since discovered themselves to be otherwise, and having mixed the works of the Law with the Gospel as *means* of grace, is at enmity against the Brethren. Envy is not extinct in him. His heroes falling every day into

* *Æneid*, i., 122—"some scattered swimmers in the vast abyss."

† C. Wesley's "Journals," i., 239.

poor sinners frightens him; but at London the spirit of the Brethren prevails against him. I desired him simply to keep to his office in the body of Christ, *i.e.*, to awaken souls in preaching, but not to pretend to lead them to Christ. But he will have the glory of doing all things." The latter sentence explains the former. Wesley was to gather in converts; the Brethren were to stamp their own likeness upon them. It was no wonder that Wesley was "resolved to *do* all things himself." If he had neglected that, his labour would soon have been undone. We have seen how calmly and patiently he treated the Moravians. His heroes were turned into poor sinners, Hutton says; that is, they were led to deny the work of grace which had been wrought in their hearts. James Hutton's feelings were far different from those he once cherished towards the man who led him to Christ.

Molther and the disturbers at Fetter Lane were teaching doctrines opposed to the spirit of their own Church. On September 29th, 1740, Wesley earnestly called upon the Moravian Church, and Count Zinzendorf in particular, to correct him if he had misunderstood their tenets. He had learnt from them, as well as from the English Church, that a man might have a degree of justifying faith before he is wholly freed from doubt and fear, and might use the ordinances of God before he gained the full assurance of faith. Molther and his supporters entirely denied this. Wesley's Society soon outstripped the Moravian Church. In 1743, when the Methodists in London numbered 1,950 members, the Moravians of the metropolis were only about seventy-two.

On his return from Hernhuth in 1738, Wesley began a letter to his friends there in which he says, "But of some things I stand in doubt, which I will mention in love and meekness. . . . Is not the Count all in all among you?

Do you not magnify your own Church too much? Do you not use guile and dissimulation in many cases? Are you not of a close, dark, reserved temper and behaviour?" * The letter was not sent, but it shows that Wesley had already detected some germs of that spirit which afterwards led to the separation. In September, 1741, Wesley and Zinzendorf had an interview at Gray's Inn Walk; but it led to no practical result. When Mr. Stonehouse read the conversation, he remarked, "The Count is a clever fellow; but the genius of Methodism is too strong for him." † Four years later Zinzendorf inserted an advertisement in the *Daily Advertiser* to the effect that the Moravians had no connection with the Wesleys. A prophecy was added that the brothers would "soon run their heads against the wall." "We will not if we can help it," was Wesley's comment.‡ The Count's later life fully justified Wesley's position. His influence on the Moravian Church was singularly unhealthy, and Antinomianism spread among the English members of the community. Wesley's painful experience did not prevent him from paying a high tribute to his old friends. "Next to the members of the Church of England," he says, "the body of the Moravian Church, however mistaken some of them are, are in the main, of all whom I have seen, the best Christians in the world." §

Before the breach with the Society at Fetter Lane, signs of a still more painful struggle had appeared. The Calvinistic controversy separated the Wesleys from George Whitefield, who had long been as their own soul, and divided Methodism into two camps. Grave and long was

---

* Works, viii., 381.
† Moore, i., 489.
‡ Tyerman, i., 477; Hutton, 143.
§ Works, viii., 379.

the strife of opinion. No other subject has so profoundly stirred Latin Christianity as the question of free-will and Divine sovereignty. From the days of St. Augustine this has been the great theological battle-ground of the West. Even in Reformation times, when the struggle with Rome assumed its most terrible proportions, this controversy rent Protestantism into two hostile sections, and turned Lutheran and Calvinist into deadly foes. It is no wonder, therefore, that such a controversy divided the workers of the Evangelical Revival into two parties. As early as 1725 Wesley had corresponded with his mother on this subject, and had taken up his own position. He was not, therefore, likely to abandon his views nor even to keep them to himself, as Whitefield suggested that he should do.

In 1740 Wesley published his sermon on "Free Grace." He sums up the doctrine of "election, preterition, predestination, or reprobation" in one sentence: "The sense of all is plainly this—by virtue of an eternal, unchangeable, irresistible decree of God, one part of mankind are infallibly saved, and the rest infallibly damned; it being impossible that any of the former should be damned, or that any of the latter should be saved." Mrs. Wesley, in a striking letter on election in 1725, tells her son, "I think you reason well and justly against it." Then she expresses her own views. "I firmly believe that God from eternity has elected some to eternal life; but then I humbly conceive that this election is founded on His foreknowledge, according to Romans viii. 29, 30. Whom, in His eternal prescience, God saw would make a right use of their powers, and accept of offered mercy, He did predestinate and adopt for His children." Such were substantially the views Wesley held in his famous sermon. So early as July 2nd, 1739, Whitefield had urged him to "keep in" his "sermon on predestination." He went to America soon afterwards, whence he wrote several letters to his friend on the subject in controversy. In the States he found himself among ministers who were zealous for Calvinism. He read the books which they recommended, so that his own convictions became stronger. When Wesley published his sermon on "Free Grace" in 1740, he told his readers in a brief "Address" that nothing save the strongest conviction that he was indispensably obliged to declare this truth to all the world could have induced him to oppose the sentiments of those whom he esteemed so highly for their works' sake. He begged any one who might feel bound to contest his views to do so in love and meekness. Charles Wesley was perfectly in accord with his brother. He wrote a hymn of thirty-six verses which was printed at the end of the sermon.

And shall I, Lord, confine Thy love
  As not to others free?
And may not every sinner prove
  The grace that found out *me*?

Doom them an endless death to die,
  From which they could not flee
O Lord, Thine inmost bowels cry
  Against the dire decree!

Whitefield was much disturbed by the publication of this sermon. During his voyage to England, in an affectionate letter to Charles Wesley, dated February 1st, 1741, he says, "My dear, dear brethren, why did you throw out the bone of contention? Why did you print that sermon against predestination? Why did you in particular, my dear brother Charles, affix your hymn, and join in putting out your late hymn-book? How can you say you will not dispute with me about election, and yet print such hymns, and your brother send his sermon over to Mr. Garden and others in America?" The answer was simple. The Wesleys felt it their duty to speak plainly. They mentioned no names, but quietly set forth their own views. All must allow that the leaders of the greatest popular revival ever known in this country were not at liberty to be silent. Whitefield might argue that he did not know the elect, and was therefore bound to offer the Gospel to all. But such an argument would not satisfy the Wesleys. Calvinism was spreading. Antinomianism was creeping into their Societies. There was no time to lose in coping with the growing mischief.

Whitefield brought with him from America an answer he had prepared to Wesley's sermon. This manuscript letter he submitted to Charles Wesley, asking his advice whether he should print it or not. Charles returned it endorsed, "Put up again thy sword into its place." Whitefield, however, did not take this advice, but published his letter. John Wesley had no objection to fair argument; but he considered Whitefield's letter a burlesque upon an answer. He also greatly regretted that Whitefield should have mentioned him and his brother by name, so that it seemed like a public attack upon his old friends. Whitefield began to preach against the Wesleys by name in Moorfields and other places. Once, when invited to the Foundery, he preached the absolute decrees in the most peremptory and offensive manner. Some thousands of people were present, and Charles Wesley sat beside him. The rupture was soon complete. Whitefield refused to hold any connection with those who believed in free grace. The Society at Kingswood was rent asunder by this controversy, so that it did not look up again for years. John

Cennick, the schoolmaster there, was one of Wesley's lay-preachers, and owed his position entirely to his kindness. Yet Cennick did not scruple to use all his influence to spread dissension. When two women publicly railed against Charles Wesley, he did not even attempt to interpose. One day in May, 1741, when Charles Wesley was passing the Bowling Green in Bristol, a woman cried out, "The curse of God light upon you," with such uncommon bitterness that he turned to speak to her. He stayed heaping coals of fire upon her head, till at last she said, "God bless you all." When he visited Wales one man publicly left the room because he would not reprove Howel Harris for his Calvinism. Such facts show the bitterness of feeling that was aroused by this painful controversy.

The brothers were now left alone. Whitefield refused to work with them; their companions in Georgia—Ingham and Charles Delamotte—had become Moravians. Stonehouse, Gambold, Westley Hall, Hutton, and others also joined the Germans. For a time Wesley feared that his brother would follow their example. Charles had said, "No English man or woman is like the Moravians." John tells him, "The poison is in you: fair words have stolen away your heart." Charles seemed to have forgotten the struggle against stillness, in the bitterness of the more recent controversy, and drew comparisons favourable to the Germans. Whatever his danger may have been, his preaching soon showed that he was as much opposed to their doctrine of "stillness" as ever. About this time a reunion with the Moravians was discussed, but when the "bands" met together to consider the matter, all agreed that the time had not come. The erroneous doctrines were not renounced, and the Fetter Lane Society spoke with such guile that scarcely any one could tell what they really believed. Wesley did not give up hope of a reconciliation. In August, 1743, he summoned his brother Charles in haste from Cornwall to a conference with Whitefield and the Moravians. He was even willing to make unjustifiable concessions for the sake of peace; but as neither Whitefield nor the Moravians would take part in the conference, the whole matter fell through.

CHAPTER X.

THE METHODIST SOCIETIES.

WESLEY was familiar with the religious Societies of the Church of England. He found there congenial spirits, to whom he often expounded the Scriptures, after his return from Georgia. Dr. Horneck, curate at the Savoy and Canon of Westminster, Mr. Smithies, curate of Cripplegate, and William Beveridge, the great Oriental scholar, who was Rector of St. Peter's, Cornhill, and afterwards Bishop of St. Asaph, were the founders of these Societies. Their popular and awakening ministry led to the conversion of many young men, whom they advised to meet together once a week to edify each other. The members related their religious experience, and maintained a fund to relieve the poor, pay the debts of prisoners, and educate children. In 1678, a year after the formation of the Societies, two stewards were elected to manage the charities. The religious Societies were under a cloud during the reign of James II., when every private gathering was an object of suspicion to the authorities; but a great step in advance was taken by the reading of public prayers every night at eight o'clock in St. Clement Danes Church. A crowded congregation attended. A monthly lecture which was established also became very popular.

After the Revolution a rule was passed that every member should try to gain others. The numbers now grew so rapidly that Societies were formed in all parts of London. Great care was taken that no one should be admitted who would lower the religious tone of the meetings. The Societies and those who sympathised with them then set themselves to check the scandalous vice of the times. The Lord Mayor and other London magistrates lent their countenance to the scheme. The Society for the Reformation of Manners* was thus formed. Sunday markets were closed, houses of ill-fame shut up, and great success crowned the work. John Wesley's father preached a sermon on behalf of this Society in 1698. In 1735 it was stated that the number of prosecutions for debauchery and profaneness in London and Westminster since the foundation of the Societies had been 99,380. Abuses sprang up, however, in connection with this detective work, and the Society soon sank into insignificance.† James Hutton, in his narrative of the awakening in England, says that the religious Societies "had so settled down into lifelessness, that the majority of their members were altogether slumbering or dead souls, who cared for nothing but their comfort in this world, and as they had once joined this connection, they were willing to continue in this respectable pastime on Sunday evenings, by which, at small expense, they could enjoy the pleasure, and fancy themselves better than the rest of the world who did not do the like." ‡

On May 1st, 1738, the Wesleys and their friends in London, acting on the advice of Peter Böhler, had formed a little religious Society. They were to meet together every week to confess their faults and pray for one another. The Wesleys were no strangers to the bless-

* Josiah Woodward's "Account of the Religious Societies."

† Lecky, ii., 547.

‡ Benham's Life of James Hutton, p. 9.

ing of religious fellowship. The Oxford Methodists had found that the only way in which they could keep alive their zeal and spirituality was to meet frequently together. A serious man, whom John Wesley took a long journey to visit, about the time when Methodism arose at Oxford said to him, "Sir, you are to serve God and go to heaven. Remember you cannot serve Him alone; you must, therefore, find companions, or make them; the Bible knows nothing of solitary religion." On board the *Simmonds*, the little party of Methodists met several times every day to pray and help each other. In Savannah * Wesley advised the serious part of his congregation to form themselves into a Society, which should meet once or twice a week, in order to promote spiritual life. Out of their number Wesley selected some for a more intimate union with each other. These he met himself on Sunday afternoons. Peter Böhler's suggestion, therefore, being in harmony with Wesley's whole course, recommended itself to him at once. Wesley says the first rise of Methodism was at Oxford, in November, 1729, when four friends met together, the second at Savannah, in April, 1736, when twenty or thirty met at his house, the third when the Society in London was formed. The members first met at the house of young James Hutton, near Temple Bar. When that became too small they removed to the chapel at 32, Fetter Lane.† The original number of members was ten. Three years after the Society was formed, a reunion was arranged. Seven of the first members thus met together; one was sick; two were unwilling to attend. Peter Böhler, who had returned from America, was present.

* Whitehead, xiii., 305. † Life of James Hutton.

Three years had brought great changes. The Wesleys had withdrawn from Fetter Lane; Whitefield had separated from the Wesleys. "Surely," says Wesley, "the time will return when there shall be again 'union of mind, as in us all one soul.'" When Wesley got back from the Continent in September, 1738, the Society at Fetter Lane had increased to thirty-two. By the beginning of 1739 it had about sixty members. Up to the time of Molther's arrival it made steady progress, fed continually by the Wesleys' preaching in London.

The Society at Fetter Lane was not a Moravian Society. On May 2nd, 1738, the day after its formation, James Hutton wrote to Zinzendorf asking that Peter Böhler might remain in England as a Moravian preacher on his return from Carolina. The petition was signed by himself and thirteen others, but neither of the Wesleys joined in the request. The Society had no connection with the Moravians except in the personal friendship and sympathy of its leading members till Molther's arrival. He could scarcely speak in English, but four weeks after his arrival in this country, on October 18th, 1739, he made an attempt to preach. He told Count Zinzendorf that the Society had been mainly under the care of the Wesleys until this time.* Wesley states that he was only a private member; but there is no doubt that his influence † was considerable, and that the converts of the early Methodist preaching added to the numbers of the Society. James Hutton says, "In June, 1740, he" (Wesley) "formed his Foundery Society, in opposition to the one which met at Fetter Lane, and which had become a Moravian Society." Wesley's journals and his letters to the Rev. Mr. Church expressly state that "the 'reasoning and disputing,' the

* Life of James Hutton, 53, 54. † Works, viii., 424.

'biting and devouring one another,'" which he found on his arrival from Bristol on December 19th, 1739, was not among "the Moravians, but the English brethren of Fetter Lane before their union with the Moravians."* The Wesleys, therefore, were never Moravians nor members of a Moravian Society, as has been so often stated. Molther's visit to England marks the beginning of the conversion of the Fetter Lane Society into a Moravian Society.

About fifty women and twenty-five men followed Wesley to the Foundery in July, 1740. A nucleus had already been gathered there. In the latter part of 1739, seven months before the breach with the Fetter Lane Society, eight or ten persons, who appeared deeply convinced of sin, and earnestly groaning for redemption, came to Wesley. Many who were awakened under the Methodist preaching had already spoken to him. They were surrounded by difficulties; every one sought to weaken, none to strengthen their hands. Wesley's advice was always, "Strengthen you one another. Talk together as often as you can. And pray earnestly with and for one another, that you may 'endure to the end and be saved.'" They wished him to counsel and pray with them himself. Wesley, therefore, asked for their names and addresses. He soon found that the number was too great for him to visit them at their own homes. "If you will all of you come together," he said, "every Thursday, in the evening, I will gladly spend some time with you in prayer, and give you the best advice I can." This important step was taken at the end of 1739. Their number increased daily. Wesley gave them counsel, always closing "with prayer suitable to their necessities." When Wesley began to

* Works, viii., 424.

preach in Bristol in the spring of 1739, a few persons agreed to meet weekly like those in London. After the meeting-house there was built several small Societies, which already met in various parts of the city, were joined to the Methodist Society. Those at Baldwin Street and Nicholas Street are specially mentioned in the arrangements for building the room in the Horse Fair. As the work spread Methodist Societies were also formed at Kingswood and Bath.*

The Wesleys visited these Societies, but there was as yet no adequate provision for pastoral oversight. Financial necessities at Bristol led to one great step in advance. A large debt still remained on the room in the Horse Fair. On February 15th, 1742, many of the friends met together to consult about its payment. A Captain Foy stood up and suggested that every member should give a penny a week till the debt was paid. Some one objected that many of the people could not afford to do this; but he replied, "Then put eleven of the poorest with me; and if they can give anything, well: I will call on them weekly; and if they can give nothing, I will give for them as well as for myself. And each of you call on eleven of your neighbours weekly; receive what they give, and make up what is wanting." The person who took charge of the contributions was called a leader, the company under his care a class. After this arrangement was made the visitors sometimes reported to Wesley that certain members did not live as they ought. He at once saw that this was the very thing he had long been wanting. He called the leaders together and desired each to make particular inquiry into the behaviour of those whom he visited weekly. By this means many "disorderly walkers" were detected. Some

* Works, xiii., 308.

turned from the evil of their ways; others were put out of the Society. The new organisation was introduced into the metropolis and all other places as soon as possible. It bore the best fruit. In London especially it was a vast gain.* On February 1st, 1742, there were already eleven hundred members of the Society scattered from Wapping to Westminster. Wesley could not easily discover what their life was in their own homes and their own neighbourhood. Some who were inconsistent did much harm before he was aware of it. The pastoral care of the Societies had till then rested entirely on the Wesleys. The first step towards transforming the leaders into a lay pastorate was taken when Wesley requested them to make special inquiries about the Christian consistency of those from whom they collected contributions. It was soon found to be inconvenient for the leaders to visit the members at their own homes. It took up more time than many of them could spare. In some cases masters and relatives were much opposed to these visits. There was no opportunity for the members to strengthen each other's hands, or meet face to face for the removal of any misunderstandings that arose. It was therefore arranged that the members of each class should meet together for an hour or two every week.†

By these means Methodism was provided with an organisation which remains unchanged to this day. The secret of its endurance and of the high spiritual tone which it has maintained among its members is to be found here. Wesley abundantly recognised the blessing of these weekly meetings to the Society. "It can scarce be conceived what advantages have been reaped from this little prudential regulation. Many now happily ex-

* Works, i., 356. † *Ibid.*, viii., 253, etc.

perienced that Christian fellowship of which they had not so much as an idea before. They began to "bear one another's burdens," and naturally to "care for each other." As they had daily a more intimate acquaintance with, so they had a more endeared affection for, each other. Objections were raised, of course. "Many were at first extremely averse to meeting thus." Some looked on the class as a restraint; others said they were ashamed to speak before company. When any one objected that there were no such meetings when he joined the Society, Wesley replied, that it was a pity that they had not been held at first, but that the need and benefit of them was not then known. He regarded it as one of the great advantages of Methodism that it was able to change whatever could be changed for the better, and to learn by every day's experience. He set himself to answer the more plausible objection that the leaders had neither gifts nor grace for such work by meeting them once a week for counsel. If any one was remarkably deficient in qualifications, Wesley promised that he would try to exchange him for a better leader if the objectors spoke to him of such cases. He took care, however, to point out that God had greatly blessed the work even of humble leaders.

These arrangements were introduced into Methodism during the year 1742, when the great extension of Wesley's itinerancy took place by his visit to Newcastle. It provided a lay pastorate at the time when the growth of the work made it essential to have a vastly increased staff. Restless as was the itinerancy of the brothers, they could only pay occasional visits to the country Societies. The leaders lived on the spot, and met their classes every week at the appointed hour. By this means the work made steady progress, even when the brothers and their lay-preachers were called away to other scenes of labour. Their converts were knit together and kept from wandering back into the world. Bands had been formed at Fetter Lane consisting of not less than five or more than ten members of the Society; married men met together in one band, married women in others; single men and single women had bands of their own. It was thought that greater freedom and fuller help would be secured by grouping them thus. The "Select Society" or "Band" at the Foundery formed an inner circle composed of the more advanced Christians, to whom Wesley gave advice which might help them to "go on unto perfection." The visitation of the classes once a quarter by Wesley or his preachers and the use of a ticket of membership which might secure the discipline and privacy of the Society seem to have begun in 1742.* In August, 1737, Wesley joined with the Germans in Georgia in one of their lovefeasts. Wesley was greatly interested in these survivals of the ancient Church. He, therefore, introduced them into his own Societies.† At first they were only open to the Methodist bands, but by-and-bye all the Society joined in them. After partaking of bread and water, the meeting was devoted to religious experience.

Wesley early resolved, by the grace of God, not "to strike a blow" in any place where he could not follow it up.‡ At Mullingar, in Ireland, on July 10th, 1750, for instance, he declined an invitation to preach made by the sovereign of the town (the Irish title for mayor). "I had little hopes," he says, "of doing good by preaching in a place where I could preach but once, and where none but me could be suffered to preach at all." When he visited a

---

* Myles' "Chronological History," 19.

† *Ibid.*, 19. ‡ Works, i., 416.

new place and found that those who had been awakened desired to join his Society, Wesley used to explain its purpose, and receive those who were willing to become members. At Newport, in the Isle of Wight, in 1781,* he says, "After preaching, I explained the nature of a Methodist Society, of which few had before the least conception." Sometimes the whole congregation begged to remain to his Society meetings. They crowded in with the members, or exhibited such eagerness to hear that Wesley could not refuse them admittance.† He was well repaid at Barnard Castle in June, 1763. "It was a day of God's power. They all seemed to take the kingdom by violence, while they besieged heaven with vehement prayer." The financial affairs of the Society were under the care of stewards. This arrangement was first made in London. A few days after the Foundery was taken, some of the friends told him that they would not sit under him for nothing. When Wesley replied that his fellowship supplied all his needs, they reminded him of the expenses of the lease and repairs of the Foundery. One man offered to receive the subscriptions and pay accounts.‡ Wesley thus found his first steward. The number was afterwards raised to seven. They met every Thursday morning at six, and distributed all the money paid them up to the previous Tuesday night. All the finance of his Societies was thus placed under the management of suitable persons chosen from their own number. As the growth of Methodism called for division of labour, it was simply made on these lines.

The watchnight service, which has been adopted by so many evangelical Churches, was first kept in 1740, at

* Works, iv., 218. † *Ibid.*, iii., 135, 161, 197.
‡ *Ibid.*, viii., 311.

the suggestion of a Kingswood collier. Before their conversion the colliers used to spend their Saturday night at the public-house. Now it was devoted to prayer and praise. Wesley heard that they met thus in Kingswood School. Some advised him to put an end to such meetings, but he could see no cause to forbid them. Rather he believed the watchnight might be introduced elsewhere. He sent word that he would join in the service on the Friday nearest full moon, and on the previous Sunday announced that he would preach. Methodism thus gained one of its most popular and useful services. At first watchnights were held once a month, then once a quarter, from half-past eight to twelve. The service is now confined to the last night of the year.

Wesley felt himself responsible for every side of his people's life. He was not content to be their adviser in spiritual matters only, but laboured to make them model citizens and subjects. In March, 1755, on a visit to the west of England, Wesley "found Bristol all in a flame; voters and non-voters being ready to tear each other to pieces." He was suffering from a severe cold, and had not recovered his voice so as to preach or even to speak to the whole Society, but he desired those members who were "freemen" to meet him. He mildly and lovingly informed them "how they ought to act in this hour of temptation," and had good reason to believe that the greater number profited by the advice. What his election rules were may be seen from another record. At Bristol, on October 3rd, 1774, he says, "I met those of our Society who had votes in the ensuing election, and advised them—

"1. To vote, without fee or reward, for the person they judged most worthy.

"2. To speak no evil of the person they voted against.

"3. To take care their spirits were not sharpened against those that voted on the other side."

Extracts might be multiplied to show how necessary and how effectual such counsels were.

Wesley was equally careful to preserve his Society from defrauding the revenue. Smuggling was carried on in all parts of the country in those days to an extent which now appears almost incredible.* Wesley states that "the numbers concerned therein, upon all our coasts, are far greater than can be imagined." In 1744 it was estimated that not less than four thousand five hundred horses were employed in the trade in Suffolk alone.† In July, 1753, the stewards of West Cornwall met at St. Ives. When Wesley began to examine the Society he soon found that he could not proceed. "Well-nigh one and all bought or sold uncustomed goods." In the evening he met all together, and told them they must put away this abomination or see his face no more. All promised to do so, and the plague seemed to be stayed.‡ At Sunderland in 1757 he warned the Society that he would no more suffer smuggling, than robbing on the highway. Next day he examined every member on this subject. A few would not promise to refrain, so that he was obliged to cut them off. Two hundred and fifty were of a better mind. Two years later § he spoke to each of the Society there again on this matter. "Most of the robbers, commonly called smugglers, have left us," he says, "but more than twice the number of honest people are already come in their place. And if none had come, yet should I not dare to keep those who steal either from the King or subject." In a letter written from

* Works, ix., 225.

† Tyerman, i., 216.

‡ Works, ii., 413.

§ *Ibid.*, ii., 490.

Chatham to Joseph Benson, who was grappling with smuggling at Sunderland, Wesley says, "'The Word to a Smuggler' is plain and homely, and has done much good in these parts." The tract thus aptly described was published in 1767. There is no escape from its reasoning. It shatters every subterfuge, and proves that all who buy uncustomed goods are as guilty as the actual smuggler himself. Those who excused themselves by saying, "But I do not know that it was run," did not escape. "No! Did not he that sold it tell you it was? If he sold it under the common price, he did. The naming the price was telling you, 'This is run.'" He points out that those who defrauded the revenue increased the burden of taxation on all honest men. "Therefore every smuggler is a thief-general, who picks the pockets both of the King and all his fellow-subjects."

Any one who studies Wesley's relation to his Societies will soon see how resolutely he set himself to grapple with the vices of his day. Wherever Methodism was planted it contributed in no small degree to a general reformation of manners. It made its members better citizens, and raised the whole standard of morality. No truce was ever made with sin. At Rye, in January, 1778, Wesley preached, as usual, to a crowded congregation. "How large a Society would be here could we but spare them in one thing! Nay, but then all our labour would be in vain. One sin allowed would intercept the whole blessing."

London was the choicest of Wesley's Societies. At Manchester, in May, 1783, he was greatly delighted with the select Society. "I believe there is no place but London where we have so many souls so deeply devoted to God." *

* Works, iv., 247, 273, 280.

A year later at Whitby he says, "I met such a select Society as I have not seen since I left London. They were about forty, of whom I did not find one who had not a clear witness of being saved from inbred sin. Several of them had lost it for a season, but could never rest till they had recovered it. And every one of them seemed now to walk in the full light of God's countenance." Such a tribute helps us to understand the high character of the London Society. The old preachers often trembled when they were called to labour among the experienced and devoted Methodists of the metropolis. Not a few came with reluctance. But they soon found that their hands were borne up by the people, so that their work prospered, and the happy fellowship with some of the oldest and best members Methodism possessed proved no small blessing to them. For both the Wesleys London Methodism cherished the warmest affection. Charles felt so deeply the loving interest of the Society at the time of his marriage, that he writes, "Surely both Jesus and His disciples are bidden." Nowhere was he more beloved or more happy than at London. It was the same with his brother. In December, 1741, he met the Society. "We scarce knew how to part, our hearts were so enlarged toward each other." Years only deepened the love and sympathy with which London Methodism regarded its founder. This was, indeed, true of all the Societies. Wesley had sacrificed everything—ease, wealth, honour—to give himself wholly to the work of God; and he was honoured not only by the abounding success of Methodism, but by the reverence and love of all his people.

CHAPTER XI.

THE EXTENSION OF THE WORK.

WESLEY'S journey to Newcastle in 1742 forms an important stage in his itinerant life. He had been much exercised during the early successes of field-preaching at Bristol in 1739 about the unusual manner of his ministration there. After much prayer and careful weighing of all objections, he felt that he could still adhere to the views expressed in a letter to his friend, the Rev. James Hervey, some time before, and printed in his journal.* In that letter occurs the famous phrase on the memorial tablet erected to the Wesleys in Westminster Abbey: "I look upon all the world as my parish." The practical outcome of this principle was gradually exhibiting itself. Up to the spring of 1742 Wesley's labours had been confined mainly to London and Bristol. At Oxford he was a frequent visitor, and many places on the road between the two Methodist centres enjoyed his ministry. Wales and various adjacent towns and villages had been visited from Bristol. He had also found his way to the Moravian Societies in Nottingham and other places. The year 1742 saw the boundaries of his great circuit stretched to the extreme north of England. John Nelson, who had been converted under Wesley's first sermon in Moorfields, afterwards returned to his home at Birstal, in

* Works, i., 200; "Oxford Methodists," 412.

Yorkshire. His labours soon changed the face of the whole town. So many came to hear him read and exhort that he had to stand at the door of his house and talk to the crowd that stood within and without. Six or seven people were converted every week, and the greatest profligates and drunkards in the county were changed. Nelson begged Wesley to come to his help. The Countess of Huntingdon was also anxious that the colliers on the Tyne should share the blessing which the colliers of Kingswood had already found.

The immediate cause of Wesley's journey, however, was a summons from Leicestershire to visit his dying friend Miss Cowper, who lived with the Countess of Huntingdon. He had arranged to start for Bristol on the day this call reached him, but set off to the north at once. From Donnington Park he pushed on to Birstal, and sent for Nelson to his inn. Wesley now heard from the heroic stonemason the story of his fifteen months' labour, and himself preached to the people. On May 28th he reached Newcastle. He found that he had not come too soon. In his first walk through the town he says, "I was surprised: so much drunkenness, cursing, and swearing (even from the mouths of little children), do I never remember to have seen and heard before in so small a compass of time. Surely this place is ripe for Him 'who came not to call the righteous, but sinners, to repentance.'" He could find no one who appeared to care for religion. At seven o'clock on the Sunday morning, he walked down to Sandgate, the poorest and most contemptible part of the town, with his travelling companion, John Taylor. Standing alone at the end of the street, they began to sing the hundredth Psalm. Three or four people came out to see what was the matter. Soon the number increased to four or five hundred, and before the service was over twelve or fifteen hundred assembled. Wesley's text was, "He was wounded for our transgressions; He was bruised for our iniquities; the chastisement of our peace was upon Him; and by His stripes we are healed."

When the sermon was over, the people stood gaping and staring at the preacher in profound astonishment. Seeing their amazement, he said, "If you desire to know who I am, my name is John Wesley. At five in the evening, with God's help, I design to preach here again." At the appointed hour, the hill on which he intended to stand was covered from top to bottom. Neither at Moorfields nor at Kennington Common had he seen such an audience. Wesley knew that even his voice, strong and clear though it was, could not reach one half of this vast concourse; but he stood where he had all in view, ranged on the side of the hill. Then he explained and applied that promise, "I will heal their backsliding; I will love them freely." Wesley had never received such a welcome as he found in the metropolis of the north. The poor people, he says, were ready to tread him under foot out of pure love and kindness. For some time he was quite unable to get out of the press. When at last he reached his inn, several people were waiting there who "vehemently importuned" him to stay at least a few days, or even one day longer. Wesley had promised to be at Birstal on Tuesday, so that he could not comply with their request. But about two months later Charles Wesley took his brother's place. Before the year was out Wesley himself was with them again.

He set out from Newcastle after his first visit at three o'clock on the Monday morning. He was welcomed everywhere. The mistress of the inn at Boroughbridge where he stayed for the night, begged that she and her family might join in Wesley's evening devotions. Next morning, between four and five, she joined them again at prayers. Riding through Knaresborough, where they had no intention of stopping, a young man begged Wesley to go to his house. There he learned that some words spoken to a man as he and his companion passed through the place on their way to Newcastle had set many in a flame. A sermon they had given him had travelled from one end of the town to the other. Just then a woman begged to speak with Wesley. At her house he found five or six of her friends, one of whom had long been under deep conviction. They spent an hour together in prayer with great blessing. Such incidents were God's call to thrust in the sickle, for the harvest was ripe.

The most interesting part of this preaching tour was Wesley's visit to Epworth. After spending a few days in the neighbourhood of Birstal, he rode on to his native place. He does not seem to have been at Epworth since he consulted his mother about his mission to Georgia seven years before. Not knowing, as he says, whether there were any left who would not be ashamed of his acquaintance, Wesley took up his quarters at an inn in the middle of the town. Here an old servant of the Parsonage, with two or three other poor women, found him out. When he asked if she knew any in the place who were in earnest to be saved, she answered, "I am, by the grace of God; and I know I am saved through faith." Many others, she assured him, could rejoice with her. In this happy way Wesley spent his Saturday night at Epworth. Next morning he offered to assist Mr. Romley, either by preaching or reading prayers. But the drunken curate would have none of his help. The old church was crowded in the afternoon in consequence of a rumour that Wesley would preach. Mr. Romley gave them a sermon on "Quench not the Spirit," in which he said that enthusiasm was one of the most dangerous ways of doing this, and enlarged in a very florid and oratorical manner on the character of an enthusiast. Every one knew the application he had in view.

As the people flocked out of church they learned that they were not to be disappointed. John Taylor stood in the churchyard and gave notice, "Mr. Wesley, not being permitted to preach in the church, designs to preach here at six o'clock." When the hour came such a congregation assembled as Epworth had never seen before. Wesley stood near the east end of the church, upon his father's tombstone, and cried, "The kingdom of God is not meat and drink, but righteousness, peace, and joy in the Holy Ghost." He was urged to visit the neighbouring villages, and though very anxious to pursue his journey, he could not resist the appeal. Through the influence of Moravian teachers in the district, many had forsaken church; others were plunged in doubt. Wesley yielded to their entreaties, and remained for seven days more. He visited the neighbouring villages, and preached every evening on his father's tomb. During the week he went to see a justice of the peace in a neighbouring town who had shown a candour and good feeling which were rare in those days. A waggon-load of the new heretics had been carried before him by their angry neighbours. When he asked what these people had done, there was deep silence. No one seemed to have thought of such an insignificant matter. One of the accusers at last found a voice. He informed the magistrate that they pretended to be better than other people, and prayed from morning to night. "But have they done nothing beside?" he inquired. "Yes, sir," said an old man; "an't please your worship, they have *convarted* my wife. Till she went among them, she had such a tongue! And now she is quiet as a lamb." "Carry them back, carry them back," replied the justice, "and let them convert all the scolds in the town."

On the Saturday evening many in the churchyard congregation dropped down as dead. Wesley's voice could scarcely be heard for the cries of those who were seeking rest; but their sorrow was soon changed to praise. One gentleman, who had not been at public worship for more than thirty years, stood there as motionless as a statue. His chaise was outside the churchyard; his wife and one or two servants were with him. Wesley, seeing him stand thus, asked abruptly, "Sir, are you a sinner?" With a deep and broken voice, he answered, "Sinner enough." He "continued staring upwards till his wife and a servant or two, all in tears, put him into his chaise and carried him home." This touching scene has a happy sequel. The impression then made was never effaced. Ten years later, in April, 1752, Wesley says, "I called on the gentleman who told me he was 'sinner enough' when I preached first at Epworth on my father's tomb, and was agreeably surprised to find him strong in faith, though exceeding weak in body. For some years, he told me, he had been rejoicing in God, without either doubt or fear, and was now waiting for the welcome hour when he should 'depart and be with Christ.'"

On the last Sunday of this visit, Wesley preached morning and evening at Wroot, where John Whitelamb, his brother-in-law, was Rector. He had been Samuel Wesley's amanuensis whilst he was writing his book on Job, and was afterwards John Wesley's pupil at Oxford. Mary Wesley, his wife, only lived nine or ten months after their marriage. Whitelamb had been in Wesley's congregation on the first Sunday when he preached in Epworth churchyard. The little church at Wroot would not hold the people who came from all the district to hear their old friend and minister, who had laboured among them for two years with such acceptance. After three other services on the Sunday Wesley took his stand at six o'clock on his father's tomb. A vast multitude had assembled from all parts. "I continued among them for near three hours; and yet we scarce knew how to part." His reflections upon the work at Epworth have peculiar interest. "Oh, let none think his labour of love is lost because the fruit does not immediately appear. Near forty years did my father labour here; but he saw little fruit of his labour. I took some pains among this people, too; and my strength also seemed spent in vain. But now the fruit appeared. There were scarce any in the town on whom either my father or I had taken any pains formerly, but the seed sown so long since now sprang up, bringing forth repentance and remission of sins."

Five weeks later, after visiting Sheffield and Bristol, Wesley returned to London. He found his mother on the borders of eternity. She had no doubt or fear. Her one desire was to depart and be with Christ. Wesley's description of the work at Epworth must have filled his mother's heart with joy. Her Rectory services had borne witness to her intense desire for the salvation of the people. Her labour also was bearing fruit. After the account of her burial, Wesley inserted in his journal the letter to her husband in which she justifies her services. She also had been, he reminds his readers, in her measure and degree, a preacher of righteousness. She died on Friday, July 23rd, three days after her son's return. Her five daughters were with her. Charles Wesley, who was absent on one of his evangelistic tours, was the only member of her family who was not at her side. Her children, standing around her bed, fulfilled her last request, made just before she lost her speech: "Children, as soon as I am released, sing a psalm of praise to God."

Mrs. Wesley had spent her last days at the Foundery, where she lived in her son's apartments. She was thoroughly identified with all the early phases of the Great Revival. Samuel Wesley had ventured to offer some remonstrance because she was present at John's open-air service at Kennington in September, 1739. Three or four weeks before that service, whilst her son-in-law, Mr. Hall, handed her the cup at the Sacrament, with the words, "The blood of our Lord Jesus Christ, which was given for thee," the words, she said, "struck through my heart, and I knew God, for Christ's sake, had forgiven *me* all *my* sins." On the Monday before she went to Kennington she told John Wesley the blessing she had found. When he asked whether her father, Dr. Annesley, had not the same faith, she replied that he had it himself, and declared shortly before his death that for more than forty years he had no darkness, no fear, no doubt at all of his being "accepted in the Beloved," but he never preached explicitly on the subject, and Mrs. Wesley had scarcely ever heard such a thing mentioned as having forgiveness of sins now, or the witness of the Spirit. From the time of this service her heart was filled with peace. She took part in the consultation held at the Foundery before Wesley read his final protest on his withdrawal from the Fetter Lane Society. She also rendered important service when the subject of lay-preaching was exercising Wesley's mind.

On Sunday, August 1st, 1742, she was buried in Bunhill Fields, close to the Foundery. An innumerable company of people gathered at five o'clock in the afternoon. Great was the mourning when Wesley read, "I commit the body of my dear mother to the earth." * He afterwards spoke from the words, "I saw a great white throne, and Him that sat on it, from whose face the earth and the heaven fled away; and there was found no place for them. And I saw the dead, small and great, stand before God; and the books were opened. And the dead were judged out of those things which were written in the books, according to their works." "It was one of the most solemn assemblies I ever saw, or expect to see on this side eternity." The mother lived on in her sons and in the glorious work which they were doing for God and their country. Her name has become one of the household names of the world. Isaac Taylor says, with great justice,† "The Wesleys' mother was the mother of Methodism in a religious and moral sense; for her courage, her submissiveness to authority, the high tone of her mind, its independence, and its self-control, the warmth of her devotional feelings, and the practical direction given to them, came up and were visibly repeated in the character and conduct of her sons."

Wesley spent the three months after his mother's death between London and Bristol. He travelled over the high-road between the two cities five times in these months. On November 8th he set out from Bristol to Newcastle. Charles Wesley had just left on his way to London, after a few weeks' visit. The work at Newcastle was different from any that Wesley had yet seen. He says, "The grace of God flows here with a wider stream than it did at first either at Bristol or Kingswood. But it does not sink so deep as it did there. Few are thoroughly convinced of sin, and scarce any can witness that the Lamb

* Stevenson, "Wesley Family," p. 226.

† "Wesley and Methodism," p. 19.

of God has taken away their sins." A week later he adds that he never saw a work of God so evenly and gradually carried on. It constantly increased. So much did not seem to be done at any one time as had often been accomplished in Bristol or London, but the work always made steady advance both in the Society and in individual members. Wesley spent nearly seven weeks in Newcastle, preaching constantly in the town and the outlying district. He was detained by the endeavour to find a site for a preaching-place. At last Mr. Stephenson, a merchant in Newcastle, whose descendant, an ex-mayor of the city, is one of its best-known Methodists, offered a plot of ground, forty-eight by ninety feet, for forty pounds. Next day Wesley signed an agreement. Within a week he had taken a lodging near the ground, but the intense frost made it impossible to begin the building. Wesley never felt such cold. His desk stood within a yard of the fire, yet he could not write for a quarter of an hour together without his hands being quite benumbed.

The first stone of the "house" was laid on December 20th. People flocked from all parts. Three or four times during the evening service Wesley was forced to pause in his sermon that the congregation might pray and give thanks. The cost of building was estimated at seven hundred pounds. Many asserted that it would never be finished, or that Wesley would not live to see it covered in. "I was of another mind," he says, "nothing doubting but, as it was begun for God's sake, He would provide what was needful for the finishing it." Wesley's courage will be better appreciated when it is known that he began to build with only twenty-six shillings in hand. His confidence was not disappointed. Soon afterwards a Quaker, who had heard of his scheme, sent him the following letter:—

"FRIEND WESLEY,—I have had a dream concerning thee. I thought I saw thee surrounded with a large flock of sheep, which thou didst not know what to do with. My first thought when I awoke was, that it was thy flock at Newcastle, and that thou hadst no house of worship for them. I have enclosed a note for one hundred pounds, which may help thee to provide a house." * Supplies came in from time to time, so that the work was pushed on rapidly. Wesley called it "The Orphan House," apparently after Francke's schools at Halle, which he had seen with great interest during his Continental journey in 1738.

Wesley preached his farewell sermon on December 30th to a vast congregation. Men, women, and children hung upon him, so that he could not disengage himself. When at last he got to the gate and took horse, one woman kept her hold, and ran by his side down to Sandgate. Seven weeks later he returned, as the work at Newcastle needed special oversight during the building of the Orphan House. At last, on March 25th, 1743, he preached in the shell of the building on "The Rich Man and Lazarus." A great multitude assembled and kept a watchnight there. The Orphan House stood just outside Pilgrim Street Gate. It had a blessed history. Its school, under the care of a master and mistress, provided for forty poor children. One of the first Sunday-schools in the north, with a thousand scholars, met there; it had its Bible Society before the British and Foreign Bible Society was established. In its choir, one of the best in the country, the sons of Mr. Scott, afterwards the celebrated Lord Eldon and Lord Stowell, were sometimes found. The colliers and keelmen of the district were so eager to hear the Wesleys that they would lie down

* Moore, i., 551.

on the benches after evening service and sleep till the hour for the early morning preaching. The Newcastle of Wesley's time was very different from the city of to-day.* Sir William Blackett's mansion then stood in its extensive pleasure-grounds on what is now the centre of the place. When Wesley visited the town in June, 1759, he found it in all its summer beauty. It called forth from him the high tribute, "Certainly, if I did not believe there was another world, I should spend all my summers here, as I know no place in Great Britain comparable to it for pleasantness." "The Newcastle of Wesley's time," says a recent writer, "must have been indeed one of the most beautiful spots under the canopy of heaven, with its castle and its churches and quaint groups of red-tiled, old-timbered houses, nestling amongst orchard trees, with patches of meadow and garden here and there, and all hemmed in by the encircling wall, with its gateway, towers, and its turrets, which, an old writer tells us, was the finest town-wall in Europe, and very like those of Avignon and Jerusalem in appearance." †

During the year 1742 many Methodist Societies were formed in Northumberland, Somersetshire, Wiltshire, Gloucestershire, Leicestershire, Warwickshire, and Nottinghamshire, as well as in the southern parts of Yorkshire.‡ Charles Wesley's journal for this year has not been preserved, but glimpses of him may be caught in Newcastle, Bristol, and London. He was devoting himself to the labours of an itinerant's life with an ardour and success scarcely, if at all, inferior to his brother's. Whitefield was now working on his own lines, but the

* Tyerman, i., 385.

† R. J. Charleton, in *English Illustrated Magazine*, November, 1885.

‡ Works, xii., 311.

Wesleys had already gathered a band of lay-preachers around them, who were rendering inestimable service in extending and consolidating the work.

We may here refer to Wesley's connection with his old university after his return from Georgia. He was a frequent visitor to Oxford, and some important steps of his preparation for the Great Revival were taken there.

Two pleasant glimpses of Wesley, at Lincoln College, are given in his journal. On Saturday, December 8th, 1739, he came into his old room, "from which I went to Georgia. Here, musing on the things that were past, and reflecting how many that came after me were preferred before me, I opened my New Testament on those words (oh, may I never let them slip!), 'What shall we say, then? That the Gentiles, which followed not after righteousness, have attained to righteousness. But Israel, which followed after the law of righteousness, hath not attained to the law of righteousness. Wherefore? Because they sought it not by faith, but, as it were, by the works of the Law.'"* A month later he was in his room once more, looking over the letters he had received for sixteen or eighteen years. Few traces of inward religion were found there. Only one of all his correspondents declared that the love of God was shed abroad in his heart. Wesley did not then understand his words. He adds, "He was expelled out of his Society as a madman, and, being disowned by his friends, and despised and forsaken of all men, lived obscure and unknown for a few months, and then went to Him whom his soul loved." Wesley preached before the University in 1738 and 1741. He was bound to take his turn in the

* Rom. ix. 30—32.

pulpit, or pay three guineas for a substitute. His last sermon was on Friday, August 24th, 1744. The races brought many strangers to Oxford, who swelled his congregation at St. Mary's. The Vice-Chancellor, the Proctors, and most of the heads of houses were present. Charles Wesley, Mr. Piers, and Mr. Meriton had come down to support the preacher. The little band of friends walked together to and from this memorable service. "Never have I seen a more serious congregation," Charles Wesley wrote. "They did not let a word slip them. Some of the heads stood up the whole time, and fixed their eyes on him." The Vice-Chancellor sent the beadle for Wesley's notes, which he sealed and forwarded to him immediately. Wesley admired the wise providence of God in this request. By this means every man of eminence in the University read his sermon. He was not allowed to preach again. But the beautiful description of Scriptural Christianity and the touching appeal to the venerable men who were more especially called to form the tender minds of youth show how unworthy and unfounded were the "false and scurrilous" accounts of it which, Wesley tells us, were published in almost every corner of the nation. Gibbon and Adam Smith both bear witness how deeply Oxford then needed reformation. Serious religious instruction or efficient tuition was almost unknown. Wesley was never more faithful, more tender, or more truly Scriptural in his teaching than in the sermon which led to his exclusion from the pulpit of his university. Dr. Conybeare, the learned Dean of Christ Church, said on the day of the sermon, "John Wesley will always be thought a man of sound sense, though an enthusiast." * Dr. Kennicott, the Hebrew

* *Methodist Magazine*, 1866, p. 44.

scholar, then an undergraduate at Wadham College, heard this sermon. He says Wesley's "black hair, quite smooth, and parted very exactly, added to a peculiar composure in his countenance, showed him to be an uncommon man." He speaks of the agreeable emphasis with which the preacher read his text. Kennicott did not like Wesley's reflections on the University, but was greatly impressed by his sermon. "Had these things been omitted, and his censures moderated, I think his discourse as to style and delivery would have been uncommonly pleasing to others as well as to myself. He is allowed to be a man of great parts." *

Wesley resigned his Fellowship on June 1st, 1751, wishing the Rector and Fellows "constant peace and all felicity in Christ." From November 6th, 1739, his leave of absence had been regularly renewed every six months, till November 6th, 1750, when he asked this favour for the last time. His place was not filled till May 10th, 1754, because there was no candidate duly qualified by county. Robert Kirke, B.A., of Lincoln College, was then chosen as his successor.

* *Methodist Magazine*, 1866, p. 44.

CHAPTER XII.

ENCOUNTERS WITH THE MOB.

NO man was so familiar with the English mobs of his day as John Wesley. In almost every place he visited opposition was, sooner or later, stirred up against the despised Methodists. We have already seen how Beau Nash tried to silence him at Bath in June, 1739. Next day Wesley was at Priest Down. He stood in the open air, where two men, hired for the purpose, began to sing a ballad. Wesley spoke a few mild words, but as they were without effect, he and his friends were compelled to sing a psalm, which drowned the voices of the disturbers, and utterly silenced them. Prayer was then offered, and the men seemed utterly confounded.* In London and Bristol violent opposition broke out both from high and low. "The beasts of the people," Wesley says, "were stirred up almost in all places to 'knock these mad dogs on the head at once.'" At first no magistrate would listen to any complaints against this brutal violence. On April 1st, 1740, however, the rioters in Bristol, who had long disturbed the Methodists, were so increased as to fill, not only the court before the place of meeting, but a considerable part of the street. The Mayor sent them an order to disperse; but they set him at defiance. He then ordered several of his officers to take the ringleaders into custody.

* Works, i., 199.

These received a severe reprimand at the Quarter Sessions. When they began to excuse themselves by saying many things against Wesley the Mayor cut them short, saying, "What Mr. Wesley is is nothing to you. I will keep the peace; I will have no rioting in this city." The Methodists of Bristol thus found a deliverer.

London was soon as quiet as Bristol. One Sunday evening in September, 1740, when Wesley stepped out of the coach at the Foundery, the mob, who had gathered in great numbers about the door, quite closed him in. He blessed God that the time he had long looked for was come, and at once began to speak on "righteousness and judgment to come." The noise was so great that at first only a few heard, but the silence spread from the little ring around him, till even those on the skirts of the crowd were perfectly quiet. Wesley withdrew from this novel congregation amid general marks of goodwill. "They all showed me much love, and dismissed me with many blessings." The following Tuesday, many who came into the Foundery like lions were quickly subdued. Tears trickled down the faces of those who had just before blasphemed and contradicted. On the Thursday a great number of men got into the Foundery and disturbed the service; but they were soon silent, and did not hear in vain. "I wonder," Wesley says, "that the devil has not wisdom enough to discern that he is destroying his own kingdom. I believe he has never yet, any one time, caused this open opposition to the truth of God without losing one or more of his servants, who were found of God while they sought Him not." A fortnight later these scenes were repeated, but Wesley's tact and self-possession secured a complete victory. Experience gave him perfect facility in handling disturbers. In October, 1740, a London crowd came to drown his voice by shouting. No sooner had they begun than he turned upon them, "and offered them deliverance from their hard master. The word sank deep into them, and they opened not their mouth."

On December 31st, 1741, Sir John Ganson, the chairman of the Middlesex bench, called upon Wesley, and said, "Sir, you have no need to suffer these riotous mobs to molest you, as they have done long. I and all the other Middlesex magistrates have orders from above to do you justice whenever you apply to us." Two or three weeks later the Methodists did apply for redress. Justice was done, though not with rigour, and from that time the persecuted people had peace in London. Sir John referred to George II. when he spoke of "orders from above." Wesley told Henry Moore, late in life, that one of the Oxford Methodists, who had become a Quaker, settled at Kew.* He was rich and much respected. Permission was given him to walk in the royal gardens, where he often had conversation with the King. One day the monarch asked him if he knew the Wesleys when he was at Oxford, adding, "They make a great noise in the nation." The Quaker replied, "I know them well, King George, and thou mayst be assured that thou hast not two better men in thy dominions, nor men that love thee better, than John and Charles Wesley." When the troubles of the Methodists were discussed by the Council, the King took a firm stand: "I tell you, while I sit on the throne, no man shall be persecuted for conscience' sake." †

Wesley had been in considerable peril at Long Lane, Southwark, in February, 1741, where the mob threw many large stones, one of which went just over his shoulder

---

* Moore, ii., 3. † Works, vi., 393.

On January 25th, 1742, whilst speaking from the words, "He that committeth sin is of the devil," the rabble made all the noise they could, and pushed violently against the hearers. They struck some of them, and broke down part of the house. Wesley had instructed the Methodists to keep their seats and not answer the disturbers. They carefully observed his counsels. When, however, their enemies began to throw large stones, which forced their way through the roof, and fell with the tiles among the people, Wesley saw that the people were really in peril of their lives. He then told the rioters, "You must not go on thus; I am ordered by the magistrate, who is, in this respect, to us the minister of God, to inform him of those who break the laws of God and the King. And I must do it if you persist herein; otherwise I am a partaker of your sin." This appeal only made them more outrageous. Wesley then said, "Let three or four calm men take hold of the foremost, and charge a constable with him, that the law may take its course." One man was brought in cursing and blaspheming in a dreadful manner. Five or six men took him to Justice Copeland, who bound him over to appear at the next sessions at Guildford. When the rioter was brought into the house some of his companions shouted, "Richard Smith! Richard Smith!" This man was one of their stoutest champions. Now, however, he made no response. He had been deeply convinced of sin, and came into the room with a woman who also had been actively promoting the disturbance. This woman fell upon her knees and urged Smith never to forget the mercy God had shown him. The prosecution against the man, who had been carried before the magistrate, was suffered to drop, as he submitted and promised better behaviour.

When Methodism began to spread over England in

1742, persecution and riot were the order of the day. Staffordshire has won for itself unenviable notoriety as the headquarters of opposition. In January, 1743, Wesley visited Wednesbury, where his brother had spent a few days. He preached in the Town Hall morning and evening, and also in the open air. About a hundred members were gathered into Society, who increased within two or three months to between three and four hundred. Mr. Egginton, the Vicar, was at first friendly to the Methodists, and told Wesley that the oftener they came the better he should be pleased. Wesley heard him preach a plain, useful sermon, and almost all the congregation at the church went down to the preaching-place, a large hollow half a mile from the town, which would hold four or five thousand people. They stood in a semicircle, tier above tier. The hollow would not contain the multitude gathered from all parts, so that they overflowed on all sides. When Wesley returned in April he found things surprisingly altered. The inexcusable folly of Mr. Williams, one of Wesley's preachers, had transformed the Vicar into a bitter enemy. Williams had abused the clergy and aroused their hatred by his unworthy spirit. But though the Vicar was thoroughly enraged, he had not yet won over the people. They were extremely quiet and attentive to Wesley's preaching. On the Sunday he says that he had never heard so wicked a sermon, and delivered with such bitterness of voice and manner, as the Vicar preached. Wesley tried to prepare the members of Society for the storm which he was must soon break upon them. Whilst he was speaking "a gentleman rode up very drunk, and after many unseemly and bitter words, laboured much to ride over some of the people." The trouble seemed nearer when he learned that this man was also a clergyman in the district. A month later Charles

Wesley was with "our dear colliers at Wednesbury." He consecrated a piece of ground given for a preaching place by singing a hymn upon it, and ventured to Walsall, where, he says in his graphic way, the street was full of fierce Ephesian beasts.

In June the storm burst on the poor Methodists. Wesley received the news of the terrible six days' riot on Saturday, June 18th. It was necessary for him to stay in London for his Sunday services, but he set out early next morning to assist them as far as he could. He rode over to Tamworth to consult Counsellor Littleton whether his people could be protected from such outrage. This gentleman told him that there was an easy remedy if the persecutors were rigorously prosecuted. Three months later Wesley visited the sufferers once more. He had preached unmolested at mid-day in the centre of Wednesbury. In the afternoon, whilst he was busy writing at the house of one of the Methodists, a cry arose that the mob had gathered before the door. The friends prayed that God would disperse the mob, and in half an hour all had melted away. Wesley now said this was the time for him to go, but the people were so urgent that he sat down again. Before five o'clock his worst fears were realised. The mob beset the house in greater numbers than ever. One and all shouted, "Bring out the minister; we will have the minister." Wesley asked some one to take their captain by the hand and lead him in. After a few words the lion became a lamb. Wesley now asked him to bring one or two of the bitterest opponents inside. He soon returned with a couple who "were ready to swallow the ground with rage; but in two minutes they were as calm as he." After such skilful preparation, Wesley went out, and calling for a chair, asked, "What do any of you want with me?" They told him that they wanted him to go with them to the magistrate. "That I will," said Wesley, "with all my heart." The few words he spoke had such effect that the mob shouted, "The gentleman is an honest gentleman, and we will spill our blood in his defence." Wesley now set out for the magistrate's house with two or three hundred rioters; the rest dispersed to their homes. Darkness and heavy rain came on in less than half an hour, but they pushed on another mile to the justice's house at Bentley Hall. He sent word that he was in bed, and advised them to go home and be quiet. The charge as stated to the magistrate's son was ridiculous enough. "Why, an't please you, they sing psalms all day; nay, and make folks rise at five in the morning." They now went to another magistrate at Walsall. He also sent word that he was in bed. These very magistrates had just issued an order calling all officers of justice to search for and bring to them any Methodist preacher found in the district. Fifty of the rioters now undertook to convey Wesley home. They had not gone a hundred yards, when the mob of Walsall burst upon them. It was between seven and eight o'clock. Wesley's convoy were weary and greatly outnumbered. They tried to stand against the new-comers, but many were knocked down, and the rest ran away, so that Wesley was left in the hands of his new enemies. The woman who led the first mob, however, ran into the thickest of the Walsall rioters, and knocked down three or four of them, but she was overpowered and held down by three or four men, who beat her with all their might. She would probably have been killed had not "honest Munchin," the leader of the Walsall rioters, interposed. She was then allowed to crawl home as well as she could.

It was in vain for Wesley to speak, for the noise was

like the raging of the sea. He was dragged along to the town. When he attempted to enter an open door, a man caught him by the hair and pulled him back. He was then hurried through the main street from one end of the town to the other. This was the town which Charles Wesley had found full of "fierce Ephesian beasts" five months before. Their hour had now come. Wesley felt neither pain nor weariness, but continued to speak to all who could hear. At last he stood at the door of a shop and gained a hearing. When he asked them to let him speak, many cried out, "No, no! knock his brains out; down with him! kill him at once." Others said, "Nay, but we will hear him first." For a quarter of an hour Wesley spoke. Then his voice failed, and the tumult began once more. His voice soon returned, and he broke out in prayer. The man who led the mob now turned and said, "Sir, I will spend my life for you. Follow me, and not one soul here shall touch a hair of your head." Two or three of his companions confirmed this, and got close to Wesley; the gentleman in the shop, who had prevented his entrance lest the mob should pull it to the ground, shouted, "For shame! for shame! Let him go," and an "honest butcher" pulled back four or five of the fiercest rioters. The mob now fell back, and Wesley passed through them, surrounded by his champions. On the bridge the opposition rallied again. Wesley and his friends therefore went down one side, crossed the mill-dam, and a little before ten o'clock safely reached Wednesbury. During these five terrible hours Wesley was as self-possessed as if he had been in his study. It came into his mind once that if he were thrown into the river, the papers in his pockets would be spoiled, but he knew that he could swim across, as he had a thin coat and light boots. Though he had to go downhill on a slippery road.

he never stumbled nor made the least slip. A lusty man just behind him struck at the back of his head several times with a large oaken stick, but every time the stroke was turned aside. He escaped many blows through his low stature, and his enemies were knocked down by them. One man raised his arm to strike, but suddenly dropped it, and stroked his head, saying, "What soft hair he has!" The gentleman in the shop where Wesley stopped was the mayor. Wesley, of course, was not aware of this, but the mob knew the chief magistrate, and were somewhat checked by his presence. The first whose hearts were touched were the captains of the rabble, one of whom had been a prizefighter at the bear-garden of the district.

Four members of Society—three men and one woman—stood by Wesley from first to last. None received a blow save William Sitch, who held Wesley's arm from one end of the town to the other. He was knocked down, but soon got to his friend's side again. Wesley asked him what he looked for when the mob came upon them. "To die for Him who had died for us," was his noble answer. Joan Parks, the heroic young woman who shared Wesley's perils, was as free from fear as if she had been quietly at home. All through the struggle she felt a confident persuasion that God would deliver them. Wesley lost one flap of his waistcoat and a little skin from his hand in this tumult. The flap of the other pocket, in which was a bank-note, was only half torn off. Wesley had been hardened by encounters with the mob. Two years before, he says, a piece of brick grazed his shoulders; a year later a stone struck him between the eyes at the Great Gardens; a month before his Walsall experiences he received a blow in a riot. This night he received two: one as the rioters bore him into Walsall, the other as he came out. One man struck him on the breast with all his might, another hit him in the mouth with such force that the blood gushed out, yet he felt no more pain from either blow than if, to use his own illustration, they had touched him with a straw. When he reached Wednesbury the friends were praying for him in the house from which he had started. His sufferings awoke general sympathy. Many whom he had never seen came to rejoice in his escape. Next morning, as he rode through the town, he says, "Every one I met expressed such a cordial affection that I could scarce believe what I saw and heard." Charles Wesley met him at Nottingham. He says that his brother "*looked* like a soldier of Christ. His clothes were torn to tatters." Charles Wesley, who went straight from Nottingham to the scenes of the rioting, adds some interesting particulars. The greatest profligate of the country was his brother's deliverer, and carried him through the river on his shoulders. This man, "honest Munchin," Charles Wesley admitted on trial into the Methodist Society five days after the riot. Since that night he had been constantly under conviction of sin. Charles asked what he thought of his brother. "Think of him?" was the answer; "that he is a mon of God; and God was on his side, when so mony of us could not kill one mon." The real name of this convert was George Clifton. He died in Birmingham in 1789, two years before Wesley, at the age of eighty-five. He was never weary of telling the story of the night when God saved him from laying his hand on His servant.*

Cornwall vied with Staffordshire in the fierceness of its opposition to the Methodists. But the brunt of the Cornish opposition was borne by Charles Wesley. The story of his visit to St. Ives in July, 1743, is one of

* Tyerman, i., 413.

the most interesting pages of his itinerant life. The resolute mayor of that town saved the Methodists from outrages such as their brethren in Staffordshire groaned under. Wesley, who was at St. Ives two months later, had one brush with the mob. They rushed into the room where he was preaching, roaring and striking those that stood in the way. He tried to inspire his friends with his own calmness, but they were not so familiar with such scenes. Finding the uproar increase, he went into the midst and brought the captain of the mob up to the desk. Wesley received one blow on the side of the head. He and the leader of the rabble reasoned together, till the man was quite won over, and undertook to quiet his companions. When Wesley visited the place again in April, 1744, he found that the mob had pulled down the preaching-place, "for joy that Admiral Matthews had beat the Spaniards." "Such," he adds, with his keen satire, "is the Cornish method of thanksgiving. I suppose if Admiral Lestock had fought too, they would have knocked all the Methodists on the head." For a time there was great peace, but Wesley received news from Cornwall six months later which made him say that the war against the Methodists was "everywhere carried on with far more vigour than that against the Spaniards."

The riot at Falmouth in July, 1745, was one of the most serious Wesley ever faced. His tact and courage were never more conspicuous. He escaped without the slightest injury. "I never saw before," he says—"not at Walsall itself—the hand of God so plainly as here." At Bolton, in Lancashire, Wesley had also to face bitter opposition. But the disturbers came in for the worst blows themselves. Wesley took his stand at the Cross in August, 1748, when the great wild mob tried to throw him down from the steps on which he stood. They pushed him off once or twice, but he stepped up again and continued his discourse. Stones now began to fly. Some of the rioters got behind Wesley on the Cross to thrust him down. They thus enjoyed the sweets of persecution. One man was bawling at Wesley's ear, when a stone struck him on the cheek, and he was still. Another was forcing his way down to push the preacher off, when a missile struck him on the forehead. The blood ran down from the wound, and his course was stayed. A third man had got close to Wesley and stretched out his hand, when a sharp stone hit him smartly on the joints of his fingers. He was thus effectually disabled.

Fourteen months later Wesley gained a signal victory over the Bolton mob. He had come from Rochdale, where multitudes of people filled the streets, "shouting, cursing, blaspheming, and gnashing upon us with their teeth." Their rage had compelled him to abandon his intention of preaching in the street, and to hold his service in a large room. He found, however, that the people at Rochdale were but lambs compared with those at Bolton. "Such rage and bitterness," he says, "I scarce ever saw before in any creatures that bore the form of men." They followed in full cry to the house where Wesley stayed, and filled the street from end to end. When there was a slight lull in the storm, one of the party ventured out, but he was rolled in the mire by the rioters, so that when he scrambled into the house again he could scarcely be recognised. The friends inside heard the ringing of a bell which summoned all the forces together, and quietly awaited the attack. Wesley was upstairs when news was brought that the mob had rushed into the house. Two of his friends were busy reasoning with them. Wesley quietly walked down into their midst. They had filled every room below. The scene can only be described in his own words. "I called for a chair. The winds were hushed, and all was calm and still. My heart was filled with love, my eyes with tears, and my mouth with arguments. They were amazed; they were ashamed; they were melted down; they devoured every word. What a turn was this! Oh, how did God change the counsel of the old Ahithophel into foolishness, and bring all the drunkards, swearers, Sabbath-breakers, and mere sinners in the place to hear of His plenteous redemption." Next morning the preaching-place was crowded to excess at five o'clock. Wesley spoke a good deal longer than he was accustomed to do. But the people were not satisfied. He therefore promised to preach again at nine, in a meadow near the town. Hearers flocked from all sides. Wesley adds, "Oh, how have a few hours changed the scene. We could now walk through every street of the town, and none molested or opened his mouth, unless to thank or bless us."

The Irish mobs sometimes gave Wesley a warm reception on his visits to their country. At Cork, in 1750, the mayor sent the town drummers and his sergeants to disturb the congregation. They came down to the preaching-place with an innumerable mob. The drummers were noisy enough, but Wesley continued his discourse. When he went out he asked one of the sergeants to keep the peace; but he answered, "Sir, I have no orders to do that." The rabble threw whatever came to hand, but nothing hit the preacher. He walked forward quietly, looked every man in the face, the rioters opening right and left as he passed along. When he reached his friend's house a Papist stood in the door to prevent his entrance. Just then one of the mob aimed a blow at Wesley, which knocked this woman down flat. He had nothing to do but step in. No one followed him. Ten days later another immense mob assembled near the barracks in Cork, where Wesley was preaching. When he had done seven or eight of the soldiers marched in front, and a whole troop behind, so that he passed safely through the rabble with his military body-guard.

Wesley never failed in tact and resource during his encounters with the rioters. It was his rule, confirmed by long experience, always to look a mob in the face.* However much the mob threatened, he never swerved. In Cornwall, in July, 1745, as he stood preaching on a high wall, the rabble appeared. He kept his eye steadily on them. Many were softened, and grew calmer and calmer. One of their champions, however, who feared that all their plans were going to be defeated, went round and suddenly pushed Wesley off the wall. He fell on his feet without any hurt, and finding himself beside one of the warmest opponents, who was on horseback, took hold of his hand and reasoned with him. The man refused to be convinced, but he and all the rest grew much milder, and parted from the preacher with great civility. At Bath, in February, 1742, many noisy persons were gathered at one end of the room. Wesley slipped from his place and took up a position amongst them. Seeing this, the greater part of them stole to the end from which Wesley came, and began to cry aloud again. He paused to give them full scope, then began "a particular application," which very soon put them to silence. His congregations were sometimes disturbed by a single noisy opponent. In the market-place at Nottingham a man thus began to contradict and blaspheme. He was standing close to the preacher's back, but when Wesley turned he slunk

* Works, ii., 19, 33.

behind a pillar and disappeared. The opposer sometimes played his part so badly that even his comrades disowned * him or thrust him out of the place.†

As Wesley became known throughout the kingdom, the people themselves disposed of the disturbers. One man at Lisburn, in July, 1756, contradicted him while he was preaching, but the mob handled him so roughly that he was soon glad to hold his peace. A clergyman at Bandon‡ planted himself near Wesley in the main street, with a large stick in his hand, and interrupted the service. Before he had uttered many words two or three women dragged him into a house and sent him away through the garden. This maudlin opponent was about to indulge in familiarities with the woman who conducted him, and she had to cuff him soundly before she could escape. A young gentleman of the town next presented himself, along with two companions, who had pistols in their hands, but the people quietly bore him away. A third disturber was more furious, but a butcher of the town, who was not a Methodist, effectually cooled his courage by two or three hearty blows on the head. At Grimsby a young gentleman and his companions once quite drowned Wesley's voice, so that his large audience was kept without a sermon. A poor woman at last disposed of him by reciting a few passages of his life so wittily and keenly that the laugh of his companions was turned against him, and he was only too glad to slink away. A popish miller at Athlone § got up once to preach just opposite to Wesley, but when some of his comrades threw a little dirt at him he leaped down to fight them, and was roughly handled in the fray. A few days later Wesley

* Works, i.. 478.
† *Ibid.*, i., 467.
‡ Works, ii., 189
§ *Ibid.*, iii., 229

met with more noise and stupid, senseless impudence than he had experienced since he left England; but the chief man of the town silenced one of the disturbers, and another was knocked down by a hearer who was not a Methodist, so that the congregation soon had peace.* At another place a gentleman gave those who would not attend to his signs a stroke on the head with his stick, and thus effectually quieted a congregation that was inclined to be noisy.† At Burnley in 1784, high and low, rich and poor, flocked from all quarters to hear Wesley. All were eager to listen save the town-crier, who began to bawl amain. His wife, however, ran up, clapped one hand on his mouth, and seized him with the other, so that he could not utter a word.‡

Wesley's chaise-boy figures honourably in this record. His master had preached to a crowded congregation in a colliery village near Pembroke, when a gentleman broke in and ordered the people to go home and mind their business. As he used some bad words, the driver reproved him. He replied fiercely, "Do you think I need to be taught by a chaise-boy?" The "boy" had been an apt pupil. "Really, sir, I do think so," was the answer.§ Every form of opposition was tried during Wesley's long itinerancy. Mill-dams were let out;‖ church bells were jangled;¶ drunken fiddlers ** and ballad-singers †† were hired; organs pealed out; drums were beaten. From such encounters Wesley generally came off victorious. Once a man was sent to cry fresh salmon ‡‡ at a little distance from a multitude of "unawakened" hearers at

* Works, iii., 230.
† *Ibid.*, iii., 365.
‡ *Ibid.*, iv., 284.
§ *Ibid.*, iv., 106.
‖ Works, i., 494.
¶ *Ibid.*, ii., 21, 495
** *Ibid.*, ii., 22.
†† *Ibid.*, i.
‡‡ Works, iii., 407.

Leicester, but no one regarded him. On another occasion a Papist began to blow a horn as soon as Wesley gave out his text; but a gentleman stepping up, snatched away his horn, and without ceremony knocked him down.*

Wesley's caution was not less conspicuous than his courage. A good illustration of this may be drawn from the account of his visit to Pocklington in April, 1752. It was fair-day. There was no Society, and scarcely any one in the town was awakened. The room provided for preaching was only five yards square, and Wesley was anxious to have a bigger place. Some one suggested a yard. But when he went to see it he found that "it was plentifully furnished with stones, artillery ready at hand for the devil's drunken companions." Fortunately a gentleman offered a large barn, where the tears of Wesley's congregation fell as the rain. His long experience in such matters had just been supplemented at Hull the previous day. Clods and stones flew about him on every side, but nothing touched him. When he finished his sermon he found that his coachman had driven quite away. A lady kindly offered Wesley and his wife a place in her coach. It had nine occupants, three on each side and three in the middle. The mob formed an escort, throwing in at the windows whatever came first to hand. Wesley quaintly adds, "But a large gentlewoman, who sat in my lap, screened me, so that nothing came near me." One of Wesley's preachers took the mob in hand at Norwich with the best results. John Hampson was a man of splendid physique, the very ideal of a muscular Christian. Once, when Wesley left the preaching-place, the rioters assumed a threatening attitude. Hampson came forward as his champion. Wesley wished him to

* Works, iii., 278.

withdraw, but his preacher answered with a thundering voice, "Let me alone, sir; if God has not given you an arm to quell this mob, He has given me one, and the first man who molests you here, I will lay him dead." Hampson's loud voice and big threat answered the purpose. The mob took care to keep at a safe distance.

Wesley's character and work, joined to the consistent lives of his members, gradually won happier days for the persecuted Methodists. Peace was not, however, secured without further appeals to law. Sometimes a threat was enough. In March, 1745, as Wesley was walking up Pilgrim Street, Newcastle, a man called after him. Wesley stood still. The fellow came up, used much abusive language, pushed Wesley once or twice, and then went away. Wesley found that this man had long annoyed the members of the Orphan House. Next day, therefore, he sent the following note:—

"ROBERT YOUNG,—I expect to see you between this and Friday, and to hear from you that you are sensible of your fault; otherwise, in pity to your soul, I shall be obliged to inform the magistrates of your assaulting me yesterday in the street.

"I am, your real friend,
"JOHN WESLEY."

Within two or three hours the offender came and gave ample promise of amendment. In 1751 the Methodists of Wrangle, in Lincolnshire, were violently assaulted by the mob, their goods destroyed, and their lives endangered. The magistrate refused redress. Wesley wrote a calm remonstrance, but "Mr. B——" was not wise enough to accept advice. The sufferers, therefore, applied to the Court of King's Bench, and he was afterwards glad to let them worship God in their own way.* A mob at Stalbridge was effectually quieted by the same means. The rioters got the hearing of the case postponed for eighteen months on one pretext after another, but this only increased their bill of costs when they were found guilty. The Methodists were now left in peace.† At Faversham, where he was informed that the mob and the magistrates had agreed to drive Methodism out of the town, Wesley told the people after his sermon what they had been constrained to do with the magistrate at Rolvenden, who perhaps would have been richer by some hundred pounds had he not meddled with the Society. "Since we have both God and law on our side," he concluded, "if we can have peace by fair means, we had much rather; we should be exceeding glad; but if not, we *will* have peace."

The journals often allude to the attitude of the magistrates. Wesley says that the baser sort stood at a distance, but made no disturbance, when he preached at Colchester in 1758, because they knew that the magistrates were determined to suffer no riot.‡ He gratefully acknowledges the quiet enjoyed at Scarborough, "since God put it into the heart of an honest magistrate to still the madness of the people." § When speaking of a Gloucester magistrate who had tamed the rioters, he adds, "So may any magistrate, if he will; so that wherever a mob continues any time, all they do is to be imputed not so much to the rabble as to the justices." ‖ At Manchester in 1759 ¶ he notes that wretched magistrates, who, by refusing to suppress, encouraged the rioters, had long occasioned

* Works, ii., 240, 256.
† *Ibid.*, iii., 263.
‡ *Ibid.*, ii., 462.
§ Works, iii., 168.
‖ *Ibid.*, iii., 313.
¶ *Ibid.*, ii., 477.

constant trouble, but some were now of a better mind. In the later years of Wesley's itinerancy it was rare to find an unfriendly magistrate. At Drogheda, in June, 1785, the mayor and several of the magistrates took care that no one should disturb his congregation. At Waterford, in May, 1787, a file of musketeers paraded at the door of the Court House, where he preached, at the order of the mayor. At Newark, in February of the same year, Wesley deferred his service for half an hour at the request of the mayor, who wished to attend with some of the aldermen. At Congleton, in April, 1790, the minister, mayor, and all the heads of the town were at the service. The mayor of Bristol invited Wesley to preach at his chapel and dine with him at the Mansion House.* Everywhere Wesley now found a welcome. The reproach of the Cross had ceased, for him at least, long before his itinerancy closed. His visits to all parts of the country assumed the character of public holidays, when all classes united to welcome the venerable itinerant. The particulars grouped together in this chapter illustrate Isaac Taylor's verdict, "When encountering the ruffianism of mobs and of magistrates, he showed a firmness as well as a guileless skill which, if the martyr's praise might admit of such an adjunct, was graced with the dignity and courtesy of the gentleman." †

* Works, iii., 409.
† "Wesley and Methodism," p. 50.

CHAPTER XIII.

WESLEY AS A TRAVELLER.

WE have already referred to Wesley's life in Georgia and his visit to Germany in 1738. His range was afterwards more limited, but he knew the United Kingdom better than any man of his time. In the summer of 1731 he walked from Oxford to Epworth. On his return to the University he learned that four or five-and-twenty miles was an easy and safe day's journey, in hot weather as well as cold. Then also he made another discovery, that it was easy to read as he walked for ten or twelve miles. It beguiled the journey,* and caused no additional fatigue. Wesley was no mean pedestrian. The year before he sailed to Georgia he walked a thousand and fifty miles † to preach in the churches round Oxford. A large part of his travelling on the Continent in 1738 was done on foot. Wesley never lost his zest for walking. In Ireland in 1758, when a horse was brought for him without saddle or bridle, he set out on foot.‡ A saddle was then found, and some one galloped after him at full speed with the horse. Ten years later § he walked on seven or eight miles before his servant overtook him with his carriage. At Bristol, in September, 1788, he says that his friends, more kind than wise, would scarce suffer him to walk. "It seemed so sad a thing to walk five or six

---

* Works, xii., 6.

† Whitehead, i., 453.

‡ Works, ii., 447.

§ *Ibid.*, iii., 348.

miles! I am ashamed that a Methodist preacher, in tolerable health, should make any difficulty of this." The old man of eighty-five had not lost his enjoyment of a good walk. Most of Wesley's journeys were made on horseback. There were no turnpikes in the north of England, and the London stage-coach went no further than York.* In many parts of the northern counties neither coach nor chaise had ever been seen. It was not till 1773 that Wesley began regularly to use a carriage. He travelled between four and five thousand miles a year. Mr. Hampson says,† "He was a hard but unskilful rider; and his seat was as ungraceful as it appeared uneasy, with a book in his hand and his hands up to his head." Notwithstanding Mr. Hampson's criticism, Wesley was no mean horseman, though his habit of reading may have made him appear ungraceful. In June, 1750, he mentions ninety miles as his longest day's journey on horseback. He started at four o'clock that morning, and was not in bed till twelve. He had been nearly twenty hours in the saddle. His own horse grew tired, so that he left it behind and borrowed that of his companion.

Wesley was familiar with all the discomforts of the road. His horses fell lame or were maimed by incompetent smiths. Sometimes there were more serious accidents. In July, 1743, he and John Downes rode from Newcastle to Darlington. They had young horses, which were quite vigorous the day before, but now both seemed unwell. The ostler went in haste for a farrier, but both animals died before they could discover what was the matter with them. In June, 1752, a young strong mare which Wesley borrowed at Manchester fell lame before he reached

* Southey, i., 407. † Life of Wesley, iii., 191.

Grimsby. Another was procured, but he was "dismounted" again between Newcastle and Berwick. When he returned to Manchester, he found that his own mare had lamed herself whilst at grass. He intended to ride her four or five miles, but some one took her out of the ground. Another which he had lately bought ought to have been forthcoming, but she had been taken to Chester. In one journey his horse became so exceeding lame that it could scarcely set its foot to the ground. Wesley could not discover what was amiss. He rode thus seven miles till he was thoroughly tired, and his head ached more than it had done for months. He says, "What I here aver is the naked fact. Let every man account for it as he sees good. I then thought, 'Cannot God heal either man or beast by any means, or without any?' Immediately my weariness and headache ceased, and my horse's lameness in the same instant. Nor did he halt any more that day or the next. A very odd accident this also!"

Wesley had some remarkable escapes during his long itinerancy. At Bristol, in June, 1739, his horse suddenly pitched upon its head, and rolled over and over.* He only received a little bruise on the side, and preached without pain to six or seven thousand people. A few months later some one riding sharply came full against him, and overthrew both Wesley and his horse, but they received no hurt.† Once the fall of his horse upon him ‡ brought one or two women out of a neighbouring house, who kindly helped him in to rest. Here he found three people who had gone astray, and was the means of restoring them all. An accident in 1747 was more dangerous.§ Wesley

* Works, i., 206.

† *Ibid.*, i., 227.

‡ Works, i., 343.

§ *Ibid.*, ii., 41.

was riding through St. Nicholas' Gate, Bristol, when a cart came swiftly down the hill. There was just room for it to pass, but the carman was walking beside his waggon, and filled up all the space. Wesley called to him to go back, but the man took no heed, so that Wesley was obliged to hold in his own horse. The shaft of the cart came against his horse's shoulder with such violence as to force it to the ground. Wesley was shot over its head like an arrow out of a bow, and lay with arms and legs stretched out against the wall, he knew not how. The wheel ran by close to his side, but only dirtied his clothes. A man took Wesley into his shop, where he cleaned himself a little, and set out again for Wick. He returned to Bristol in time to preach. A report that he was killed had spread far and wide, so that his friends received him with great rejoicing. His shoulders, hands, sides, and legs were a little bruised; his knees and his right thigh were more painful. Some warm treacle, he says, took away all the pain in an hour, and the lameness in a day or two. A restive horse once ran backward and tumbled head over heels with Wesley in the saddle. He rose unhurt and went on his journey on the same animal, which was sobered at last.* At Canterbury his mare was struck on the leg with such violence by a stone that sprang out of the pavement that she dropped down at once. Wesley kept his seat, but his horse, in struggling to rise, fell again and rolled over him. His right leg seemed powerless, and he was very sick, but an honest barber came out, lifted him up, and helped him into his shop. Wesley felt very sick, but took a glass of water, and was soon able to proceed. On the way to Shoreham, in December, 1765, his horse fell in the Borough, Southwark, with Wesley's leg

* Works, ii., 91.

under it. He managed to go on in the coach, but for many months he suffered from the effects of this accident.

Wesley was out in some terrible storms. His northern journey in February, 1745, was the roughest he had ever had up to that time. There were, as we have seen, no turnpike-roads then in the north, and the causeways were like glass. The horses often fell down while Wesley and his companion were leading them. Gateshead Fell was a pathless waste of snow. No roads could be seen, but a Newcastle man overtook the travellers and guided them safely into the town. "Many a rough journey have I had before," says Wesley, "but one like this I never had, between wind, and hail, and rain, and ice, and snow, and driving sleet, and piercing cold." Next February, on his way from Birmingham to Stafford, the driving snow crusted him and his companion over from head to foot in less than an hour. A man who lived at the edge of the moors said, "Sir, 'tis a thousand pound to a penny that you do not come there to-day." He told them that it was four miles across, and even in a clear day he himself could not always go straight over. Wesley nevertheless pushed on, and, though all the roads were covered with snow, did not go ten yards out of the way till he reached Stafford. The same month in 1747 found him in similar circumstances. Snow covered everything, and the wind seemed as if it would overturn both man and beast. A violent storm of rain and hail which they met whilst passing across an open field drove through their coats and boots, freezing as it fell even upon their eyebrows. They had scarce strength or motion left when they reached their inn at Stilton. On Stamford Heath the snow-drifts almost swallowed them up. Next morning the servant reported that there would be no travelling that day, as the roads were quite filled up by a fresh fall of snow. "At least, we can walk twenty miles a day, with our horses in our hands," said Wesley.

Such particulars will show what a bold and untiring traveller Wesley was. In April, 1770, when he was in the Highlands, he pushed on to Inverness, though three young women who attempted to cross the mountain which he had to climb had been swallowed up in the snow. He was brought to a stand at the top by the snow-drifts, but dismounted, and striking warily out of the way, sometimes to the right, sometimes to the left, reached his destination safely, after many a stumble. In his eighty-third year he was the same fearless traveller as at the beginning of the Great Revival. An old inhabitant of Helston used to tell with great pride a story about Wesley. This man was then ostler at the London Inn, and drove the traveller on to St. Ives, as his own coachman did not know the road. When they reached Hayle, they found the sands between that town and St. Ives covered by the rising tide. A sea-captain earnestly begged Wesley not to venture across, but he had arranged to preach at a certain hour. Looking out of the carriage window, Wesley shouted, "Take the sea, take the sea." Before long the horses were swimming. Wesley put his head out of the window to encourage the driver, who feared every moment that they would be drowned. His long white hair was dripping with the sea-water. "What is your name, driver?" he asked. The man told him it was Peter. "Peter," was the answer, "fear not: thou shalt not sink." When they were safely in St. Ives, Wesley first saw that his driver had warm clothing, refreshment, and fire; then he himself went on to the chapel to preach to the people.

Wesley's stages were carefully arranged, so that he might hold as many services as possible on the way. Notice was given of his coming, and sometimes whole villages and towns flocked to hear him. It was necessary for him to adhere carefully to his plan. Sometimes he did break through it, as at Epworth, when he held his eight days' mission in the churchyard. But this was a striking exception to his rule. At Bedford, in March, 1758, after his sermon on "The Great Assize," the judge sent Wesley an invitation to dine. He had promised to be at Epworth on Saturday, and as it was now Friday, he was compelled to send an excuse. Wesley had already been detained for twenty-four hours by a change in the day appointed for his sermon. Between one and two in the afternoon he set off in haste. Thirty miles of rough travelling lamed the horses, but he took a post-chaise early next morning. He might have spared himself the expense, for driving on the frosty road was so tedious that Wesley's companion reached Stamford with the lame horses as quickly as the post-chaise. He made the next stage on horsebark, then hired another post-chaise. The waters were out in the Isle of Axholme. Fortunately, Wesley had heard of a man in the neighbourhood who knew the roads. Under his guidance, he reached Epworth between nine and ten on Saturday night. "After travelling more than ninety miles, I was little more tired than when I rose in the morning." This characteristic incident illustrates Wesley's determination to keep his engagements at all costs.

Wesley read his history, poetry, and philosophy on horseback. He says in 1770 that thirty years before he had wondered how it was that no horse stumbled while he was reading. He could find no other reason than that at such times he threw the reins upon his horse's neck. After more than a hundred thousand miles of such travelling, he scarcely remembered any horse, except two "that were always falling head over heels," that fell or made any serious stumble while he rode with a slack rein. He was convinced that a slack rein would prevent stumbling if anything could do so.*

In March, 1772, Wesley says, "I met several of my friends, who had begun a subscription to prevent my riding on horseback, which I cannot do quite so well since a hurt which I got some months ago. If they continue it, well; if not, I shall have strength according to my need." When he set up his carriage, the itinerancy of Wesley's later life became more easy than the long rides of former years. He spent ten hours a day as much alone as if he had been in a wilderness, and always had a store of books with him. In 1786 he travelled seventy-six miles in one day, and preached three times. "Still I was no more tired than when I rose in the morning." Three years later he refers to two other days' travelling of eighty and seventy-eight miles.† Riding on horseback became difficult from want of practice. Whilst in the Dales, in June, 1784, he was forced to ride.‡ "Being but a poor horseman, and having a rough horse, I had just strength for my journey, and none to spare; but, after resting a while, I preached without any weariness." § In 1773 he took chaise from Salisbury at two in the morning, and in the evening came to London. Six months later, whilst at Congleton, he received a letter which called him in haste to Bristol. He spent two hours in that city, and was back at Congleton on the Friday afternoon. He left on the Wednesday at one in the afternoon, so that he had travelled two hundred and eighty miles, "no more tired (blessed be God) than when I left." In August, 1768, he made a similar journey between Bristol

* Works, iii., 392.
† *Ibid.*, iv., 334, 448, 467.
‡ Works, iv., 96.
§ *Ibid.*, iv., 3.

and London. He reached the metropolis at one in the morning, found that his wife was out of danger, and after staying an hour came the same afternoon—"not at all tired"—to Bristol. In October, 1782, he took chaise from Portsmouth at two in the morning, and reached London in the afternoon. Such were some of Wesley's feats in travelling.

His chaise sometimes stuck fast, so that he had to borrow a horse and ride on,* or the axle-tree broke and overturned the carriage; † his chaise-springs ‡ suddenly snapped, but the horses instantly stopped, and he stepped out without the least inconvenience. On the way to Sligo in 1778 his carriage got well through two sloughs.§ By the help of seven or eight countrymen, one of whom carried Wesley over on his shoulders, they struggled through the third. The fourth was more difficult. Wesley was helped out, and walked forward. His friends with the stronger horse managed to get the chaise through, but with great difficulty. In December, 1784, a snow-storm upset all Wesley's plans. His carriage could scarcely get on. He walked great part of the way from Tunbridge Wells to Robertsbridge, which he reached after the time appointed for his service. An hour after nightfall he came to Rye, but the preaching-place was filled with serious hearers, so that he did not repent of his labour. Next day, even with two pairs of good horses, it was hard work to do fifteen miles in five hours. This record was outdone in his journey to Wrestlingworth thirteen days later. "Having a skilful guide, who rode before the chaise, and picked out the best way, we drove four miles in only three hours." In October, 1785,

* Works, iv., 46, 267; iii., 382.
† *Ibid.*, iv., 431.
‡ Works, iv., 67.
§ *Ibid.*, iv., 123.

Wesley was told that he could not get over the Ely roads. They ran between two banks, and had many bridges, where the coachman must "drive to an inch." Wesley was anxious to reach London, and pushed forward at once. A further glimpse of the Fen-country is given in his journal for November, 1774. A gentleman met him with a chaise when he went to Ely. "Oh, what want of common-sense! Water covered the high-road for a mile and a half. I asked, 'How must foot-people come to the town?' 'Why, they must wade through,'" was the answer. Two days later a friend led the horse in a place where water and mud reached up to his mid-leg. "We fenmen do not mind a little dirt," he said. Wesley had by-and-bye to take to horseback, as the chaise could not go on. Then a boat, twice as large as a kneading-trough, was called into requisition. In his later years Wesley sometimes took the whole coach for himself and his friends. In August, 1787, he thus engaged the coach from Bolton to Birmingham. They had six inside and eight outside, so that the conveyance broke down. It was patched up, and went on to Congleton, where another was obtained. This also broke down, and one of the horses was so tired that it could scarcely set one foot before the other. Wesley was two hours late, and stepped from the coach into the pulpit. A large congregation was awaiting him. Once, when he had taken the coach from Bristol, the clerk "faced him down" that he had secured it for another day. But Wesley's friends spoke so strongly that another coach was soon provided. Sometimes the coach was already full, so that he had to take a post-chaise,* or make the best arrangement he could.

* Works, iv., 359, 366, 432.

All Wesley's plans were exactly mapped out. He once sent to take two places in the coach for Lynn, where he was to preach "in their new house." The messenger, "mending my orders," took them in the diligence, which only reached the place between nine and ten at night, so that Wesley was robbed of one of the three evenings which he intended to give the people. We have one pleasant picture of a night journey. Two years before his death, Wesley took the night mail-coach for Bristol. "Having three of our brethren, we spent a comfortable night, partly in sound sleep and partly in singing praise to God." Some journeys were trying. One diligence * in which Wesley travelled let in air on all sides, so that he and his friends could scarcely preserve life.

He never lost an opportunity of doing good in these journeys. On the way to Colchester in the stage-coach, in November, 1771, he "met with two agreeable companions, whose hearts were quite open to instruction." A counterpart to this is found in the journal for February, 1779. "I went to Norwich in the stage-coach, with two very disagreeable companions called a gentleman and gentlewoman, but equally ignorant, insolent, lewd, and profane." A young officer with whom he once travelled swore incessantly. Wesley quietly asked if he had read the Book of Common Prayer, for if he had, he might remember the collect which began, "Almighty and everlasting God, who art always more ready to hear than we to pray, and art wont to give more than either we desire or deserve." The young fellow was effectually cured for that journey at least by this neat reproof.

It will easily be understood that Wesley never had a

* Works, iv., 297, 343.

moment to lose. Once, when he was kept waiting for his chaise, he was heard to say, "I have lost ten minutes for ever." He always expected his coachman to be ready at the precise moment fixed. "Have the carriage at the door at four," he said to him at Hull in 1788. "I do not mean a quarter or five minutes past, but four." In the later years of his life Wesley's visits to all parts of England were gala-days. Friends often trooped out to meet the venerable patriarch and escort him to the place in triumph. When he returned to London, they sometimes came out to meet him as far as Cobham or Hatfield.* Dublin welcomed him in like manner, and Cork sent out thirty horsemen to escort him to the city.† In the June before his death he had preached at Beverley in the afternoon, and was to be at Hull the same evening. About forty friends from Hull met and dined with him at Beverley. The pleasant conversation made them quite forget the time. Wesley suddenly pulled out his watch, bade his friends good-bye, and was gone before they had recovered from their surprise. They just managed to overtake the punctual traveller before he reached Hull.

Wesley's most perilous ride was in the neighbourhood of Newcastle in 1774. Mr. Hopper, one of his preachers, and Mr. Smith, who had married Wesley's stepdaughter, were on horseback; Mrs. Smith and her two little girls were with Wesley in the chaise. On the brow of a hill both the horses suddenly started off without visible cause, and flew down like an arrow out of a bow. In a minute Wesley's man fell off the box. "The horses went on full speed, sometimes to the edge of the ditch on the right, sometimes on the left." They avoided a cart, dashed over a narrow bridge, and rushed through an

* Works, iv., 51, 495. † *Ibid.*, iv., 305, 315, 385.

open gate more skilfully than if the man had been holding the reins. A gate on the far side of the farmer's yard into which they rushed was shut. Wesley thought this would certainly stop them, but the end of the chariot-pole struck the centre of the gate, and the horses dashed through as if it had been a cobweb. They were now galloping over a cornfield. The little girls cried out, "Grandpapa, save us!" Wesley replied, "Nothing will hurt you; do not be afraid." He felt as calm as if he had been sitting in his study. The horses were fast approaching the edge of a precipice. Just then Mr. Smith, who had been in full pursuit, managed to overtake them. He rode in between the runaway horses and the precipice. The horses stopped in a moment. Had they gone on ever so little, all must have been dashed over the brink together. The coachman received no hurt by his fall, so that the marvellous deliverance was complete.

No account of Wesley's travel would be complete without some reference to his experience at sea. He crossed the Atlantic twice, paid three visits to the Continent, and sailed forty-two times across the Irish Channel. His voyages across the Atlantic prepared him for many a rough passage between England and Ireland, or across the Solent and to the Isle of Man. Wesley was a good sailor. A strong gale and rolling sea made most of the passengers sick enough near Holyhead in 1773, but did not affect him at all.* He was not so fortunate in July, 1778. A strong north-easter made the sea so lumpy, that it affected him as much as a storm. He lay down at four in the afternoon and slept most of the time till four in the morning. Like all passengers in those days, he had some weary waiting for change of wind. In 1748, when he reached

* Works, iii., 489.

Holyhead, all the ships were on the other side. He was detained twelve days. The time was not wasted. He preached several times, and read prayers at his inn. He also wrote "A Word to a Methodist," at the request of a clergyman, who said he would take it as a favour if Wesley would write some tract advising his members not to leave the Church and not to rail against the clergy. The delay, however, tried his patience. He says, "I never knew men make such poor, lame excuses as these captains did for not sailing. It put me in mind of the epigram,

> 'There are, if rightly I methink,
> Five causes why a man should drink,'

which, with a little alteration, would just suit them :—

> 'There are, unless my memory fail,
> Five causes why we should not sail :
> The fog is thick ; the wind is high ;
> It rains, or may do by-and-bye ;
> Or—any other reason why.' "

After a week of waiting he made a little tour into the country. There was no more probability of a passage than when they reached Holyhead. This was on Wednesday. On the following Monday Wesley found all the packet-boats still there. He took lodgings in a private house, as he was determined not to stay any longer at the inn.* At midnight, however, the wind changed, and he was soon on his way to Dublin. Two years later he was delayed quite as long.† Their little vessel was twice driven back by the storm, and they had to wait several days for better weather. Wesley found it useful to be in suspense,‡ so that he might learn to "lean absolutely on His disposal

* Works, ii., 86. † *Ibid.*, ii., 179. ‡ *Ibid.*, ii., 268.

who knoweth and ruleth all things well." * After his plans had been thus deranged in 1760, he says, "Oh, how good it is to have no choice of our own, but to leave all things to the will of God." † Wesley's passages were made in all kinds of vessels. Some were little and uncomfortable. But signs of improvement appear in his later years. He speaks of the *Kildare* in 1771 as "abundantly the best and cleanest ship which I have sailed in for many years." ‡ She was eclipsed by the *Hawk.* § "So fine a ship I never sailed in before. She never shipped one sea, and went more steady than I thought was possible."

His services on board ship are pleasant features of Wesley's busy life. His fellow-passengers generally treated him with signal respect. One exception must be made. In March, 1750, "the famous Mr. Gr——, of Carnarvonshire, a clumsy, overgrown, hard-faced man," was on board the vessel in which he sailed for Dublin. When Wesley was about to lie down, this man tumbled in, pouring out a volley of ribaldry, obscenity, and blasphemy. Wesley retired to his own cabin, and some of Mr. G——'s companions took him away. When the vessel was driven back to Holyhead, this man came with a rabble of gentlemen to disturb Wesley's service. He burst open the doors, struck the old landlord several times, "kicked his wife, and with twenty full-mouthed oaths and curses, demanded, 'Where is the parson?'" The landlord put Wesley into another room. Mr. G—— climbed on a chair to look if Wesley were on the top of a bed, but fell full length on the floor. The bully now retired for a time. About nine he came again with his friends. The

* Works, iii., 14.
† *Ibid.*, ii., 382.
‡ Works, iii., 425.
§ *Ibid.*, iv., 41.

landlord's daughter, who was standing in the passage with a pail of water when he burst open the door, covered him with it, either intentionally or in her fright, from head to foot. This cooled his courage, so that when the landlord slipped past him and locked the door, he was very glad to pledge his word of honour that if he was allowed to go out, none of his friends should come in. Such an incident is a marked exception to the usual civility and seriousness of passengers and crew when Wesley was on board. Sometimes he was asked to pray with the passengers. In July, 1762, the captain of the vessel in which Wesley crossed over from Dublin asked him if he would not read prayers to them on the Sunday morning. "All who were able to creep out were willingly present" at prayers and sermon. One week-day in July, 1771, many gentlemen were on board, and begged for a sermon. All listened with deep attention.* On his way to Holland in 1786 he received the same request, and found his congregation "all attention." †

The most interesting of these services on board ship was in March, 1758. Wesley embarked at Liverpool for Dublin. In addition to his own party, consisting of himself and four friends, there were seven other cabin passengers and "many common ones." "So good-natured a company," he says, "I never met with in a ship before. The sea was as smooth as glass, the sun shone without a cloud, and the wind was small and quite fair." About nine Wesley prayed with the passengers, and then lay quietly down. Next day they were becalmed off Holyhead. Wesley and his party seized the opportunity to speak to their fellow-passengers. From that time no oath, no immodest or passionate word, was heard while they

* Works, iv., 300, 344. † *Ibid.*, iii., 489.

were on board. Next day the calm continued. Wesley and his companions assembled on the quarter-deck, where they no sooner began to sing a hymn than both passengers and sailors gladly assembled. Such is Wesley's account. Francis Okeley, who had been a Moravian, was travelling with him. A letter sent by this friend to Dr. Byrom,* whom he visited in Manchester shortly before, gives another description. "I think I may say we had one of the most agreeable voyages from Liverpool to Dublin that could be wished, ship, captain, passengers, as agreeable as could be expected, and a smooth, calm sea and clear, serene sky throughout. Mr. Wesley preached on the quarter-deck to all in the ship between Penmenmawr hills, on the Welsh coast, and Holyhead. They were attentive, serious, and satisfied. In a word, we did and said what we pleased, which was, I believe, usefully improved." This beautiful record may close this sketch of Wesley's half-century of travel. Wherever he went, on foot or on horseback, in coach or in sailing vessel, he was a pleasant companion, who generally won all hearts, and never lost an opportunity of doing good.

---

* Byrom's "Journals."

CHAPTER XIV.

WESLEY'S PREACHERS.

NO leader of a great religious movement was ever more happy in his helpers than Wesley. It would be hard indeed to find a finer band of men than the early Methodist preachers. They generally travelled their circuits mounted on horseback, with saddle-bags, containing their scanty wardrobe and a stock of Methodist books for sale in the Societies. The horse was scarcely less important than his master in days when the preacher's "round," or circuit, sometimes embraced a county or two. For a quarter of a century Thomas Olivers rode one horse that a friend purchased for five pounds and gave to him when he went to his first circuit. He travelled comfortably upon it not less than a hundred thousand miles. This, however, was a model horse, "such another as, in many respects, none of my brethren could ever boast of." * John Pritchard was less fortunate. His horse became sick, and the poor itinerant had to travel on foot during one winter and spring about twelve hundred miles.† The early minutes, which may be said to contain the "whole duty of a Methodist preacher," do not forget one cardinal point. It is asked in 1765, "Are all the preachers merciful to their beasts?" "Perhaps not. Every one

* "Early Methodist Preachers," ii., 73. † *Ibid.*, vi., 267.

ought—1. Never to ride hard. 2. To see with his own eyes his horse rubbed, fed, and bedded."

Wesley's first preachers had a daily baptism of privation and persecution. Mob and magistrate conspired to drive them out of the towns and villages where they came to labour. One of Wesley's itinerants wrote to him in October, 1744, about the violence of the Cornish mob, and informed him that Mr. Westall had been committed to the House of Correction at Bodmin as a vagrant. "I pray you," says Wesley, "for what pay could we procure men to do this service? to be always ready to go to prison, or to death?" Nelson, Maxfield, and others were pressed as soldiers. Thomas Mitchell was thrown repeatedly into a deep pond till he was insensible; then his clothes were covered with paint. These pioneers of Methodism had a hard and long struggle with the mob. Even after Wesley's position and character had begun to command general respect his humble itinerants had to face much rough usage; but they were true heroes, who counted all troubles light in order to win men for Christ.

In addition to all other privations, the early preachers had a long struggle with poverty.* John Downes' widow had only one sixpence in the world at the time of her husband's death; John Jane's clothes scarcely sufficed to pay the thirty-seven-and-threepence which his modest funeral cost.* At first the circuits provided for any preacher who laboured among them. His wife, if he had one, was without any provision. Four shillings a week was the sum allowed for a wife at first, with a sovereign per quarter for each child. When the husband was at home eighteen-pence a day was allowed for his board, a deduction being made if he went out for a meal.†

* See p. 223. † Southey's "Wesley," ii., 61.

In 1752 it was arranged that the preachers should receive stipends of twelve pounds a year,* in order to provide themselves with clothes, etc. Board and lodging was found by the Societies. "Two meals and horse one night, 1*s.*," an entry in the accounts of "The Dales" circuit, shows the average cost of entertainment. Up to this time the stewards of the various Societies provided the preachers with what they needed, and sometimes gave them a trifle † for travelling expenses. Ten years after this date, however, we find that Thomas Taylor, then stationed in Wales, had neither quarterage nor travelling expenses. He was generally entertained by the friends. Sometimes a shilling or half a crown was put into his hand. Fortunately he had a little money of his own, on which he drew for expenses. His horse, with its saddle and other equipments, cost him nine pounds. Some of the first preachers supported themselves by the labour of their own hands; others married wives with property, or, like Taylor, had a little stock of their own. By the year 1763 what is called "a competent provision" had been made for the preachers' wives and a weekly allowance for their little children. Kingswood School provided education and clothing for the elder boys.‡ Out of the collection for the school some money allowance was also made to a few sons and daughters of the preachers. The failure of many circuits to raise the usual allowance for the preachers' wives threw such a heavy burden on the Contingent Fund that in 1788 Wesley made a special appeal to the Societies to provide for those who laboured among them. The Contingent Fund was raised by a yearly collection

* Myles' "Chronological History."

† Tyerman, iii., 551.

‡ "Minutes of the Conference," i., 590.

in the classes to meet law expenses and reduce chapel debts, etc. The year after this appeal the call upon it was reduced from nine hundred and three pounds to five hundred and sixty-eight, but the relief was temporary. In 1790 it rose to one thousand pounds.

The school for preachers' sons at Kingswood was one of Wesley's favourite institutions. In 1739 the foundation of a school for the colliers' children had been laid by Mr. Whitefield, but the whole burden of its building and maintenance fell on Wesley. He hoped to make it a school for his people, and for many years several of the Methodist families sent their children. In 1748 it was enlarged, and a public collection was made for it in the Societies, which has been continued ever since. Wesley prepared school-books for use there, and watched over the religious life of the inmates with constant care. Every sign of religious quickening cheered him, but he often mourned that he could not make Kingswood all he wished. He planted two rows of trees in the grounds, and lived long enough to preach under their agreeable shade in the summer-time.

The three names that head the list of Wesley's lay-preachers are John Cennick, Joseph Humphreys, and Thomas Maxfield. Wesley says, "Joseph Humphreys was the first lay-preacher that assisted me in England, in the year 1738." * There was at this date no distinctively Methodist Society, so that Humphreys' help must have been given in the Society at Fetter Lane. On September 1st, 1740, he first began to assist Mr. Wesley at the Foundery. John Cennick, schoolmaster-elect at Kingswood, had begun to preach there in June, 1739. He had gone from Bristol to hear a young man read a sermon under a sycamore tree in Kingswood, but the reader did

* Works, iv., 493.

not come, and Cennick reluctantly took his place. Wesley was asked to forbid his preaching, but he encouraged him to proceed, so that Cennick was constantly employed in the neighbourhood of Bristol. Humphreys and Cennick both left Wesley during the Calvinistic controversy in 1741. Thomas Maxfield's name, though it does not stand first, is associated with the most remarkable incident in the early history of lay-preaching. He was one of Wesley's converts at Bristol. On May 20th, 1739, he began to roar and beat himself on the ground so violently, that it took six men to hold him. With a single exception, Wesley never saw any one "so torn of the evil one." Maxfield found peace whilst Wesley was praying with him. He seems to have travelled for some time with Charles Wesley as a companion and servant. Once he was left in London to meet and pray with the members at the Foundery during Wesley's absence. Insensibly he passed from prayer and exhortation to preaching sermons. His word led to many conversions. When the news reached Wesley, he hurried to London to check this irregularity. His mother, then living at the Foundery, asked him the reason of his evident dissatisfaction. "Thomas Maxfield has turned preacher, I find," was his answer. She reminded him of her own objections to lay-preaching, and then added, "John, take care what you do with respect to that young man, for he is as surely called of God to preach as you are. Examine what have been the fruits of his preaching, and hear him yourself." The Countess of Huntingdon also wrote to say how much she was astonished by Maxfield's power both in preaching and in prayer. When Wesley heard for himself, he could only say, "It is the Lord; let Him do what seemeth Him good." Thomas Westall, another of the first preachers, also found a friend in need. Wesley thought of silencing him, but a pious old lady at Evesham, Mrs. Canning, said, "Stop him at your peril! He preaches the truth, and the Lord owns him as truly as He does you or your brother." *

Maxfield's recognition as a lay-preacher prepared the way for the extension of Methodism throughout the United Kingdom. Without such machinery the Great Revival could only have been local; now its "circuits" began to stretch all over the country. Dr. Barnard, Bishop of Londonderry, who visited Bath for his health, ordained Maxfield. Wesley had recommended him warmly to his Lordship, and the Bishop told him,† "Sir, I ordain you to assist that good man, that he may not work himself to death." Maxfield remained with Mr. Wesley more than twenty years. He was intimately associated with George Bell, the Life Guardsman, whose extravagancies caused so much mischief in the London Society in 1763. Maxfield was appointed to take a service at the Foundery on April 28th, 1763, but refused to do so. Wesley had gone to Westminster to preach, but walked back to the Foundery as soon as he heard this news, and preached from Jacob's complaint, "If I am bereaved of my children, I am bereaved!" Maxfield's position as one of Wesley's helpers had led to his marriage to a lady of considerable fortune, but he had no sense of gratitude. In later years, however, Wesley did not refuse to renew the intercourse. He preached at Maxfield's chapel in Ropemaker's Walk, Little Moorfields, in 1783, but he reports soon afterwards that Maxfield was clearly convicted by the testimony of unexceptionable witnesses of lying and slandering his old friends for twenty years.

A finer man than Maxfield was John Nelson, the Birstal mason. Southey says he "had as high a spirit and as

* Moore, ii., 11. † Works, iii., 131.

brave a heart as ever Englishman was blessed with." He came to London to work at his trade, and found peace under Wesley's first sermon in Moorfields. He had long been grappling with the great questions of life, and attended all places of worship where he thought he might find guidance. He slept little, and awoke from horrible dreams shivering with terror. Whitefield's preaching did not relieve his distress. At last he heard Wesley. When the preacher ascended the pulpit, Nelson says, "My heart beat like the pendulum of a clock, and when he spoke, I thought his whole discourse was aimed at me." Nelson soon found the rest he sought. He was lodging with a family that objected to so much preaching and praying. They even asked him to seek another home. But before the time came for him to leave Nelson's consistency and earnestness had won them over. They went with him to Moorfields, and one of them was converted. His employer was pushing on the building for the Exchequer near Westminster Hall, and pressed Nelson to work on Sundays, but he stood firm, and won the Sunday rest for his fellow-workmen as well as for himself. He had not spoken to Wesley, but he took care to hear him or his brother every Sunday, and persuaded many of his comrades to go with him. He was so zealous for the souls of others, that he even hired one man to hear Wesley preach. It was a good speculation. The man afterwards assured Nelson that it was the best thing both for him and his wife that ever man did for them.

Nelson's first conversation with Wesley is singularly interesting. The Yorkshire mason had often wished for an opportunity to speak with one to whom he owed so much. One day he attended the Sacrament at St. Paul's, where Wesley was, and contrived to walk with him after service towards the Foundery. They talked together all the way from St. Paul's to the farther end of Upper Moorfields. "It was a blessed conference to me," says Nelson. "When we parted, he took hold of my hand, and, looking me full in the face, bade me take care I did not quench the Spirit." This was Nelson's only interview with Wesley in London. Just before Christmas he returned to Yorkshire. There he was led to tell the story of his conversion. His opinions were soon noised abroad, and people of all denominations came to hold controversy with him, so that his house used to be filled with visitors as soon as he came home from work. Some would ask questions, or argue with him; others stood by to listen. Nelson always took care to have prayer before they separated, and soon eight persons had found rest for their souls. In this humble way a great work broke out. Nelson did not attempt to preach, but read some portion of Scripture, exhorted the people to observe what they had heard, and closed his meetings with prayer. For some time six or seven were converted every week. During all this while Nelson had no correspondence with Wesley. Peter Böhler, after his return from America, visited him and greatly strengthened his hands. Nelson was at this time much troubled by some of the Moravians, and felt that he would give ten pounds, if he had it, for an hour's conversation with Wesley. One night he dreamt that both the Wesleys were sitting at his fireside. John Wesley said, "I will stay but a few days now; for I must go into the north, and return at such a time, and stay with you a week." A few months later they did visit him, and he heard the very words of his dream.

A neighbour who attended his services was going up to London, and said he would like to hear Wesley, whom Nelson called his father in the Gospel. He brought a letter from the Yorkshire mason asking Wesley's advice in his perplexities. Wesley told the man to say that he would be at Nelson's house the following Tuesday. On May 26th, 1742, Wesley met this devoted worker. From this time the brothers became frequent visitors to Birstal, and Nelson's way was soon opened to wider usefulness. He laboured in various parts of Yorkshire with great success; then Wesley called him to London. His clothes were so worn out in the Lord's service that he was not fit to obey the call, but in this emergency a tradesman of the parish brought him a piece of blue cloth for a coat and black cloth for waistcoat and breeches. The Yorkshire mason was now ready to start for London.

A neighbour who was going there allowed Nelson to ride his horse sometimes while he walked himself. In this manner the new itinerant entered the metropolis. He then pushed on to join Wesley at Bristol. Wesley was on his way to Cornwall. John Downes and Nelson went with him; but as they only had one horse between them, they generally set out before Wesley and his companion Mr. Shepherd. When they reached St. Ives, Nelson worked at his trade, preaching as opportunity served. Poor Downes was soon seized by a fever. Nelson was better able to bear the hardships of this rough life. For three weeks he and Wesley slept every night on the floor. The mason's great-coat made a fairly comfortable pillow for Wesley, but Nelson had to lay his weary head upon Burkitt's "Notes on the New Testament." One morning, about three o'clock, Wesley turned over, and finding his companion awake, clapped him on the side. "Brother Nelson, let us be of good cheer: I have one whole side yet." The skin was rubbed off the other. Hospitality was at a discount in those days. It was a rare thing for any one to offer meat or drink to the poor preachers in Cornwall. After one service Wesley stopped his horse to pick the blackberries, saying to his companion, "Brother Nelson, we ought to be thankful that there are plenty of blackberries; for this is the best country I ever saw for getting a stomach, but the worst that ever I saw for getting food. Do the people think we can live by preaching?" Nelson replied that a friend had given him a capital meal of barley-bread and honey. Wesley told him he was well off. He himself had intended to ask for a crust of bread at Morva, but forgot to do so till he got some distance from the house.

On May 4th, 1744, Nelson was pressed for a soldier by an alehouse-keeper at Adwalton, near Birstal, who felt that his craft was in danger. For a long time he could gain no redress. He refused to fight or to accept soldier's pay, and had to suffer much for his religion. Neither threats nor promises, however, could silence Nelson. He fearlessly reproved sin and preached to crowds of people wherever his regiment marched. At last a substitute was provided by his friends, and Nelson was set at liberty. He still followed his business as a mason, but was incessant in his labours as an evangelist. In 1750 he was stationed to a circuit as a regular preacher, and laboured with great blessing for twenty years. This brave soldier of Jesus Christ died on July 18th, 1774, at the age of sixty-seven.

John Downes, who shared his horse with Nelson on the way to Cornwall, was another of the zealous itinerants, who had his full share of the privations and successes of those days. He suffered so much from ill-health that in 1751 Wesley set him to superintend his printing. The journal for November 4th, 1774, pays warm tribute to the genius and devotion of this noble man. Wesley never forgot the meed of honour due to his heroic fellow-workers. On his testimony Downes is acknowledged as the mechanical genius of early Methodism. He did not hesitate to say, "I suppose he was by nature full as great a genius as Sir Isaac Newton." When he was a boy at school, he astonished his master by proving an algebraical proposition in a better way than that given in his school-book. Soon afterwards he was sent into Newcastle with a clock to be repaired. He watched the workman, then returned home, made himself tools, and soon finished a clock of his own, which went as well as any in the town. One morning whilst Wesley was shaving he noticed Downes "whittling the top of a stick." He found that the itinerant was making a likeness of his leader, which he intended to engrave on a copper plate. The second engraving which he made from a folio portrait of Wesley by Williams was prefixed to the "Notes upon the New Testament." After a long conflict with pain, sickness, and poverty, John Downes died at the age of fifty-two. Charles Wesley visited his widow. "She had one six-pence in the world, and no more." A friend had received her into her house, and her calm submission and peace of mind surprised all who saw her.*

Thomas Walsh, an Irish Papist, became one of the grandest of Wesley's lay-preachers.† He had been trained in the strictest obedience to Rome, but was led to join the Church of England through the instrumentality of an elder brother, who was trained as a priest, but forsook Popery through reading the Bible. Walsh heard the Methodist preachers, and joined the Society in September, 1749, when he was about nineteen years old. He was soon rejoicing in the love of God. When he opened his mind to Wesley about his call to preach, he

Works, iv., 34; Moore's "Wesley," ii., 262. † See p. 231.

was requested to send an account of his conversion and experience. He received the following answer :—

"MY DEAR BROTHER,—It is hard to judge what God has called you to till trial is made. Therefore, when you have an opportunity, you may go to Shronil, and spend two or three days with the people there. Speak to them in Irish."

Walsh's gifts were soon recognised. His roughness of address and his dialect offended some, but the power of God was manifest in his preaching. He had his full share of the perils of his new vocation. Seventy-eight men took an oath to oppose him. Armed with clubs, they met him a mile from the town of Roscrea, where he intended to preach, and offered to bring either a priest or a clergyman to argue with him. Walsh told them that he did not concern himself with opinions, but preached against sin of every kind. The opponents were much mollified by his appeals to their conscience, but when he refused to promise that he would not visit the place again, they determined to put him into a well, which they had prepared for that purpose. Walsh escaped this fate, but was taken by the back and thrust out of the town when he attempted to preach in the street. At Bandon, where he was cast into prison by the magistrate, who was also the Rector of the place, he preached through the window to all who could hear his voice. The people, in their sympathy for the young preacher, brought bedding and provision for him and the companions who accompanied him to prison, and the magistrate soon found it prudent to set him at liberty.

Walsh became the Apostle of Ireland. His perfect command of Erse everywhere won him a hearing, and he had a large share in the spread of Methodism in his own country. His knowledge of the Scriptures was profound. The study of Hebrew was a passion with him. Wesley says that he was the finest Hebrew scholar he ever met.

He could tell how often any word was found in the Hebrew Bible and what it meant in each place. He often attended the synagogues and conversed with the Jews, for which work his studies gave him a special fitness. Wesley calls him "that blessed man." He did not remember any preacher who in so few years had been used for the conversion of so many souls. Walsh died of consumption in 1759, in the twenty-eighth year of his age. His incessant study, his abstemiousness, and his prodigious labours, all contributed to this painful loss, but Wesley always considered Walsh a martyr to loud and long speaking. He carefully entreated his preachers to beware lest excitement should lead them to commit the same error.

Thomas Walsh was buried in Dublin, but no monument was raised to his memory. Dr. Albert S. Hunt, one of the representatives from America to the English Wesleyan Conference of 1886, has since then provided a marble tablet, which is placed in the Methodist chapel built in the Irish village of Ballingrane, where Philip Embury and Barbara Heck, the pioneers of Methodism in New York, resided before they sailed for the New World.

John Jane deserves a place in the record of Methodist martyrs. At Holyhead, in March, 1750, Wesley, on his way to Ireland, overtook Jane, who had set out on foot from Bristol with three shillings in his pocket. He had spent seven nights on the road, for six of which he was entertained by entire strangers. He reached Holyhead with one penny left. A few months later Jane's rough life closed. A walk from Epworth to Hainton on an exceedingly hot day threw him into a fever, from which he never recovered. He spent his last days at the house of a good woman, but no nursing could save him. He passed away with a smile on his face. His last words were, "I find the love of God in Christ Jesus." His clothes, stockings, hat, and wig were not thought sufficient to meet the funeral charges, amounting to thirty-seven and threepence. All the money he had was one shilling and fourpence, "enough," Wesley adds, "for any unmarried preacher of the Gospel to leave to his executors." Wesley makes another reference to this devoted man in connection with his visit to Colne in 1776. He preached to a multitude of people, and scarcely ever saw a congregation where men, women, and children stood in such rapt attention drinking in the word, "and this in the town," he adds, "wherein, thirty years ago, no Methodist could show his head! The first that preached here was John Jane, who was innocently riding through the town, when the zealous mob pulled him off his horse, and put him in the stocks. He seized the opportunity, and vehemently exhorted them to 'flee from the wrath to come.'" Jane had been dead for more than a quarter of a century, but Wesley had not forgotten his labours, nor had those labours been without the abundant blessing of God.

Another story may illustrate the poverty of the early Methodist preachers. One Saturday an itinerant rode into York, where he was to preach on the Sunday. On Monday he had to find eighteen-pence for his horse. He had no money, nor had the steward any funds, so the horse was detained. In this emergency the steward's daughter took the ribbon from her head, and sold it for nearly the amount. With some other addition Miss Harrison thus obtained one shilling and tenpence, paid the charge for the horse, and handed fourpence to the preacher, telling him she "had set him off like a gentleman." *

* "Memoir of R. Spence," p. 143.

Wesley was often compelled to employ men of little or no education. But he did his best to rouse the desire for self-improvement. During the Lent of 1749 he met at Kingswood as many of the preachers as could be spared from their circuits, and read lectures to them, as he used to do to his pupils at the University. Seventeen assembled, whom he divided into two classes. To one of these companies he read "Pearson on the Creed," to the other Aldrich's "Logic." He also read "Rules for Action and Utterance" with both. Many references to similar gatherings are found in the journals. Wesley sometimes chose a book of philosophy, and pointed out its merits or its mistakes. When he was not particularly engaged in London, he spent an hour in this way with his preachers. The work gave him great satisfaction. In November, 1764, he writes, "Many pupils I had at the University, and I took some pains with them. But to what effect? What is become of them now? How many of them think either of their tutor or their God? But, blessed be God! I have had some pupils since who well reward me for my labour. Now 'I live'; for 'ye stand fast in the Lord.'" In December, 1757, he spent some days quietly at Lewisham in finishing "A Preservative against Unsettled Notions in Religion," designed for all the Methodists, but chiefly for the young preachers. His "Christian Library," consisting of selections made from the best works on divinity, was another proof of his care for the education both of preachers and people.

James Wheatley, who was expelled in 1751 for immoral conduct, brought slanderous accusations against his brethren, which led the Wesleys to institute a careful examination into character. Charles Wesley made a tour of inquiry, with happy results. The charges were found to be groundless. From that time investigation into ministerial character has been one of the fundamental principles of Methodism. It is still made year by year.

Wesley expected his preachers to be the mainspring of his Societies. At Londonderry, in June, 1771, he met the singers, whom he had joined together two years before. The preachers had paid no attention to that part of their work, so that all Wesley's previous care was fruitless. "And no wonder," he adds; "for nothing will stand in the Methodist plan unless the preacher has his heart and his hand in it. Every preacher, therefore, should consider it is not his business to mind this or that thing only, but everything." Wesley was proud of his preachers. The first Sir Robert Peel greatly esteemed the Methodists. He often attended their chapels, and most of his Lancashire works were under the management of members of the Society, who rendered him excellent service. He once asked Wesley to breakfast with him during a Lancashire Conference. Wesley promised to do so on condition that he might bring some of his children with him. At the appointed hour he appeared, accompanied by thirty-six of his itinerant preachers.*

The health of his preachers often gave Wesley grave concern. He did not fail to point the sad moral of such losses as that of Thomas Walsh, who, "by violent straining of his voice, added to frequent colds," † brought on the consumption which snatched him away in the strength of his years. John Cowmeadow was "another martyr to loud and long preaching." Wesley tried to save his life by his favourite specific: "I took him to travel with me." But it was too late. The poor preacher revived a little, but soon relapsed. Wesley steadily set his face against "that vile custom" of one man's preaching three

* *Wesley Banner*, 1850, p. 114. † Works, ii., 451.

times a day to the same congregation week after week, which he felt was enough to wear out the body and mind both of the speaker and his hearers.* His journals and the Minutes of Conference bear constant witness to Wesley's loving watchfulness over the men who laboured with him in the Gospel. St. Paul's care for Timothy is a true picture of Wesley and his "helpers."

Wesley's rule over his preachers and people has been branded as arbitrary. Henry Moore, who was well able to judge, says that his "*arbitrary power*, so called, was exercised from first to last in keeping his associates to that *work of God*, that wholly religious design and employment, which they all professed to embrace as their duty and calling when they joined him. And from this he certainly would not consent that any of them should swerve. In everything else he was, even by their own account, a father and a friend."† Henry Moore enjoys the reputation of having contradicted Wesley more than any man in England.‡ But Wesley encouraged him to speak his mind, and only liked him the better for his plainness. Wesley administered a neat rebuke to one of his preachers, who was irritated because a young itinerant found fault with one of his seniors. "I will thank the youngest man among you to tell me of any fault you see in me; in doing so, I shall consider him my best friend."§ Wesley felt the care of his Societies a burden put upon him by Providence, which he durst not lay down. He had not sought authority, but he was determined to use what had come on him unawares as wisely as he could for the glory of God and the best interests of the Methodist people.‖ If he erred at all in the use of his power, it

* Works, iv., 493. † Moore, i., iv. ‡ Tyerman, iii., 567.
§ Tyerman, iii., 567. ‖ Works, viii., 312.

was in his forbearance. "I have been too tender of these men," he once said to Moore in reference to two recalcitrant preachers; "*you* should have opposed my receiving them again. You know I halt on that foot." The history of George Bell's fanaticism confirms Wesley's verdict upon himself. Whilst expecting his preachers to be faithful to the great evangelical doctrines which he taught, he gave them abundant liberty. He instructed Joseph Benson to say to one of his critics, "I never undertook to defend every sentence of Mr. Wesley's. He does not expect or desire it. He wishes me and every man to think for himself."

The annual Conference was the great event of a preacher's year. The first of these Conferences, held at the Foundery, opened on Monday, June 25th, 1744, and lasted for the rest of the week. The Wesleys, four other clergymen, and four Methodist preachers were present. Mr. Hodges, Rector of Wenvo, Mr. Piers, Vicar of Bexley, Samuel Taylor, Vicar of Quinton, in Gloucestershire, and Mr. Merriton, from the Isle of Man, were the clergymen; Thomas Richards, Thomas Maxfield, John Bennet, and John Downes the preachers. Downes lived and died in the ranks; the other three itinerants left Wesley. On the Sunday before this first Conference opened, a lovefeast was held, and the Sacrament was administered by five clergymen to the whole of the London Society. Next morning the Conference opened with solemn prayer. Charles Wesley preached with much power, and baptised a man called Samuel Holloway, "who felt in that moment the great burden taken off." The first Conference was thus inaugurated by a conversion. The doctrines and discipline of the Society were carefully considered. Every one was entreated to speak freely whatever was in his heart. The result of the conversations on doctrine was a body of practical divinity which must have unravelled many knotty questions for the rising theologians of Methodism. The conversation on sincerity shows the breadth of tolerance which characterised these discussions. "But can it be conceived that God has any regard to the sincerity of an unbeliever?" Answer: "Yes, so much that if he persevere therein, God will infallibly give him faith." "Is not sincerity all in all?" Answer: "All will follow persevering sincerity. God gives everything with it, nothing without it."

Wesley's name for his itinerants was "preachers" or "helpers." The preacher whose name stood first in the appointment for any circuit was the assistant, now known as the superintendent, who had oversight of all the work of the circuit. "In what view may we and our *helpers* be considered?" was another question. "Perhaps as extraordinary messengers (*i.e.*, out of the ordinary way), designed—1. To provoke the regular ministers to jealousy. 2. To supply their lack of service towards those who are perishing for lack of knowledge."

Wesley's twelve rules of a helper are still cherished as the guiding principles of a Methodist preacher:—

"1. Be diligent. Never be unemployed. Never be triflingly employed. Never *while* away time, nor spend more time at any place than is strictly necessary.

"2. Be serious. Let your motto be, 'Holiness to the Lord.' Avoid all lightness, jesting, and foolish talking.

"3. Converse sparingly and cautiously with women, particularly with young women.

"4. Take no step towards marriage without solemn prayer to God and consulting with your brethren.

"5. Believe evil of no one unless fully proved; take heed how you credit it. Put the best construction you can on everything. You know the judge is always supposed to be on the prisoner's side.

"6. Speak evil of no one, else *your* word, especially, would eat as doth a canker; keep your thoughts within your own breast till you come to the person concerned.

"7. Tell every one what you think wrong in him, lovingly and plainly, and as soon as may be, else it will fester in your own heart. Make all haste to cast the fire out of your bosom.

"8. Do not affect the gentleman. A preacher of the Gospel is the servant of all.

"9. Be ashamed of nothing but sin: no, not of cleaning your own shoes when necessary.

"10. Be punctual. Do everything exactly at the time. And do not mend our rules, but keep them, and that for conscience' sake.

"11. You have nothing to do but to save souls. Therefore spend and be spent in this work. And go always, not only to those who want you, but to those who want you most.

"12. Act in all things, not according to your own will, but as a son in the Gospel, and in union with your brethren. As such, it is your part to employ your time as our rules direct: partly in preaching and visiting from house to house, partly in reading, meditation, and prayer. Above all, if you labour with us in our Lord's vineyard, it is needful you should do that part of the work which the Conference shall advise, at those times and places which they shall judge most for His glory.

"Observe, it is not your business to preach so many times, and to take care merely of this or that Society, but to save as many souls as you can, to bring as many sinners as you possibly can to repentance, and, with all your power, to build them up in that holiness without which they cannot see the Lord. And, remember, a Methodist preacher is to mind every point, great and small, in the Methodist discipline. Therefore you will need all the grace and sense you have, and to have all your wits about you."

The early Conferences laid the foundations of Methodism on a firm basis. Its preachers were knit together by their doctrine and their discipline. Difficulties of every kind vanished when all thus met face to face. At the Conference of 1751, Wesley says, "The more we conversed the more brotherly love increased." He expected to hear many objections to the first Methodist doctrines, but none were raised. "We seemed to be all of one mind, as well as one heart." Before the session closed Wesley mentioned whatever he thought amiss or wanting in any. His words were received with love and with serious attention, so that not one seemed to go away discontented. In 1753 and 1754 the same spirit of unity and love finds emphatic recognition in the journals. The early Minutes show that the first Conferences were largely employed in considering the fundamental doctrines of Methodism and the practical work of her preachers. During the last twenty years of Wesley's life the oversight of the growing organisation occupied more and more of the attention of the Conference.

CHAPTER XV.

LOVE AND MARRIAGE.

WESLEY has sometimes been represented as an enthusiast whose asceticism and laborious itinerant life effectually crushed those tender feelings which would have made him an ardent lover or a devoted husband. That theory can be maintained no longer. We have already had occasion to refer to his feeling towards Miss Hopkey in Georgia. But this was not his earliest attachment. Wesley's first love was Miss Betty Kirkham, the younger sister of his friend Robert Kirkham, one of the earliest of the Oxford Methodists. Her father, the Rev. Lionel Kirkham, was a clergyman at Stanton, in Gloucestershire. On February 2nd, 1727, Robert Kirkham addressed a boisterous letter to his friend at Oxford, which begins, "With familiarity I write, dear Jack." Wesley had now been Fellow of Lincoln for nearly a year, and was Greek Lecturer and Moderator of his college. There was no Oxford Methodism till about two years after the date of this letter. Kirkham writes, 'Your most deserving, queer character, your worthy personal accomplishments, your noble endowments of mind, your little and handsome person, and your obliging and desirable conversation have been the pleasing subject of our discourse for some pleasant hours. You have often been in the thoughts of M. B." (Miss Betty), "which I have curiously observed, when with her alone, by inward smiles and sighs and abrupt expressions concerning you.

Shall this suffice? I caught her this morning in an humble and devout posture on her knees. I am called to read a *Spectator* to my sister Capoon. I long for the time when you are to supply my father's absence. Keep your counsel, and burn this when perused. You shall have my reasons in my next. I must conclude, and subscribe myself, your most affectionate friend—and *brother* I wish I might write—Robert Kirkham." *

No particulars of Robert Kirkham's life after he left Oxford have been caught by any Wesleyan biographer. In Mrs. Delany's Life, however, there seem to be two references. In February, 1756, she tells her sister that Miss Sally Chapone, daughter of her old friend Sarah Kirkham, had to leave her. "She is under an engagement, made for her by her uncle Kirkham, to spend three weeks or a month with a young gentlewoman that Dr. Hinckley is going to be married to." The young ladies were to stay with a Miss Prescot and then go to Charleton. This doctor, a physician at Guy's Hospital, married Miss Marcon, daughter of a merchant of Ludgate Hill, the following November.† In May, 1772, Mrs. Delany tells her nephew, the Rev. John Dewes, "Mr. Kirkham has not been heard of since I received my brother's letter, though strict inquiry has been made after him."

Wesley did not burn his friend's letter. His sister Martha wrote him on February 7th. She had been eagerly expecting to hear from him, "but when I knew that you were just returned from Worcestershire, where, I suppose, you saw your *Varanese*" (Betty Kirkham), "I then ceased to wonder at your silence; for the sight of such a woman, 'so known, so loved,' might well make

* *Wesleyan Times*, February 26th, 1866.

† Mrs. Delany's "Letters," ii., 407.

you forget me. I really have myself a vast respect for her, as I must necessarily have for one that is so dear to you." This letter shows that Wesley's feeling toward the young lady was well known to his sister. Kirkham directs his letter, "Lincoln College, Oxford, by the Worcester carrier." This will account for Martha Wesley's description of his journey as a visit to Worcestershire. It was evidently made to the Kirkhams at Stanton. For more than three years Wesley kept up a correspondence with Miss Betty Kirkham. He spoke of her in the tenderest terms, and the friendship seemed to be leading to the result the young lady's brother so ardently wished. In 1731, however, it was broken off. The probability is that she married a Mr. Wilson. Mrs. Delany writes from Killala, June 28th, 1732, "Poor Mrs. Wilson! I am sorry for the shock her death must have given Sally, whose tenderness must sometimes take the place of her wisdom; but I hope, when she considers the great advantage her sister in all probability will receive by the exchange she has lately made, that she will be reconciled to the loss of a sister that has given her more woe than happiness. Pray, has Mrs. Wilson left any children?"*

Wesley's sister Emilia wrote to him on August 13th, 1735,† "Had you not lost your dear Mrs. C——n, where had your love been fixed? On heaven, I hope, principally; but a large share, too, had been hers: you would not have been so spiritualised, but something of this lower world would have had its part of your heart, wise as you are; but being deprived of her, there went all hope of worldly happiness." "C——n" evidently refers to Mrs. Capoon or Chapone. That lady, however, was married in 1725.

* Lady Llanover's Life and Correspondence of Mrs. Delany, i., p. 360.

† Stevenson's "Wesley Family," p. 271.

Wesley's attachment was to her younger sister. It is not surprising that Emilia Wesley should have made a mistake in the name. Perhaps we may conclude that Mr. Badcock refers to a disappointment in love in one part of his letter to the *Westminster Magazine.** "By an incident of domestic life I see his genius clouded, and the clearest reason muddled in the school of Mysticism. Devoting himself to silence and solitude, he exerted all the powers of his mind on the darkest and most inexplicable dogmas of school divinity."

Wesley's correspondence with Mrs. Delany, then Mrs. Pendarves, opens up another interesting field of investigation, and throws considerable light on the young collegian's character. The lady was the elder daughter of Bernard Granville, brother of Lord Lansdowne. She had been married at the age of seventeen to Mr. Pendarves, a Cornish gentleman, who left her a widow in 1724, at the age of twenty-three. Before her marriage she had lived much at Whitehall with her aunt Lady Stanley, who had apartments there as a maid-of-honour. Her marriage to a fat, gouty, and ungainly man, forty-three years older than herself, who in his later years became addicted to intemperance, was a great trial to the young lady; but happily she was soon set free from the yoke. As a widow Mrs. Pendarves lived in London, paying visits to her friends in the country and in Ireland. She afterwards married Dr. Delany, who became Dean of Down. Lady Llanover's volumes show that she mixed in the best London society, and was greatly esteemed at Court. George III. and his queen honoured her with their intimate friendship, and even provided her a house at Windsor, that they might have daily intercourse with one whom they profoundly admired.

* 1774, p. 180.

As a girl Mrs. Delany had formed a warm friendship for Sarah Kirkham, who afterwards married Mr. Capoon or Chapone. Mrs. Chapone was a woman of brilliant wit and rare intellectual gifts. One of her letters on behalf of Mrs. Elstob, a literary lady in distress, became the leading topic of discourse at a royal drawing-room in 1730. Mrs. Pendarves says on January 4th, 1736, "Sally would shine in an assembly composed of Tullys, Homers, and Miltons. At Gloucester she is like a diamond set in jet; their dulness makes her brightness brighter." Mrs. Pendarves often spent her summers with her mother and sister at Gloucester. In this way Wesley seems to have become acquainted with this brilliant lady and her family. He corresponded with her mother and sister as well as herself. A letter to Mrs. Granville dated "Lincoln College, December 12th, 1730," shows Wesley's high esteem for her. The young tutor evidently finds it difficult to play the part of spiritual adviser. "I have, therefore, little reason to expect that He will direct any motion of mine to that end, especially when the particular end proposed relates to one who is far advanced in the great race which I am but lately entered upon, if, indeed, I am entered yet. What shall I say to such a one as is almost possest of the crown which I dimly see afar off?" He adds a postscript: "My brother joins with me in his best respects both to yourself and those good ladies whom we love to call your family."* Dr. Rigg, after a careful study of the whole subject, has reached the conclusion that Mrs. Granville's daughter, Mrs. Pendarves,† succeeded to the place Miss Betty Kirkham had held in Wesley's affection. Mr. Lecky endorses that opinion.

* Mrs. Delany's "Letters," i., 269.
† "Living Wesley," p. 56.

The correspondence with her had already begun. According to the custom of the time, the friends bear fancy titles. John Wesley is Cyrus; Charles is Araspes. Mrs. Pendarves is known as Aspasia, Miss Granville, her sister, as Selina. Betty Kirkham is Varanese, V., or Vnse. Some of the letters are given in Mrs. Delany's Life and Correspondence, but fuller extracts, as deciphered from Wesley's own manuscripts by Mr. G. J. Stevenson, will be found, with explanations of the fancy names, in the *Wesleyan Magazine* for 1863, and in Dr. Rigg's "Living Wesley." Mrs. Pendarves had been trifled with by Lord Baltimore, who won her affection and then made some pretext for breaking off the intercourse. He was married on July 20th, 1730. She bore her trial with great patience, and from that time her correspondence grew more serious. Wesley's first letter to her, dated August 14th, 1730, seems to have accompanied some copies of Miss Betty Kirkham's letters to him. "While I was transcribing the letters, these last monuments of the goodness of my dear V., I could not hinder some sighs, which, between grief and shame, would have their way. Not that I was pained at seeing my utmost efforts outdone by another's pen, but I could not, I ought not to, be unmoved when I observe how unworthy I am of that excellent means of improvement. I trust so unusual a blessing of Providence has not been utterly useless to me. To this I owe both the capacity and the occasion of feeling that soft emotion with which I glow even at the moment when I consider myself as conversing with a kindred soul of my V." On September 14th he writes, "My dear V. informs me you are going yet farther from us, but cannot inform me how soon." Other letters refer to Miss Betty's ability to write on high and serious subjects, and to her deep piety. "I do not wonder," Wesley says, "that Aspasia is thus minded, any more than I did at the temper of dear Vnese., under the sharpest pain that an embodied spirit can know. You will easily take knowledge of those words, if you have not heard them before, 'When I was in the greatest of my pains, if my strength would have allowed, I would gladly have run out into the streets to warn all I met that they should save themselves from pain sharper than mine.'"

In the early summer of 1731 Wesley had met Varanese, and enjoyed a time of almost uninterrupted conversation with her. He speaks of it with a lover's fervour. "'On this spot she sat,' 'Along this path she walked,' 'Here she showed that lovely instance of condescension,' were reflections which, though extremely obvious, could not but be equally pleasing, and gave a new degree of beauty to the charming arbour, the fields, the meadows, and Horrel itself." * This was perhaps their last meeting.

Wesley's correspondence with Mrs. Pendarves was carried on regularly till her journey to Ireland. She sought his advice for herself and her friends. Wesley pointed out the perils to religious character attendant on the gaieties of fashionable life in which she moved. "That London is the worst place under heaven for preserving a Christian temper, any one will imagine who observes that there can be none where its professed, irreconcilable enemies, 'the lust of the eye' and 'the pride of life,' are more artfully and forcibly recommended." The advice was not all on one side. When Wesley was accused of being "too strict" at Oxford in July, 1731, he asked Aspasia's opinion, and laid his defence before her. The reply was flattering. "O Cyrus, how noble a defence you make! and how are you adorned with the beauty of holiness! You really are in a

* "Living Wesley," p. 66.

state to be envied. . . . How ardently do I wish to be as resigned and humble as Cyrus. . . . Company is come, and will not allow me a long conversation. I cannot always submit to this sort of life. It encroaches too much. Adieu!" Less than three weeks afterwards she writes again. "While I read your letters I find myself carried above the world; I view the vanities I left behind with the disdain that is due to them, and wish never to return to them. But, as it is my lot to dwell among them as yet, I will at least endeavour to defend myself from their assaults; and, with your assistance, I hope to baffle and turn aside their sting. As from every evil we may extract good, so in this particular I have great consolation, that, weak and insignificant as I am, I have sometimes found means of maintaining the honour of a great God when I have heard the blasphemer say, 'Where is now their God?' At such an instant, how have I wished for a capacity equal to the mighty cause!"

In the earlier part of this correspondence, Wesley's style is cumbrous, and his compliments somewhat fulsome, but the letters on both sides bear evidence of deep religious earnestness and high mutual esteem. When Mrs. Pendarves visited Dublin in 1731, she asked Cyrus to address his letters to her mother's residence at Gloucester, but afterwards begged her sister to send him her Dublin address, that he might write direct. Readers of her Life will notice how entirely Mrs. Pendarves neglected all her correspondents save her sister during her long stay in Ireland. It is not strange therefore that Wesley shared the common fate. In March, 1732, six months after she had asked her sister to send her address to him, she tells her, "Cyrus by this time has blotted me out of his memory, or if he does remember me, it can only be to reproach me; what can I say *for* myself? What can I indeed say *to myself*, that have neglected so extraordinary a correspondent? I only am the sufferer, but I should be very sorry to have him think my silence proceeded from negligence; I declare 'tis want of time." * She still took a lively interest in Wesley's work. In a letter to her sister on April 11th, 1733, she says, "As for the ridicule *Cyrus* has been exposed to, I do not at all wonder at it; religion in its plainest dress suffers daily from the insolence and ignorance of the world; then how should that person escape who dares to appear openly in its cause? He will meet with all the mortification such rebels are able to give, which can be no other than that of finding them wilfully blinding themselves and running headlong into the gulf of perdition, a melancholy prospect for the honest-hearted man who earnestly desires the salvation of his fellow-creatures." †

In the summer of 1734, after nearly three years' silence, Mrs. Pendarves wrote again to her old friend. Her first sentence shows her self-reproach: "I never began a letter with so much confusion to anybody as I do this to Cyrus." She had been full of shame and reluctance to write after her long delay and neglect, but had broken through this feeling, and was willing to "suffer any reproach rather than lose the advantage of Cyrus's friendship." Wesley's answer shows that he had no hope of doing his correspondent further service. "Alas, Aspasia! Are you indeed convinced that I can be of any service to you? I fear you have not sufficient ground for such a conviction. Experience has shown how much my power is short of my will. For some time I flattered myself with the pleasing hope; but I grew more and more ashamed of having indulged it. You need not the support

* Life and Correspondence, i., p. 343. † *Ibid.*, i., p. 410.

of so weak a hand. How can I possibly think you do (though that thought tries now and then to intrude itself still), since you have so long and resolutely thrust it from you? I dare not, therefore, blame you for so doing. Doubtless you acted upon cool reflection. You declined the trouble of writing, not because it was a trouble, but because it was a needless one. And if so, what injury have you done yourself? As for me, you do me no injury by your silence. It did, indeed, deprive me of much pleasure, and of a pleasure from which I have received much improvement. But still, as it was one I had no title to but your goodness, to withdraw it was no injustice. I sincerely thank you for what is past; and may the God of my salvation return it sevenfold into your bosom! And if ever you should please to add to those thousand obligations any new ones, I trust they shall neither be unrewarded by Him nor unworthily received by Aspasia's faithful friend and servant, Cyrus. Araspes, too, hopes you will never have reason to tax him with ingratitude. Adieu!"

So closes this remarkable correspondence. Wesley had gained force of character since he indulged in the high-flown and scarcely orthodox compliment of his first letter. "I spent some very agreeable moments last night," he then said, "in musing on this delightful subject" (the excellencies of his fair friend) "and thinking to how little disadvantage Aspasia or Selina would have appeared even in that faint light which the moon, glimmering through the trees, poured on that part of our garden in which I was walking. How little would the eye of the mind that surveyed them have missed the absent sun! What darkness could have obscured gentleness, courtesy, humility, could have shaded the image of God? Sure none but that which shall never dare to approach them, none but vice, which shall ever be far away!"

The following letter, given in Mrs. Delany's Life,* shows that John Wesley still kept up some correspondence with her younger sister, Miss Granville, whose comparatively retired life at Gloucester gave her more leisure. Her portrait and her letters leave a pleasing impression of this charming and devout young lady on the minds of readers of her sister's Life. Lady Llanover says that the letter to Miss Granville is without signature. She does not seem to be aware that it is from John Wesley. Charles was on his voyage to England at this date, and the letter bears its writer's name in every line. The seal was a cross, and the English postmark December 7th.

"*To Mrs. Ann Granville, in Gloster.*

"SAVANNAH, 24*th September*, 1736.

"The mutual affection, and indeed the many other amiable qualities, of those two sisters one of whom is lately gone to a happier place, would not have suffered me to be unmindful of your friend and you had I had nothing else to remind me of you. I am persuaded that heavy affliction will prove the greatest blessing to the survivor which she has ever yet received. She is now very cheerful, as well as deeply serious. She sees the *folly* of placing one's happiness in *any creature*, and is fully determined to give her whole heart to Him from whom death cannot part her.

"I often think how different her way of life is at Savannah from what it was *at St. James's*, and yet the wise, polite, gay world counts her removal thence *a misfortune*. I should not be at all grieved if *you* were fallen into the *same misfortune, far removed from the pride of life,*

* I., p. 581.

and hid in some obscure recess, where you were scarcely seen or heard of, unless by a few plain Christians and by God and His angels.

"Mr. Rivington will send your letter, if you should ever have leisure to favour with a few lines

"Your sincere friend and most obedient servant.

"Do you still watch, and strive, and pray, that your heart may be right before God? Can you *deny yourself, as well as take up your cross?* Adieu!"

The two sisters were the Miss Boveys. Charles Wesley says in his journal for June 20th, 1736, "Walking in the trustees' garden" (at Savannah), "I met the Miss Boveys, whom I had never been in company with. I found some inclination to join them; but it was a very short-lived curiosity." On July 10th, Miss Becky died suddenly. Two days before Mr. Oglethorpe when with them had spoken of sudden death. She said, "If it was the will of God, I should choose to die without a lingering illness." Her sister asked, "Are you, then, always prepared to die?" She replied, "Jesus Christ is always prepared to help me. And little stress is to be laid on such a preparation for death, as is made in a fit of sickness." On the Saturday, after tea, her sister, seeing her colour change, asked if she was well. She received no answer. The doctor, who was passing by, was called in, and told them she was dying. He tried whether bleeding would restore her, but she bled about an ounce, leaned back, and died! Wesley went to the house as soon as he heard the painful news, and begged that they would not lay her out, as it might be a swoon. Any such hope, however, had soon to be abandoned. "I never saw so beautiful a corpse in my life," he says. "Poor comfort to its late inhabitant! I was greatly surprised at her sister. There was, in all her behaviour, such an inexpressible mixture of tenderness and resignation. The first time I spoke to her, she said, 'All my afflictions are nothing to this. I have lost not only a sister, but a friend. But it is the will of God. I rely on Him, and doubt not but He will support me under it.'" Almost the whole town was present at the funeral.

Edmund Burke told Dr. Johnson that Mrs. Delany "was a *truly great* woman of fashion; that she was not only the woman of fashion of the *present age*, but she was the *highest-bred woman in the world* and the woman of fashion of all ages; that she *was* high-bred, great in every instance, and *would continue* fashionable in *all ages*." * One glimpse of Mrs. Delany's feeling about the Wesleys in later life is caught in her Life.† Her friend Miss Hamilton had a long conversation with her at Bulstrode on December 4th, 1783. "She told me she *had known* the two Mr. Wesleys (the Methodist preachers); she knew them when they were young men. They lived near her sister when they were students at Oxford. They were of a serious turn, and associated with such as were so. These brothers joined some other young men at Oxford, and used to meet of a Sunday evening and read the Scriptures, and find out objects of charity to relieve. This was a *happy beginning*, but the vanity of being singular and growing *enthusiasts* made them endeavour to gain proselytes and adopt that system of religious doctrine which many reasonable people thought pernicious." Mrs. Delany had adopted the current opinion as to the motives of the Wesleys. The lady of fashion, devout as she always was, could not

* Life and Correspondence, vi., 12. † VI., 175.

understand a life spent for the salvation of the common people.

We must now pass to other scenes. When Charles Wesley was married to Miss Sarah Gwynne, the daughter of a Welsh magistrate, on April 8th, 1749, his brother, who performed the ceremony, says, "It was a solemn day, such as became the dignity of a Christian marriage." He was looking forward to similar happiness for himself. The previous August he had suffered from a troublesome bilious headache at Newcastle, where he was nursed by Grace Murray, a young widow, thirty-two years old, foremost in all Christian work there. She was born at Newcastle, but removed to London when she was eighteen. Two years later she married a sailor, who belonged to a Scottish family that had lost its estates during the rebellion of 1715. The death of her infant child led Mrs. Murray to attend the Methodist preaching. Her husband bitterly opposed her views; but she held her ground, and at last won him over. Wesley's first sermon produced a great effect on her mind. "Is there any one here," he asked, "who has a true desire to be saved?" "My heart," she says, "replied, 'Yes, I have.'" Wesley continued, "My soul for thine if thou continue lying at the feet of Jesus!" On this word she took hold, but it was some months before she found rest.

In 1742 Mr. Murray was drowned at sea. His widow returned to Newcastle, where she afterwards became housekeeper at the Orphan House,* had a hundred members in her classes, met a "band" each day of the week, and visited the neighbouring villages to read and pray with the people. At Wesley's request, she went to nurse one of the preachers at the Orphan House, but

* Life of Mrs. Bennet.

some disagreement with another inmate led her to return to her mother's. After spending six months in London she went back to the Orphan House, with the same result. Two years of great spiritual depression followed, but in the autumn of 1745 for the third time she became a member of the Methodist family. Besides her classes and her visits to the sick and to the country Societies, Grace Murray was the nurse of the preachers. She had at least seven of these hard-worked itinerants as her patients. One of them, John Bennet, was under her care for six months.

This was the woman whom Wesley resolved to make his wife. When he proposed to marry her, in August, 1748, she answered, "This is too great a blessing for me; I can't tell how to believe it. This is all I could have wished for under heaven." Ten days later, when Wesley had to leave Newcastle, he expressed his conviction that God intended her to be his wife, and hoped that when they met again they would not have to part any more. Grace Murray begged that she might not lose him so soon, so Wesley took her with him through Yorkshire and Derbyshire, where "she was unspeakably useful both to him and to the Societies." She remained at Bolton, in the circuit of Bennet, whom she had nursed at Newcastle. He was really Wesley's rival. Grace Murray vacillated strangely between her lovers, and even wrote to Wesley to say that she thought it was her duty to marry Bennet. In April, 1749, however, a week after Charles Wesley's marriage, she went with Wesley to Ireland. For three months she was his constant companion. She examined all the women in the smaller Societies, settled the female bands, visited the sick, and prayed with the penitent. She anticipated all Wesley's wants, acted as his monitor when she thought she saw anything amiss in his behaviour, and graced her position in such a way that Wesley's esteem and affection daily increased. At Dublin they entered into a solemn contract of marriage.

After their return to England, she travelled with Wesley from Bristol to London and Newcastle, so that for five months they were scarcely separated. At Epworth Bennet came and said that Mrs. Murray had sent him all Wesley's letters. Wesley was now convinced that she ought to marry Bennet, but when he wrote her a line to this effect, she ran to him "in an agony of tears, and begged him not to talk so, unless he designed to kill her." Her conduct during the next few days showed strange weakness and irresolution, but she assured Wesley, "I love you a thousand times better than I ever loved John Bennet in my life. But I am afraid, if I don't marry him, he'll run mad." At Newcastle she expressed her strong determination to live and die with Wesley, and urged him to marry her immediately. No doubt this would have been the proper course. But Wesley first wished to satisfy Bennet, to secure his brother's approval, and to inform the Societies of his intention. One of the preachers was admitted to their confidence, in whose presence they renewed their contract. This preacher then went off to satisfy Bennet in Derbyshire. Wesley wrote to his brother at Bristol. The tidings filled Charles Wesley with dismay. He had married a lady of birth and position, and was overwhelmed by the idea that John should marry a woman who before her marriage had been a servant. He started in haste for the north to avert what he considered would be nothing less than a general disaster.

From Newcastle he followed his brother into Cumberland. They met at Whitehaven. Charles told him that their preachers would leave them and their Societies would be scattered if he married so mean a woman. John replied that he wished to marry her, not for her birth, but for her own character and worth. Her neatness, her carefulness, her strong sense, and her sterling piety had won his highest esteem. She was "indefatigably patient and inexpressibly tender; quick, cleanly, and skilful; of an engaging behaviour, and of a mild, sprightly, cheerful, and yet serious temper; while, lastly, her gifts for usefulness were such as he had not seen equalled." Finding that he could not move his brother, Charles returned alone to Newcastle. At Hineley Hill he met the lady, and after kissing her, said, in his usual impulsive manner, "Grace Murray, you have broken my heart." She rode with him to Newcastle, where Bennet had arrived from Derbyshire. She fell at Bennet's feet and begged forgiveness for using him so badly. Within a week she had become his wife.

Whitefield invited Wesley to Leeds, where he broke the painful news to his friend. Next day Charles came with the husband and wife. He greeted his brother with the hard words, "I renounce all intercourse with you but what I would have with a heathen man or a publican." Whitefield and brave John Nelson, who were present at the interview, prayed, wept, and entreated till the brothers fell on each other's neck. Wesley kissed Bennet without uttering a word of upbraiding. He also made such explanations to his brother in a private interview, that Charles entirely exonerated him and laid all the blame on Grace Murray.

This disappointment was the greatest trial of Wesley's life. He opened his heart in the following touching note to Mr. Thomas Bigg, of Newcastle:—

"LEEDS, *October 7th*, 1749.

"MY DEAR BROTHER,—Since I was six* years old, I never met with such a severe trial as for some days past. For ten years God has been preparing a fellow-labourer for me by a wonderful train of providences. Last year I was convinced of it; therefore I delayed not, but, as I thought, made all sure beyond a danger of disappointment. But we were soon after torn asunder by a whirlwind. In a few months, the storm was over; I then used more precaution than before, and fondly told myself, that the day of evil would return no more. But it too soon returned. The waves rose again since I came out of London. I fasted and prayed, and strove all I could; but the sons of Zeruiah were too hard for me. The whole world fought against me, but above all my own familiar friend. Then was the word fulfilled, 'Son of man, behold, I take from thee the desire of thine eyes at a stroke; yet shalt thou not lament, neither shall thy tears run down.'

"The fatal, irrevocable stroke was struck on Tuesday last. Yesterday I saw my friend (that was), and him to whom she is sacrificed. I believe you never saw such a scene. But 'why should a living man complain, a man for the punishment of his sins?'

"I am, yours affectionately,

"JOHN WESLEY." †

Wesley saw the woman he had lost at Leeds three days after her marriage. He did not meet her again till 1788. John Bennet soon left Mr. Wesley, and took with him all the hundred and twenty-seven members at Bolton save nineteen. The whole Society at Stockport joined

* The time of the fire at Epworth. † Works, xiii., 162.

him with the exception of one woman. At Bolton Bennet spoke bitterly of Wesley, and accused him of preaching nothing but Popery. He afterwards became the pastor of a Calvinistic Church at Warburton,* near Warrington, where he died in 1759, at the age of forty-five. His widow conducted weekly meetings for prayer and fellowship, and carefully brought up her five boys. She afterwards removed to Derbyshire,† where she again joined the Methodists, and was active in good works of every kind. One of her sons became minister of a chapel on the Pavement in Moorfields. When she visited him in 1788, Thomas Olivers met her and told Wesley that she would like to see him. Henry Moore gives a beautiful description of the meeting: "Mr. Wesley, with evident feeling, resolved to visit her; and the next morning, he took me with him to Colebrooke Row, where her son then resided. The meeting was affecting; but Mr. Wesley preserved more than his usual self-possession. It was easy to see, notwithstanding the many years which had intervened, that both in sweetness of spirit, and in person and manners, she was a fit subject for the tender regrets expressed in those verses which I have presented to the reader. The interview did not continue long, and I do not remember that I ever heard Mr. Wesley mention her name afterward." Mrs. Bennet died in 1803, in the eighty-ninth year of her age. ‡

The verses to which Moore refers are entitled "Reflections upon Past Providences, October, 1749." The thirty-one stanzas, of six lines each, describe the course of Wesley's love, the history and attractions of the lady, and the cruel blow which had robbed him of his blessing.

* "Warbutton" (Life of Mrs. Bennet).
† Moore, ii., 171. ‡ *Ibid.*, ii., 171.

Wesley also bears witness to his own susceptibilitv to female charms :—

Oft, as through giddy youth I roved,
  And danced along the flowery way,
By chance or thoughtless passion moved,
  An easy, unresisting prey,
I fell, while love's envenomed dart
Thrilled through my nerves, and tore my heart.

Borne on the wings of sacred hope,
  Long had I soared, and spurned the ground,
When, panting for the mountain top,
  My soul a kindred spirit found,
By Heaven entrusted to my care,
The daughter of my faith and prayer.

In early dawn of life, serene,
  Mild, sweet, and tender was her mood;
Her pleasing form spoke all within
  Soft and compassionately good;
Listening to every wretch's care,
Mingling with each her friendly tear

I saw her run, with wingèd speed,
  In works of faith and labouring love;
I saw her glorious toil succeed,
  And showers of blessing from above
Crowning her warm effectual prayer,
And glorified my God in her.

No one can read the poem from which these verses are culled without regret that such a woman should have been torn from Wesley. Whatever weight may be allowed to Charles Wesley's objections, Grace Murray's devotion to the work of God and her rare capacity for usefulness far outweighed them. She cannot be acquitted of extreme weakness. But it must not be forgotten that her position was one of great difficulty, and at the last she was overcome by the severe pressure brought to bear upon her.

Her gifts eminently fitted her to become Wesley's helper, and the Societies lost much by her marriage. But the gravest aspect of the case is the matrimonial disaster which afterwards befell Wesley. Had he married Grace Murray, John Wesley would never have committed the fatal mistake of marrying Mrs. Vazeille.

This marriage took place on February 18th,* 1751. Wesley's bride was the widow of Noah Vazeille, a London merchant, of Fenchurch Street. She had four children and a fortune of ten thousand pounds in the three per cents., which Wesley took care to have settled on herself and her children. The marriage was a great trouble to Charles Wesley. A fortnight before it took place, his brother sent for him and told him that he was resolved to marry. "I was thunderstruck," Charles says, "and could only answer, he had given me the first blow, and his marriage would come like the *coup de grace*. Trusty Ned Perronet followed, and told me, the person was Mrs. Vazeille! one of whom I had never had the least suspicion. I refused his company to the chapel, and retired to mourn with my faithful Sally. I groaned all the day and several following ones under my own and the people's burden. I could eat no pleasant food, nor preach, nor rest, either by night or by day."

This remarkable extract shows that Charles Wesley objected to his brother's marriage in itself, quite apart from any considerations about the lady. He did not even inquire who was to be his sister-in-law. His own marriage must have shown him how hard it was to leave home for weeks and months together. Mrs. Vazeille was no stranger to him. He had met her in July, 1749, at the house of Edward Perronet, on the very day that his brother

* At Wandsworth Parish Church (*Gentleman's Magazine*, 1751).

embarked from Ireland with Grace Murray. His description of her as "a woman of a sorrowful spirit" shows that she sought spiritual help in Methodist circles. Next May Charles took her with him to visit the Gwynnes at Ludlow. She then returned with him and his wife to London, by way of Oxford, where he showed her the buildings and gardens. Mr. and Mrs. Charles Wesley were afterwards her guests for eight or nine days in London.

His marriage to Mrs. Vazeille was hastened by an accident which Wesley had on the middle of London Bridge. In hastening from the Foundery to Snowsfields to take leave of the congregation before he started on his northern journey, his feet slipped on the ice. He fell with great force, the bone of his ankle striking on the top of a stone. With much pain and difficulty, he took his work at Snowsfields and at West Street, but he could not preach at the Foundery. The journey to the north was now quite out of the question. Wesley took up his quarters at Mrs. Vazeille's, in Threadneedle Street, where he "spent the remainder of the week partly in prayer, reading, and conversation, partly in writing an Hebrew Grammar and 'Lessons for Children.'" The conversation interests us most. It no doubt led to Wesley's marriage on the following Monday. He was not able to set his foot to the ground, and preached kneeling on Sunday, the 17th, and on the Tuesday after, so that he must have been a remarkable bridegroom.

A fortnight later he set out for Bristol, "being tolerably able to ride, but not to walk." His wife remained in London. Charles Wesley had met his sister-in-law before John left town. During his brother's absence he called and assured her that he was perfectly reconciled. He also brought his wife to see her, and took all opportunities of showing his sincere respect and love. Such was the state of things when Wesley returned to London. He stayed a few days to settle the business which had brought him back. Then he set out for the north. "I cannot understand," he says, "how a Methodist preacher can answer it to God to preach one sermon or travel one day less in a married, than in a single state." He told Henry Moore that he and Mrs. Wesley agreed before the marriage that he should not preach one sermon or travel one mile the less on that account." "If I thought I should, my dear," he told her, "as well as I love you, I would never see your face more."

This marriage was soon seen in its true light. At Bristol, only four months after the wedding, Charles Wesley found his sister-in-law in tears. He expressed his love and desire to help her, heard her complaints about his brother, took her to his own home, and sent her away not a little comforted. Next day he had further conference with her and his brother, which "ended in prayer and perfect peace." Mrs. Wesley travelled with her husband extensively during the first four years of their marriage. She accompanied him to the north of England, to Cornwall, and to Scotland. In April, 1752, Wesley was able to report to his friend Mr. Blackwell, the banker, "My wife is, at least, as well as when we left London; the more she travels, the better she bears it." He was afraid that she would not understand the behaviour of a Yorkshire mob, but there had been no trial of that kind up to the time he wrote. "Even the Methodists are now at peace throughout the kingdom." Eight days later she had her "baptism of fire" at Hull, where the mob attended their carriage, throwing in whatever they could lay their hands on. Wesley tells us that he was himself screened by the large gentlewoman who sat on his lap; he says nothing about Mrs. Wesley.

The efforts which Charles Wesley made to secure peace at Bristol were successful for the time, but in November, 1752, the venerable Vicar of Shoreham says that for many months Mrs. Wesley had nursed her warmth and bitterness; he also mourns over her angry and bitter spirit. When Wesley was thought to be dying of consumption in 1753, he begged his wife and his brother to forget all that was past. Charles was quite ready to do so, but added a significant hope that Mrs. Wesley "will do as she says." Two years later he tells his wife, "I called, two minutes before preaching, on Mrs. Wesley at the Foundery; and in all that time had not one quarrel." * He was evidently afraid of her malice. He begs his wife to be courteous without trusting her. Mrs. Wesley's absurd jealousy of her husband acted like fuel to her violent temper. When Wesley was in Cornwall in 1755, he sent a packet of letters to Charles Perronet, which she opened. She fell into a passion when she found there a few simple lines addressed to Mrs. Lefevre. In February, 1756, Wesley wrote to his friend Sarah Ryan, "Your last letter was seasonable indeed. I was growing faint in my mind. The being constantly watched over for evil; the having every word I spoke, every action I did, small and great, watched with no friendly eye; the hearing a thousand little tart, unkind reflections in return for the kindest words I could devise,

> Like drops of eating water in the marble,
> At length have worn my sinking spirits down.

Yet I could not say, 'Take Thy plague away from me,' but only, 'Let me be purified, not consumed.'"

In January, 1758, after many severe words, Mrs. Wesley

* C. Wesley's "Journals," ii., 213, 217, 247.

left her husband, vowing that she would never see him more. In the evening, while he was preaching at the chapel, she came into the chamber where he had left his clothes, searched his pockets, and read a letter she found there addressed to Sarah Ryan. Wesley afterwards found her in such a happy temper as he had not seen her in for years. But though the letter had touched her deeply, she was not cured. She seized Wesley's papers, and put them into the hands of his enemies; she interpolated words to make them bear a bad construction, and published them in the papers. She once shut up Charles Wesley and her husband in a room, and began to tell them their faults with such detail and force as made Charles call her "my best friend." He won their release at last by quoting Latin poetry—a device which he had once tried with good effect on his voyage from Georgia—till their keeper was glad to let her prisoners escape. In her fits of jealousy, Mrs. Wesley would order a chaise and drive a hundred miles to see who was with her husband in his carriage when he entered a town.* John Hampson, one of Wesley's preachers, told his son that he once went into a room in the north of Ireland where he found Mrs. Wesley foaming with rage. Her husband was on the floor. She had been dragging him about by his hair, and still held in her hand some of the locks that she had pulled out of his head in her fury.† Hampson found it hard to restrain himself when he saw this pitiable sight. "More than once she laid violent hands upon him and tore those venerable locks which had suffered sufficiently from the ravages of time." ‡

A letter published in the *New York Critic* during the summer of 1885 will show what Mrs. Wesley was :—

* Hampson, ii., 127. †Tyerman, ii., 110. ‡ Hampson, ii., 127.

"COLEFORD, *October 23rd,* 1759.

"DEAR MOLLY,—I will tell you simply and plainly the things which I dislike. If you remove them, well. If not, I am but where I was. I dislike your showing any one my letters and private papers without my leave. This never did any good yet, either to you or me, or any one. It only sharpens and embitters your own spirit. And the same effect it naturally has upon others. The same it would have upon me but that (by the grace of God) I do not think of it. It can do no good. It can never bring me nearer, though it may drive me further off. And should you do as you often threaten me, then the matter is over. I know what I have to do. In all this you are fighting against yourself. You are frustrating your own purpose if you want me to love you. You take just the wrong way. No one ever was *forced* to love another. It cannot be: love can only be won by *softness;* foul means avail nothing. But you say, 'I have tried fair means, and they did not succeed.' If they do not, none will. Then you have only to say, 'This evil is of the Lord; I am clay in His hand.'

"I dislike (2) not having the command of my own house, not being at liberty to invite even my nearest relations so much as to drink a dish of tea without disobliging *you.* I dislike (3) the being myself a prisoner in my own house, the having my chamber door watched continually, so that no person can go in or out but such as have your good leave. I dislike (4) the being but a prisoner at large even when I go abroad, inasmuch as you are highly disgusted if I do not give you an account of every place I go to and every person with whom I converse. I dislike (5) the not being safe in my own house. My house is *not* my castle. I cannot call even my study, even my bureau, my own.

They are liable to be plundered every day. You say, 'I plunder you of nothing but papers.' I am not sure of that. How is it possible I should? I miss money too, and he that will steal a pin will steal a pound. But were it so, a scholar's papers are his treasure, my journal in particular. 'But I took only such papers as relate to Sarah Ryan and Sarah Crosby.' That is not true. What are Mr. Landey's letters to them? Besides, you have taken parts of my journal which relate to neither one nor the other. I dislike (6) your treatment of my servants (though, indeed, they are not properly mine). You do all that in you lies to make their lives a burden to them. You browbeat, harass, rate them like dogs, make them afraid to speak to me. You treat them with such haughtiness, sternness, sourness, surliness, ill-nature, as never were known in any house of mine for near a dozen years. You forget even good breeding, and use such coarse language as befits none but a fishwife.

"I dislike (7) your talking against me behind my back, and that every day and almost every hour of the day; making my faults (real or supposed) the standing topic of your conversation. I dislike (8) your slandering me, laying to my charge things which you know are false. Such are (to go but a few days back) 'that I beat you,' which you told James Burges; that I rode to Kingswood with Sarah Ryan, which you told Sarah Rigby; and that I required you, when we were first married, never to sit in my presence without my leave, which you told Mrs. Lee, Mrs. Fry, and several others, and stood to it before my face. I dislike (9) your common custom of saying things not true. To instance only in two or three particulars. You told Mr. Ireland 'Mr. Vazzilla * learnt Spanish in a fort-

* Mr. Vazeille, her former husband.

night.' You told Mr. Fry 'Mrs. Ellison was the author as to my intrigue in Georgia.' You told Mrs. Ellison 'you never said any such thing; you never charged her with it.' You also told her, 'that I had laid a plot to serve you as Susannah was served by the two elders.' I dislike (10) your extreme, immeasurable bitterness to all who endeavour to defend my character (as my brother, Joseph Jones, Clayton Carthy), breaking out even into foul, unmannerly language, such as ought not to defile a gentlewoman's lips, if she did not believe one word of the Bible.

"And now, Molly, what would any one advise you to that has a real concern for your happiness? Certainly (1) to show, read, touch those letters no more, if you did not restore them to their proper owner; (2) to allow *me* the command of my own house, with free leave to invite thither whom I please; (3) to allow me my liberty there, that any one who will may come to me, without let or hindrance; (4) to let me go where I please, and to whom I please, without giving an account to any; (5) to assure me, you will take no more of my papers, nor anything of mine, without my consent; (6) to treat all the servants where you are (whether you like them or no) with courtesy and humanity, and to speak (if you speak at all) to them, as well as others, with good-nature and good manners; (7) to speak no evil of me behind my back; (8) never to accuse me falsely; (9) to be extremely cautious of saying anything that is not strictly true, both as to the matter and manner; and (10) to avoid all bitterness of expression till you can avoid all bitterness of spirit.

"These are the advices which I now give you in the fear of God, and in tender love to your soul. Nor can I give you a stronger proof that I am your affectionate husband, JOHN WESLEY."

Mrs. Wesley often left her husband, but returned again in answer to his entreaties. At last she went off with part of his journals and various papers, which she would not restore. On January 23rd, 1771, he writes, "For what cause I know not, my wife set out for Newcastle, purposing 'never to return.' *Non eam reliqui; non dimisi; non revocabo.*" Mrs. Wesley seems to have remained with her daughter, Mrs. Smith, at Newcastle till the following year, when her husband visited the town. She then returned with him to Bristol. She might have been very useful but for her vile temper. At a little inn on the Yorkshire moors she spoke a few words to the woman of the house while Wesley talked to an old man. Both of these were deeply affected. In 1774 a petulant letter shows that she was still with her husband, but still of the same spirit. She died at Camberwell in 1781, when Wesley was in the west of England. On October 14th he says, "I came to London, and was informed that my wife died on Monday. This evening she was buried, though I was not informed of it till a day or two after."

She left her money, which had been reduced from ten to five thousand pounds, to her son. To Mr. Wesley she simply bequeathed a ring. The stone erected over her grave in Camberwell churchyard described her as "a woman of exemplary piety, a tender parent, and a sincere friend."* Whatever she may have been in these respects, she was one of the worst wives of whom we have ever read. She darkened thirty years of Wesley's life by her intolerable jealousy, her malicious and violent temper. Wesley would never sacrifice his duty to personal feeling, but though he

* The part of Camberwell churchyard in which Mrs. Wesley was buried has been taken into the main road, so that no trace of her grave is now to be found.

was a roving husband, a more tender or pleasant companion no woman could desire. He repeatedly told Henry Moore that he believed God overruled this prolonged sorrow for his good ; and that if Mrs. Wesley had been a better wife, and had continued to act in that way in which she knew well how to act, he might have been unfaithful to his great work, and might have sought too much to please her according to her own desires.

The most charitable view of Mrs. Wesley's conduct is that she suffered from some mental unsoundness. Scores of papers * in her own handwriting, bearing witness to her violent temper, seem to warrant this conclusion. She had begun life as a domestic servant,† and her querulous, discontented spirit under the inconveniences of itinerant life showed that she never gained any true refinement or good feeling.

* Jackson's "Charles Wesley," ii., 569. † Tyerman, ii., 115.

CHAPTER XVI.

WESLEY'S JOURNALS.

WESLEY'S journals form the finest picture that we possess of the Evangelical Revival in its whole compass and extent. His own history and the history of Methodism are alike found in those wonderful pages. Letters and papers embedded there preserve some of the most important incidents in the life of the Epworth parsonage. The persecutions and labours of his preachers and members there described show how many humbler workers shared the enthusiasm and the reproach of the Wesleys. The journals, however, are not merely a history of the Great Revival and of Wesley's life; they also form a storehouse of information about English manners during the eighteenth century. The modes of travel, the perils and hardships of the road, the aspect of English towns, the characteristics of English society, are all illustrated here. Wesley's extensive reading and his fine critical insight also make his journals a treasure-house of literary notes. His epitomes of books, with salient facts told in one or two bright sentences, his keen criticism or warm commendation, must have been an intellectual stimulus to hosts of readers who would never have heard of such subjects had it not been for his luminous remarks. His Societies thus had the full benefit of his wide and judicious reading. Jeremy Taylor's "Holy Living and Dying" first led Wesley to take a more exact account of his time. He wrote down in a shorthand diary the way in which he spent every hour. His time of rising, his preaching, his studies before breakfast, all labours of the day in fact, were faithfully recorded here. On the first page of these diaries he always wrote, "I resolve, 'Deo juvante'—

"1. To devote" (to retirement and private prayer,) "an hour morning and evening—no pretence or excuse whatsoever.

"2. To converse *κατὰ Θεόν*" (in the sight of God); "no lightness; no *εὐτραπελία*" (jesting).*

Moore says that this diary was in after-years distinct from his journal. The preface to the first published journal, however, states that the variety of scenes which Wesley passed through during his mission to Georgia induced him to transcribe the more material parts of his diary, adding here and there such reflections as occurred to his mind. In this way the journals were prepared. The earlier parts were published in the interest of Methodism, that the calumny and slander then rife might be silenced by a plain narrative of the facts as to its founding and its purpose. The complete journals, still preserved in twenty-six bound volumes, have never been printed. Copious extracts were made by Wesley himself and issued in twenty-one parts, the successive instalments being eagerly expected by a host of readers. The first entry of the published journals is on October 14th, 1735, when Wesley took boat to join the *Simmonds;* the last, on October 24th, 1790, describes his services at Spitalfields Church and St. Paul's, Shadwell.

The literary criticisms are well illustrated by Wesley's trenchant judgment on Machiavel, whom he read on his

* Moore, ii., 433.

return from Savannah in 1737. He says, "In my passage home, having procured a celebrated book ('The Works of Nicholas Machiavel'), I set myself carefully to read and consider it. I began with a prejudice in his favour, having been informed he had often been misunderstood and greatly misrepresented. I weighed the sentiments that were less common; transcribed the passages wherein they were contained; compared one passage with another, and endeavoured to form a cool, impartial judgment. And my cool judgment is, that if all the other doctrines of devils which have been committed to writing since letters were in the world were collected together in one volume, it would fall short of this; and that should a prince form himself by this book, so calmly recommending hypocrisy, treachery, lying, robbery, oppression, adultery, whoredom, and murder of all kinds, Domitian or Nero would be an angel of light compared to that man."* When he read Mandeville's "Fable of the Bees," in April, 1756, Wesley felt that "Machiavel had been far outdone. The Italian only recommends a few vices, as useful to some particular men, and on some particular occasions; but the Englishman loves and cordially recommends vice of every kind, not only as useful now and then, but as absolutely necessary at all times for all communities!"

Wesley's freedom from prejudice and breadth of view may be illustrated by two other critiques. In riding from Evesham to Bristol in August, 1742, he read over the Life of Ignatius Loyola,† "surely one of the greatest men," he says, "that ever was engaged in the support of so bad a cause. I wonder any man should judge him to be an enthusiast. No; but he knew the people with whom he had to do; and setting out (like Count

* Works. i., 44.

† *Ibid.*, i., 393.

Z——) with a full persuasion that he might use guile to promote the glory of God or (which he thought the same thing) the interest of His Church, he acted in all things consistent with his principles." Wesley's comment on "The History of the Puritans" is another of those calm, judicial summings-up which must have helped so largely to promote a true understanding among his people of the problems of religious history. He says, "I stand in amaze: first, at the execrable spirit of persecution which drove these venerable men out of the Church, and with which Queen Elizabeth's clergy were as deeply tinctured as ever Queen Mary's were; secondly, at the weakness of those holy confessors, many of whom spent so much of their time and strength in disputing about surplices and hoods or kneeling at the Lord's Supper." Baxter's "History of the Councils," which he read in August, 1754, led him to use strong words: "What a company of execrable wretches have they been (one cannot justly give them a milder title) who have almost in every age since St. Cyprian taken upon them to govern the Church! How has one Council been perpetually cursing another, and delivering all over to Satan, whether predecessors or contemporaries, who did not implicitly receive their determinations, though generally trifling, sometimes false, and frequently unintelligible or self-contradictory! Surely Mahometanism was let loose to reform the Christians! I know not but Constantinople has gained by the change." The history of the Church of Scotland called forth the forcible remark, "The work of God does not, cannot need the work of the devil to forward it. And a calm, even spirit goes through rough work far better than a furious one."*

* Works, iii., 254.

Wesley's reading was of wide compass. We catch glimpses of him in the library of his own college and of the Bodleian at Oxford.* He also seems to have availed himself of the books he found in the homes of friends in all parts of the country. In Ireland he studied local histories, so that he was in full sympathy with the surroundings of the people. Anson's and Cook's voyages, Rollin's and Robertson's histories, and kindred works were read and noticed in his journals. Philosophy and divinity were carefully studied. Wesley also took a lively interest in science. Huygens' "Conjectures on the Planetary World," which he read on the way from Canterbury to London, convinced him that the moon was not habitable. Everything was set at the service of his Societies. He translated a beautiful story from Ephraim Syrus, whom he considered to be "the most awakening writer of all the ancients," for their benefit, and did his utmost to awaken among them a love of knowledge.

His historical criticisms are singularly interesting. Wesley doubts "whether Judas claims so hot a place in hell as Alexander the Great," whose deliberate murder of his old friend Clitus "was a virtuous act in comparison of his butchering poor Philotas and his good old father, Parmenio, and even this but a little thing compared with the slaughter of thousands, both in battle and in and after taking cities, for no other crime than defending their wives and children." He was convinced of the innocence of Mary, Queen of Scots, and pronounced Elizabeth "as just and merciful as Nero, and as good a Christian as Mahomet." Mr. Woodrow's "History of the Sufferings of the Church of Scotland" led him to say of Charles II., "Bloody Queen Mary was a lamb, a mere

* Works, i., 317.

dove, in comparison of him!" Mr. Walpole's "Historic Doubts" convinced him that Richard III. was extremely handsome, and was clear from all the atrocities laid to his charge. Whatever may be said of these opinions, they must have helped to stimulate historic inquiry. Wesley's singularly candid mind was always open to receive fresh light on every subject.

Poetry has its fair place in these criticisms. On September 5th, 1769, he notes that he read over large part of Homer's *Odyssey* during his Cornish journey. He had always imagined it was like Milton's *Paradise Regained*, "the last faint effort of an expiring muse." He now found out his mistake. After alluding to some blemishes, he adds, "But his numerous beauties make large amends for these. Was ever man so happy in his descriptions, so exact and consistent in his characters, and so natural in telling a story? He likewise continually inserts the finest strokes of morality (which I cannot find in Virgil); on all occasions recommending the fear of God, with justice, mercy, and truth. In this only he is inconsistent with himself: he makes his hero say 'Wisdom never lies,' and—

> 'Him, on whate'er pretence, that lies can tell,
> My soul abhors him as the gates of hell.'

Meantime he himself, on the slightest pretence, tells deliberate lies over and over, nay, and is highly commended for so doing, even by the goddess of wisdom." Wesley commonly read history, poetry, and philosophy on horseback, having, as he said, other employment at other times.* When he travelled in his own carriage in later life, he always took books with him. He thus spent ten hours a day as retired as if he had been in a wilderness.

* Works, iii., 393.

When he was not travelling, he never spent less than three hours, often ten or twelve, alone.*

Wesley in early life seems to have been a connoisseur of pictures, but he soon denied himself every luxury to help the starving poor. One art-criticism is worthy of Ruskin.† In August, 1780, he says, "While I was at Bath, I narrowly observed and considered the celebrated Cartoons, the three first in particular. What a poor *designer* was one of the finest painters in the world! 1. Here are two men in a boat, each of them more than half as long as the boat itself. 2. Our Lord, saying to Peter, 'Feed My sheep,' points to three or four sheep standing by Him. 3. While Peter and John heal the lame man, two naked boys stand by them. For what? Oh, pity that so fine a painter should be utterly without common sense!" After preaching at Winchester in October, 1781, he went with great expectation to see the celebrated painting in the cathedral of the "Raising of Lazarus." "I was disappointed," he said. "I observed—1. There was such a huddle of figures, that, had I not been told, I should not ever have guessed what they meant. 2. The colours in general were far too glaring, such as neither Christ nor His followers ever wore. When will painters have common sense?"

The journals are crowded with entries which throw light upon the England of the eighteenth century. At Allandale Town in 1748 he mentions that he had a very large congregation when he preached near the Cross,‡ "it being the general pay-day, which is but once in six months."§ He was at Alnwick in 1753 on the day when sixteen or seventeen youths who had completed their

* *Methodist Magazine*, 1799, p. 564.

† Works, iv., 189.

‡ Works, ii., 106.

§ *Ibid.*, ii., 288.

apprenticeship were made free of the Corporation. These unfortunates were compelled to walk through a great bog, expressly preserved for this purpose, which took some of them up to the neck, and many of them to the breast. In May, 1765, he was amazed at the honesty of Londonderry. Such a thing as theft was scarcely heard of. No one hesitated to leave his house open all day, and the door on the latch at night.

Few men watched the growth of towns so carefully as Wesley. In April, 1755, he describes Liverpool as one of the neatest, best-built places he had seen in England. "I think it is full twice as large as Chester; most of the streets are quite straight. Two thirds of the town, we were informed, have been added within these forty years. If it continue to increase in the same proportion, in forty years more it will nearly equal Bristol. The people in general are the most mild and courteous I ever saw in a seaport town, as indeed appears by their friendly behaviour, not only to the Jews and Papists who live among them, but even to the Methodists (so called)." * Bath has also an honourable place. He thought that there were no buildings in England like those recently erected in that city. They had not only added a second Crescent, with two beautiful rows of houses, near Ludstown, but a whole town on the other side of the city, which was swiftly increasing every day. Birmingham in 1790 seemed three times as large as when he saw it fifty years before.†

Wesley availed himself of every opportunity afforded by his itinerant life to see the fine scenery or the historic scenes of the country. His visits to the Land's End must serve as an illustration of his interest in the grand sights

* Works, ii., 326. † *Ibid.*, iv., 482.

of nature. After service one Sunday evening in September, 1743, he says, "We went down, as far as we could go safely, toward the point of the rocks at the Land's End. It was an awful sight! But how will these melt away when God ariseth to judgment! The sea between them does indeed 'boil as a pot.' 'One would think the deep to be hoary.' But 'though they swell, yet can they not prevail. He hath set their bounds, which they cannot pass.'"* Fourteen years later he was there again.† "We rode to the Land's End. I know no natural curiosity like this. The vast ragged stones rise on every side, when you are near the point of land, with green turf between, as level and smooth as if it were the effect of art. And the rocks which terminate the land are so torn by the sea, that they appear like great heaps of ruins." When he was eighty-two, he clambered down the rocks to the very edge of the water. "I cannot think but the sea has gained some hundred yards since I was here forty years ago." ‡

Westminster Abbey was familiar ground to Wesley. We catch a pleasant glimpse of him there in March, 1771, with a friend from the country, to whom he was showing the tombs. A few years before he had taken a "serious walk" there. § "What heaps of unmeaning stone and marble! But there was one tomb which showed common sense, that beautiful figure of Mr. Nightingale, endeavouring to screen his lovely wife from death. Here indeed the marble seems to speak, and the statues appear only not alive." This entry throws light on the later visit. "The two tombs with which I still think none of the others worthy to be compared are that of Mrs. Nightingale

* Works, i., 431.
† *Ibid.*, ii., 424.
‡ Works, iv., 319.
§ *Ibid.*, iii., 160, 424.

and that of the Admiral rising out of his tomb at the resurrection day. But the vile flattery inscribed on many of them reminded me of that just reflection,—

> If on the sculptured marble you rely,
> Pity that worth like his should ever die!
> If credit to the real life you give,
> Pity a wretch like him should ever live!"

In December, 1780, we find him at the British Museum with some friends who had begged him to accompany them. "What an immense field is here for curiosity to range in! One large room is filled from top to bottom with things brought from Otaheite, two or three more with things dug out of the ruins of Herculaneum. Seven huge apartments are filled with curious books, five with manuscripts, two with fossils of all sorts, and the rest with various animals." He adds a comment that lays him open to criticism: "But what account will a man give to the Judge of quick and dead for a life spent in collecting these?" Sir Ashton Lever's museum, which he visited the previous January, greatly interested him. He thought that for natural curiosities it was not excelled by any museum in Europe. All the beasts, birds, reptiles, and insects were so admirably arranged and preserved, "that if you saw many of them elsewhere, you would imagine they were alive. The hippopotamus in particular looks as fierce as if he were just coming out of the river; and the old lion appears as formidable now as when he was stalking in the Tower."

Wesley found time to make one curious experiment. On the last day of 1764, "remembering how surprisingly fond of music the old lion at Edinburgh was," he determined to try whether this was the case at the Tower. He went there with some one who played the German flute. This friend "began playing near four or five lions; only one of these (the rest not seeming to regard it at all) rose up, came to the front of his den, and seemed to be all attention. Meantime a tiger in the same den started up, leaped over the lion's back, turned and ran under his belly, leaped over him again, and so to and fro incessantly. Can we account for this by any principle of mechanism? Can we account for it at all?" A pleasant half-holiday this for the busy itinerant!

Wesley's interest in natural history is familiar to all readers of his journals. Nothing escaped his notice. In 1774 Wesley rode from Glasgow to Greenock with two of his preachers. One of them, Thomas Rutherford, had often travelled that road, but when Wesley asked him the name of a gentleman's seat, he was compelled to say that he did not know. The old man taught his young friend a fine lesson. "When I can learn nothing else," he said, "I like to learn the names of houses and villages as I pass them." Between Northampton and Towcester, in October, 1773, he met with the largest elm he ever saw. It was twenty-eight feet in circumference, six feet more than one there was some years before in Magdalen College walks at Oxford. The passion for gardening had now taken firm hold of England.* At Mr. Gordon's curious garden in Mile End, "the like of which, I suppose, is hardly to be found in England, if in Europe,"† Wesley learned the real nature of the tea-tree, and gives a careful description of the difference between green tea, Bohea, and Paraguay.‡ He had seen the most celebrated gardens in England, but gave the palm to Mr. Hoare's at Stourton.§ At Dumfries in 1788 ‖ he found five very large public gardens, which yielded greens and fruit in abundance. When he was

* Lecky, i., 524. † Works, iv., 39. ‡ *Ibid.*, iv., 47. § *Ibid.*, iv., 87. ‖ *Ibid.*, iv., 418.

first in Scotland, he says that "even at a nobleman's table, we had only flesh meat of one kind, but no vegetables of any kind; but now they are as plentiful here as in England."

Pages might be filled with Wesley's descriptions of his visits to noblemen's seats and other mansions in all parts of the kingdom. He was familiar with all the great houses of England: Wentworth House, the splendid seat of the Marquis of Rockingham,* Lord Salisbury's seat at Hatfield,† the Duke of Abercorn's in Ireland,‡ and Hampton Court, "far the finest palace which the King of England has," he visited in the later years of his life. His friends in Bristol took him, in September, 1788, to see Blaise Castle § and Lord Clifford's seat near King's Weston.|| Such visits were happy breaks in his constant round of labour. One Irish proprietor wins a high tribute. In May, 1787, Wesley took a walk with some friends to Castle Barnard. The improvements made by its owner had given it, he says, almost as pleasant a situation as Rockingham House, in Yorkshire ¶ (evidently "Wentworth House," the seat of the Marquis of Rockingham). "Mr. Barnard much resembles, in person and air, the late Sir George Saville. Though he is far the richest person in these parts, he keeps no racehorses or hounds, but loves his wife and home, and spends his time and fortune in improving his estate and employing the poor. Gentlemen of this spirit are a blessing to their neighbourhood. May God increase their number!"

Wesley's journal shows that he visited Lord George Gordon, in answer to two urgent messages from that unfortunate nobleman begging for an interview. On Tuesday,

* Works, iv., 340.
† *Ibid.*, iv., 353.
‡ Works, iv., 459.
§ *Ibid.*, iv., 438.
|| Works, iv., 132.
¶ *Ibid.*, iv., 340.

December 19th, 1780, he spent an hour with him in his room at the Tower. The conversation was upon Popery and religion. Lord George seemed well acquainted with the Bible, and had quite a library of books in his apartment. "I was agreeably surprised," Wesley says, "to find he did not complain of any person or thing; and cannot but hope his confinement will take a right turn, and prove a lasting blessing to him." In June, 1787, he writes, "I had the pleasure of a conversation with Mr. Howard, I think one of the greatest men in Europe. Nothing but the mighty power of God can enable him to go through his difficult and dangerous employments. But what can hurt us, if God is on our side?"

Remarkable instances of genius were especially interesting to Wesley. His tribute to John Downes has been already given.* In May, 1776, he saw at Carlisle "a very extraordinary genius, a man blind from four years of age, who could wind worsted, weave flowered plush on an engine and loom of his own making, who wove his own name in plush, and made his own clothes and his own tools of every sort. Some years ago, being shut up in the organ-loft at church, he felt every part of it, and afterwards made an organ for himself, which, judges say, is an exceeding good one. He then taught himself to play upon it psalm tunes, anthems, voluntaries, or anything which he heard.† I heard him play several tunes with great accuracy, and a complex voluntary. I suppose all Europe can hardly produce such another instance. His name is Joseph Strong. But what is he the better for all this if he is still 'without God in the world'?"

Wesley's journals bear witness to his life-long interest in the "supernatural." In August, 1764, when he met

* P. 220.

† Works, iv., 73.

"a pious and sensible man," who had been born in the Isle of Skye, he took occasion to ask, "Tell me freely, did you yourself ever know a second-sighted man?" The stranger assured him that he had been in company with such persons when they dropped down as dead. "Coming to themselves," he added, "they looked utterly amazed, and said, 'I have been in such a place, and I saw such and such persons (perhaps fifty miles off) die in such a manner'; and when inquiry was made, I never could find that they were mistaken in one circumstance." At Darlington, in June, 1788, Margaret Barlow was brought to see him at his own request. This girl affirmed that an angel visited her and told her many things that were to come to pass. She assured Wesley that God would in a short time destroy sinners with fire from heaven. The old evangelist was much impressed by the apparent sincerity and piety of his young visitor, but subsequent events utterly discredited her prophecies.* Wesley's journals preserve many similar incidents, which he was never weary of collecting and of studying till the last day of his life.

The varied extracts we have given may illustrate the wide range of Wesley's interest in men and things. He was learning to the last day of his life. The burden of all the Churches, which rested on him for half a century, never destroyed his vivacity nor weakened his interest in men and things around him.

---

* Tyerman, iii., 536.

CHAPTER XVII.

LEADING EVENTS UP TO THE DEATH OF WHITEFIELD.

FOR fifteen years after Methodism was introduced into Newcastle, John and Charles Wesley were both full of labours. The Societies were spreading over all the country. In 1757 the age of riots and mobs was past. Methodism was organised, and was making rapid progress. Both the brothers were married. On April 8th, 1749, Charles had been married to Miss Sarah Gwynne, daughter of Marmaduke Gwynne, of Garth, an eminent Welsh magistrate, who was a warm friend of Methodism. His home at Bristol was one of the happiest to be found in that city. John Wesley's disastrous marriage was made in February, 1751.

At the end of 1756, Charles Wesley's active itinerancy seems to have come to an end. Henceforth, with some exceptions, he confined his labours to London and Bristol. By this means the burden of the Societies fell more heavily than ever on his brother. Charles Wesley had been greatly blessed during the earlier years of the Evangelical Revival. He had the happy faculty of leading his hearers to instant decision. His soul seemed aflame with devotion. His pathos and his appeal swept away every barrier. No labours had wearied him; no mob had daunted him. Now, however, there was a change. It was not easy for him to tear himself from his family. His health, too, was broken, and in some matters he was not quite agreed with his brother. All these causes seem to have combined to withdraw him from the more active itinerancy.

By the time he thus withdrew his brother's health was happily re-established. At the end of 1753, Wesley's friends thought that his days were numbered. He retired to Lewisham, near London, the home of his friend Mr. Blackwell, with all the symptoms of a rapid decline. On the night of his arrival there, "to prevent vile panegyric," he wrote his own epitaph :—

Here lieth the Body
of
JOHN WESLEY,
A brand plucked out of the burning,
Who died of consumption in the fifty-first year of his age,
Not leaving, after his debts are paid,
Ten pounds behind him,
Praying,
"God be merciful to me, an unprofitable servant."

He ordered that this, if any, inscription should be placed on his tombstone. Charles Wesley hurried to London, and did his best to take the oversight of Methodism, but he plainly told the Society there that if his brother died, he could never fill his place. After five weeks at Lewisham, Wesley went to drink the water at the Hot Well, Bristol. His health was in a precarious state for a whole year, but he was then able to resume his itinerant life. This period of retirement was fruitful. Wesley began to prepare his "Notes on the New Testament," one of the doctrinal standards of Methodism, "a work which I should scarce ever have attempted," he says, "had I not been so ill as not to be able to travel or preach, and yet so well as to be able to read and write."

When Charles Wesley retired from the more active itinerancy, there were seventy to eighty itinerant preachers labouring in the United Kingdom. These coadjutors were introducing Methodism into all parts of the country. In the summer of 1747, one of them crossed over to Ireland, where he had such success, that he urged Wesley to come without delay. On August 9th, 1747, Wesley, therefore, landed at Dublin. From this time the work rapidly spread throughout Ireland. Mr. Tyerman calculates that Wesley crossed the Channel forty-two times, and devoted at least six years of his life to Ireland.*

Four years later Wesley paid a short visit to Scotland, at the earnest entreaty of his friend Captain Gallatin. He had no intention to preach across the Border, nor did he imagine that any one would wish him to do so. But he soon learned that the Scots were eager to hear him. At Musselburgh, where his friend's regiment was then quartered, a great congregation assembled, and "remained as statues from the beginning of the sermon to the end," though they were often grossly inattentive in their own kirk. This was Wesley's introduction to Scotland.† At Edinburgh one of the bailies came with an elder of the kirk to beg Wesley to spend some days with them. His plans would not permit him to stay, but he promised that his companion Christopher Hopper should come back the next week to spend a few days. Wesley was often cheered by the rapt attention of a Scotch congregation in later years, though he was also disappointed by their apparent spiritual insensibility. Societies were formed in various places, and though they were never large, much good was done, especially in encouraging and stimulating other Churches. These were the chief events of Methodist history up to the year 1757. The relations of Methodism to the Established Church caused anxious debate at the Conference of 1755 and the following year, but that

* Tyerman, i., 557. † Works, ii., 229.

important subject must be reserved for a separate chapter.

Though Charles Wesley's more active itinerancy closed in 1756, the two historic centres of Methodism still shared his labours. In the metropolis he often stayed for months together, administering the Sacrament to the Society every Sunday, and labouring with great acceptance. His letters show that his ministry was never more blessed than in these days. His prayers at the Sacrament often seemed to open heaven, and the whole congregation was moved by his powerful appeals. About the time his brother's labours were narrowed down to the two chief centres, Wesley found one of the most valuable of all his co-workers in this second age of Methodism. On March 13th, 1757, finding himself weak at Snowsfields, he prayed that God would send him help. His Sunday work in the metropolis was equal, he says, to preaching eight sermons. The Sacramental service at West Street, his West End chapel, near the Seven Dials, was often attended by six hundred persons. Wesley's prayer for assistance was answered. As soon as he had finished his sermon at West Street, whither he hastened after preaching at Snowsfields, John Fletcher, who had that morning been ordained priest, appeared to help him. "How wonderful are the ways of God!" says Wesley. "When my bodily strength failed, and no clergyman in England was able and willing to assist me, He sent me help from the mountains of Switzerland, and a helpmeet for me in every respect! Where could I have found such another?"

Fletcher was not quite thirty. He afterwards became Vicar of Madeley, in Shropshire, married Miss Bosanquet, a native of Leytonstone, one of the saints of Methodism, and was Wesley's adviser and helper until his death in 1785. He was not spared to be Wesley's successor, for which position, save on the ground of health, he seemed so admirably qualified; but he rendered inestimable service to the cause by that seraphic piety in the presence of which all discord died away, and the hearts of the most bitter opponents were melted into love. The share he took in the Calvinistic controversy by the publication of his famous "Checks" entitles him to the high praise of being one of the keenest and at the same time most truly Christian controversialists that any Church has possessed. Isaac Taylor says,* "The Methodism of Fletcher was Christianity, as little lowered by admixture of human infirmity as we may hope to find it anywhere on earth."

Fletcher's help was the more precious to Wesley because he had many troubles at this time. Thomas Walsh died in Ireland in 1759, in the twenty-eighth year of his age. "Oh, what a man," says Wesley, "to be snatched away in the strength of his years!" Fletcher was another Thomas Walsh for Wesley. A heavier blow than Walsh's death was the defection of Thomas Maxfield in 1763. In 1760 Wesley says, "That glorious work of sanctification which had been at a stand for near twenty years" broke out among the people.† It began in Yorkshire, then spread to London and through most parts of England, till it reached Dublin, Limerick, and all the south and west of Ireland. Wherever it came, all branches of the work of God revived and increased. Wesley preached on this subject in all his Societies, and was greatly cheered by the quickened devotion of the people.

In London the movement was unhappily attended with a wild fanaticism which soon blighted all its gracious fruits, and gave the Society there a blow from which it did not recover for years. On the last day of 1762

* "Wesley and Methodism," p. 118.

† Myles' "Chronological History," p. 72.

Wesley says, "I now stood and looked back on the past year, a year of uncommon trials and uncommon blessings. Abundance have been convinced of sin; very many have found peace with God; and in London only, I believe full two hundred have been brought into glorious liberty. And yet I have had more care and trouble in six months, than in several years preceding. What the end will be, I know not; but it is enough that God knoweth." George Bell, who had been a corporal in the Life Guards, professed to find entire sanctification in March, 1761. It soon became evident that this man was a mischievous fanatic. He began to hold meetings of his own, declared that God had done with preaching and Sacraments, and that none could teach those who were renewed in love unless they enjoyed that blessing themselves. On November 24th, 1762, Wesley stood where he could hear Bell without being seen. He prayed for nearly an hour with great fervour. Wesley afterwards told him what he did not like, and treated him and his associates with characteristic moderation.

Maxfield allied himself with Bell, and caused a serious division in the Society. Some of the members went so far as to tell Wesley that they would have no more to do with him, but would follow Mr. Maxfield. A climax was reached in 1763. Bell prophesied that the world would come to an end on February 28th. Wesley did his best to counteract this mischievous prophecy, but it greatly terrified some weak people. Prayer-meetings were held through the night. Some persons remained in the fields, fearing an earthquake. Happily Bell's career as a prophet was cut short by his arrest and imprisonment. He recovered from his religious fanaticism to become an ignorant infidel and a radical reformer. Maxfield resigned his connection with Wesley at the end of April. He took with him two hundred of Wesley's members, and preached to a large congregation of his own in Little Moorfields. Wesley visited him in his last illness, and preached in his chapel, but, as we have seen, he was never able to acquit him of dishonourable conduct. The London Society lost four hundred members by this deplorable outburst of fanaticism.

Nothing, however, could long check the progress of Methodism. Before 1758 Wesley had visited every part of Ireland except the county of Sligo. He found it had the largest population of any Irish county. He counted eight villages in less than seven miles, and Sligo itself seemed as large as Limerick. He also visited the descendants of the settlers who had come from the Palatinate, half a century before. They had no minister, and were become notorious for drunkenness, cursing, swearing, and utter neglect of religion. Methodist preaching had been a great blessing to this community. An oath was now rarely heard among them, or a drunkard seen in their borders.* In 1760 Wesley found three such towns in this German settlement as could scarcely be found anywhere else. There was neither cursing, swearing, Sabbath-breaking, drunkenness, nor alehouse among them. Most of these settlers were afterwards scattered, but they carried the germs of Methodism to the New World. Wesley's ministry in Ireland was remarkable for its success among the military. "The first call of Methodism there," he said, "was to the soldiers." These brave fellows often formed Wesley's body-guard. Their officers occasionally tried to prevent their attendance at Methodist services, but they also were frequently warm friends of the work. Sometimes Wesley preached near the barracks,

* Works, ii., 451.

where no mob durst venture to molest him for fear of the soldiers. Sometimes they escorted him to his lodgings, or cleared a preaching-place and kept order whilst he spoke.

During the whole of this period, from the retirement of Charles Wesley to the death of Whitefield in 1770, Methodism spread rapidly. The Conference that met in August, 1770, reported a membership of 29,406, under the care of a hundred and twenty-one preachers, in fifty circuits. The fiftieth circuit was "America," where four preachers were now at work. There were a hundred members in New York not included in this return. Philip Embury, an emigrant from the Palatine settlement in Ireland, reached there in 1760. For five years religion languished among the early settlers. But in 1765 the zeal of a devout woman, Barbara Heck, led them to begin Methodist preaching. Captain Webb, then on military duty in the States, preached in his regimentals. He greatly strengthened the hands of the little Society, and attracted many hearers. He also wrote an account of the work to Wesley, asking for help. In the Conference of 1769 the appeal from America was presented. "Who is willing to go?" Wesley asked. Richard Boardman and Joseph Pilmoor at once volunteered, and Methodism soon struck its roots deep into American soil.

In 1767 a great effort was made to reduce the debt on Methodist chapels. There were now a hundred in all parts of the country. The debt was £11,383. Wesley drew up a statement, which he sent to his friends, with a short note asking their assistance. £5,000 was contributed the first year, £2,000 the next. Another appeal yielded £1,700 more, but as new chapels were springing up in all parts of the kingdom, fresh debt was constantly contracted. In 1770 the old debt stood at £5,671, the new at £1,287. It taxed all Wesley's resources for many years to deal with this difficulty, caused by the vast extension of Methodism.

On September 30th, 1770, George Whitefield died in America. The later years of his life had been mainly devoted to the New World. Since the Calvinist controversy of 1741 he and the Wesleys had worked apart. The breach of friendship was indeed soon healed. Whitefield preached in Wesley's chapels, and regarded both his old friends as brothers. In September, 1769, he left for America, after spending four years in England. The previous February Wesley says, "I had one more agreeable conversation with my old friend and fellow-labourer George Whitefield. His soul appeared to be vigorous still, but his body was sinking apace." Whitefield was greatly cheered on his arrival in America by the prosperity of Bethesda, his orphanage near Savannah. It was almost free from debt. Two new wings had been built, one hundred and fifty feet long, and other buildings were being pushed forward. The Governor and council of the colony received him with public honours.

His tour through the States was marked by all his old ardour. His health seemed to be restored. He lost no opportunity of preaching, and was heard with delight by enthusiastic crowds wherever he went. To Charles Wesley, whom he always loved with special tenderness, he wrote, "I can only sit down and cry, 'What hath God wrought!' My bodily health is much improved, and my soul is on the wing for another Gospel range. Unutterable love! I am lost in wonder and amazement!" The day before his death he preached for two hours to a vast open-air congregation. His feelings completely carried him away, so that he was scarcely able to stop. He afterwards went on to Newburyport, where he was expected to preach next day. Whilst he was at supper the pavement in front of his host's house and the hall of the house itself were crowded with people, who could not wait till the morrow. Whitefield was worn out. He said to a clergyman who was present, "Brother, you must speak to these dear people; I cannot say a word." Taking a candle, he hastened to his room. On the stairs he paused. He could not resist the appeal made to him by the presence of the eager people. He yielded to the impulse, and spoke on till the candle which he held in his hand burned away and died out in its socket. At two o'clock next morning Whitefield awoke his travelling companion. His asthma was coming on again. He sat in bed praying for his friends and his work, then hastened to the window, panting for breath. Medical help was called in, but all was in vain. At six o'clock the great orator of the Revival had entered into rest.

It had long been agreed between Wesley and Whitefield that the survivor should preach his friend's funeral sermon. On November 18th the solemn service was held in the Tottenham Court Road Tabernacle. An immense multitude assembled from all parts. Wesley's voice was strengthened, so that even those about the doors heard distinctly. "It was an awful season," he says. "All were as still as night. Most appeared to be deeply affected, and an impression was made on many, which, one would hope, will not speedily be effaced." He preached the sermon again at the Tabernacle in Moorfields the same afternoon, and at Greenwich on the following Friday. "Here likewise I trust God has given a blow to that bigotry which had prevailed for many years."* On January 2nd, 1771, he says, "I preached in the evening, at Deptford, a kind of funeral sermon for Mr. Whitefield. In every place I wish to show all possible respect to the memory of that great and good man."

* Works, iii., 421.

CHAPTER XVIII.

FROM THE DEATH OF WHITEFIELD TO THE DEATH OF CHARLES WESLEY.

BEFORE the news of Whitefield's death reached England, another Calvinistic controversy had broken out. At the London Conference in August, 1770, various suggestions were made for the revival of the work of God where it had grown feeble. One of these led to years of angry debate. "Take heed to your doctrine," ran the famous Minutes. "We said in 1744, 'We have leaned too much toward Calvinism.' Wherein?

"1. With regard to *man's faithfulness.* Our Lord Himself taught us to use the expression. And we ought never to be ashamed of it. We ought steadfastly to assert, on His authority, that if a man is not 'faithful in the righteous mammon,' God will not give him the true riches.

"2. With regard to *working for life.* This also our Lord has expressly commanded us. 'Labour'—ἐργάζεσθε, literally 'work'—'for the meat that endureth to everlasting life.' And, in fact, every believer, till he comes to glory, works *for* as well as *from* life.

"3. We have received it as a maxim, that 'a man is to do nothing in order to justification.' Nothing can be more false. Whoever desires to find favour with God should 'cease from evil, and learn to do well' Whoever repents should do 'works meet for repentance.' And if this is not in order to find favour, what does he do them for?

"Review the whole affair.

"1. Who of us is *now* accepted of God? 'He that now believes in Christ, with a loving, obedient heart.'

"2. But who among those that never heard of Christ? He that feareth God, and worketh righteousness, according to the light he has.

"3. Is this the same with 'he that is sincere'? Nearly, if not quite.

"4. Is not this salvation by works? Not by the *merit* of works, but by works as a *condition.*

"5. What have we then been disputing about for these thirty years? I am afraid, about words.

"6. As to *merit* itself, of which we have been so dreadfully afraid: we are rewarded *'according to our works,'* yea, *'because of our works.'* How does this differ from *for the sake of our works?* And how differs this from 'secundum merita operum,'—as our works *deserve?* Can you split this hair? I doubt I cannot.

"7. The grand objection to one of the preceding propositions is drawn from matter of fact. God does, in fact, justify those who, by their own confession, neither feared God nor wrought righteousness. Is this an exception to the general rule? It is a doubt, God makes any exception at all. But how are we sure that the person in question never did fear God and work righteousness? His own saying is not proof; for we know how all that are convinced of sin undervalue themselves in every respect.

"8. Does not talking of a justified or a sanctified state tend to mislead men, almost naturally leading them to trust in what was done in one moment, whereas we are every hour and every moment pleasing or displeasing to God, according to our works, according to the whole of our inward tempers and our outward behaviour?"

These Minutes were intended for the preachers. So that much is here taken for granted. The answer to the question, "Who of us is *now* accepted of God?" shows that works were only a *condition* of salvation. No one in the Conference had any doubt on that point. The Minutes were a counterblast to Antinomianism, which had "spread like wildfire"* among Wesley's Societies at Norwich, Manchester, Dublin, and other places. Charles Wesley's visit to Manchester in 1756 shows how the Antinomians laboured to spread their licentious teaching among the Methodists. Similar attempts were painfully familiar to Wesley's preachers. They understood clearly that whilst they preached justification by faith, they must urge all to maintain good works. Lady Huntingdon, who had become a strong convert to Calvinism, looked on these Minutes in a different spirit. Her friendship with the Wesleys was now broken off. She even went so far as to say that she could "burn against"† the Minutes. Her Ladyship had founded a college at Trevecca for training ministers, of which Fletcher was president, Joseph Benson classical tutor. In January, 1771, Benson was dismissed because he defended the Minutes. Fletcher wrote his views upon them to her Ladyship. He explained them according to Wesley's sentiments, and approved the doctrine, though he did not consider the Minutes cautiously worded at every point. He then resigned his connection with the college.

Wesley addressed a letter of expostulation to the Countess, in which he calmly pointed out certain faults which he had observed in her with great concern. As

* Fletcher's "Checks," i. and ii. † Wesley's Works, xi., 285.

the time for the next Conference approached, she and her relative and adviser—the Hon. and Rev. Walter Shirley—prepared to enter their protest. A letter was widely circulated calling on all who agreed with them to go in a body to the Conference and "insist upon a formal recantation of the said Minutes." Lady Huntingdon wrote to Charles Wesley enclosing a copy of the circular which had been issued. It bore the offensive title "Popery Unmasked." She expressed her conviction that "all ought to be deemed Papists who did not disown" the Minutes. Charles Wesley showed what he thought of this communication by endorsing it with the words, "Lady Huntingdon's LAST. UNANSWERED BY JOHN WESLEY'S BROTHER!"

The circular received so little support that her Ladyship and Mr. Shirley changed their tone. The day before the Conference met each of them addressed a letter to Wesley expressing their regret at the unbecoming language of their printed circular. They asked whether he would receive a deputation, so that a better understanding might be reached. Wesley fixed the third day of the Conference. Only eight people came, all of whom were under Lady Huntingdon's personal influence. Mr. Shirley then read the letters in which he and the Countess apologised for the language of the circular, and hoped that the "submission made was satisfactory to the gentlemen of the Conference." He at once assented to the wish of the assembled preachers that the apology should be made as public as the obnoxious circular. After further discussion Wesley and all his preachers who were present, save Thomas Olivers, who would have nothing to do with "a patched-up peace," signed a declaration expressing their entire adhesion to the doctrine of justification by faith and their abhorrence of justification by works as a most perilous and abominable doctrine. A few days later Mr. Shirley sent a written acknowledgment that he had mistaken the meaning of the Minutes.

It might now have been hoped that this controversy was ended. Fletcher, who had received one of Mr. Shirley's circulars, had carefully examined the Minutes and drawn up "Five Letters to the Hon. and Rev. Author of the Circular." This manuscript he sent to Wesley, leaving him to print it or not as he thought fit. Wesley resolved to print without delay. When Fletcher learned the result of the Conference, he wrote to a friend in Bristol to ask that the pamphlet might be kept back for the present. He felt that the Minutes must be vindicated, but wished to make some modifications that would render the letters more palatable to Mr. Shirley. Their publication, however, had been announced, and Wesley was not at Bristol to stop the press, so that the "Five Letters" soon appeared.

The controversy assumed a painful and angry form. Wesley had little share in it. Fletcher was the champion of the Minutes. His "Checks to Antinomianism," issued one after another during the prolonged struggle, are noble specimens of polemical divinity. For convincing argument, invincible charity, and high-toned courtesy, Fletcher has on all hands won the highest praise. Thomas Olivers, one of Wesley's preachers, who was now editor of his Magazine, proved himself a powerful champion on the Arminian side. Augustus M. Toplady, Sir Richard Hill, and his more famous brother Rowland Hill, were unsparing antagonists. For more than nine years Wesley was exposed to their virulent attacks. Soon after the foundation of City Road Chapel was laid in 1777, Rowland Hill published a pamphlet entitled "Imposture Detected, and the Dead Vindicated; in a Letter to a Friend; containing some gentle strictures on the false and libellous harangue, lately delivered by Mr. John Wesley, upon his laying the first stone of his new Dissenting meeting-house, near the City Road." What the strictures were may be seen from some expressions. He called Wesley "the lying Apostle of the Foundery," "a designing wolf," "a dealer in stolen wares," and asserted that he was "as unprincipled as a rook, and as silly as a jackdaw, first pilfering his neighbour's plumage, and then going proudly forth, displaying his borrowed tail to the eyes of a laughing world."

Wesley calmly pursued his work. Charles Wesley had come to live in London the same year that the little deputation of Calvinists visited the Conference at Bristol in 1770. His daughter Sarah has preserved an anecdote which shows Wesley's tranquil fidelity to his work amid all his troubles.* He had promised to take his niece with him to Canterbury and Dover some time about 1775. The day before this journey, to which the girl was looking forward with peculiar pleasure, her father learned that Mrs. John Wesley had plundered her husband's bureau and taken out some letters on which, by interpolating words and misinterpreting spiritual expressions, she had managed to put the worst construction. These she read to some Calvinists. They were to be sent to the *Morning Post.* Mr. Russell, a Calvinist, and an intimate friend of Charles Wesley's, told him of this plot. He had heard the letter read, but suspected that they were forgeries, and wished that Wesley should try to clear up the matter.

Charles Wesley, who was far more jealous of his brother's reputation than his own, at once set out for the Foundery. His daughter never forgot the manner in which he announced the result of that visit to her mother on his return to Marylebone. "He is," he said, "a most

* MS at Headingley College.

extraordinary man; I placed before him every evil consequence which could result from his leaving London, the stumbling-blocks he might cast in the way of the weak, the advantage he gave to his enemies, the importance of his character; and when I had finished, he replied with the utmost calmness, 'When I devoted to God my ease, my time, my fortune, my life, did I except my reputation? No. Tell Sally I will take her to Canterbury to-morrow.'" It was proved that the letters had been mutilated, and no scandal ensued.

Wesley had looked forward with great pleasure to his brother's removal from Bristol to London. He often wished to consult him about important matters affecting their Societies. Though they met at Bristol and London, it was very desirable that they should have closer intercourse. The benefit of this change of residence was, however, minimised in consequence of a generous offer made by one of Charles Wesley's friends. This lady, Mrs. Gumley, gave him the lease of her town house in Chesterfield Street, Marylebone. The fine house was well furnished and provided with every comfort. But it was three miles from the Foundery. This was a serious drawback. Wesley was too busy a man to spare time for frequent visits at so great a distance.

In January, 1774, a hydrocele, which had greatly troubled Wesley for a considerable time, was successfully removed in Edinburgh. In the summer of 1775, when in the north of Ireland, he lay down one extremely hot afternoon on the grass in a friend's orchard. For forty years he had been accustomed to rest in this way, and had never taken any harm. Now, however, he fell asleep on his face. When he awoke, he felt slightly unwell, but was able to preach with ease to a vast congregation. Next day his stand was so arranged that a strong, sharp wind blew full on the side of his head whilst he was preaching. This was on the Wednesday. He was soon in a high fever, and at a friend's house near Lisburn was compelled to take to his bed. His strength was utterly gone. He could not even turn himself; his memory entirely failed; his tongue was much swollen, and as black as a coal; and for some time neither heart nor pulse seemed to beat. About three o'clock on the Sunday morning he appeared to be in the agonies of death. His pulse beat about a hundred and thirty times a minute, his flesh was like fire, and he was convulsed from head to foot. Mr. Gayer* and his family were Methodists, and had abundant means. Nothing which their kindness could suggest was left untried. Joseph Bradford, one of Wesley's preachers, was his travelling companion. He nursed the invalid with a mother's care. On the Thursday after Wesley came to Mr. Gayer's, Bradford brought some medicine in a cup, saying, "Sir, you must take this." He thought, "I will, if I can swallow, to please him; for it will do me neither harm nor good." It at once caused vomiting; the heart and pulse began to play, and from that time Wesley steadily gained strength. On Saturday he was up all day, on Sunday he spent several hours in the downstairs parlour, and on Wednesday he travelled thirty miles towards Dublin. The newspapers had already announced that he was dead. John Fletcher wrote to Charles Wesley urging him to stand in the gap if his brother was removed. He suggested that a committee of the oldest and steadiest preachers might assist him to bear the burden. The blow which Fletcher feared was, in God's mercy, averted. Methodism was not yet able to spare its head, for no provision had been made for carrying on the work after Wesley's death.

* The Clerk of the Irish House of Lords.

The great event of home Methodism during this period was the erection of City Road Chapel. Since 1739 the Foundery had been the headquarters of Methodism. In 1743 Wesley had secured a West End centre, which is still standing, in West Street, near the Seven Dials. Southwark and Spitalfields had also good chapels. On April 21st, 1777, Wesley laid the foundation of his Methodist cathedral. "The rain," he says, "befriended us much, by keeping away thousands who purposed to be there; but there were still such multitudes, that it was with great difficulty I got through them to lay the first stone." In a sermon on the words, "According to this time, it shall be said, What hath God wrought!" he described the rise of Methodism at Oxford, its mission in Georgia, the exclusion of himself and his friends from the English churches; he also explained the nature of Methodism and its relation to the Church of England. All who heard the venerable preacher must have seen by what a strange path God had led him up to that memorable day.

An appeal for help in this great undertaking was sent to all the country Societies. Wesley wrote urging them to assist the parent Society, which had for many years contributed largely and willingly to their necessities. The burden of raising funds fell on Wesley himself. He made collections for the work in all parts of the country. We catch one glimpse of him and his faithful companion, Thomas Taylor, standing on either side of the path at Keighley after Wesley had preached. Hat in hand, they thus gathered seven pounds for the new chapel.* Wesley spent much time in London attending to all details of the building. Sunday, November 1st, 1778, was the opening

* Tyerman, iii., 243

day. Wesley describes his new chapel as perfectly neat, but not fine. Many were afraid that the crowds who came from all parts would have caused much disturbance. Everything was quiet and orderly, however. Wesley preached in the morning on part of Solomon's prayer at the dedication of the Temple, and in the evening on the hundred and forty and four thousand standing with the Lamb on Mount Zion. "God was eminently present."

The prayers of the Church of England were read here both morning and evening by an ordained clergyman. At first the pulpit was occupied almost entirely by Charles Wesley and other clergymen, but before long care was taken that the London preachers should not be excluded from the chief metropolitan pulpit. Many advantages were reaped by the erection of this commodious chapel. The covenant service was held there on the 1st of January, 1779. "At length," says Wesley, "we have a house capable of containing the whole Society." The dwelling-house which is still standing on the south side of the chapel (No. 47, City Road) was the home of Wesley and his preachers, to which they were glad to remove from the ruinous premises at the Foundery. In this house Wesley died. In the burial-ground behind, he rests in peace, surrounded by more than five thousand of his devoted preachers and members. The Foundery was a decaying building, quite unworthy of Methodism, which had spread over England and Ireland, found its way to Scotland, planted stations in the West Indies and the United States, and now numbered forty-seven thousand members. The time had, therefore, come when it was essential to provide some better centre than the Foundery.

The work in America was spreading rapidly. In 1776 there were 3,148 members. The war with England threw everything into confusion for a time. Whilst City Road

Chapel was being built, three of Wesley's preachers returned to England. Francis Asbury was left alone. He was the Wesley of America. For forty-five years he travelled over the rough settlements of the States as extensively as Wesley did at home. Bogs, swamps, prairies, mountains, and rivers were fearlessly crossed by this heroic itinerant. Every day he read a hundred pages, and spent three hours in private devotion. Though his colleagues had left him in 1777, there were thirty-four itinerants who had been called out to the work in America itself and nearly seven thousand members.

Methodism spread through the States by leaps and bounds. Wesley was greatly exercised by the position of his people there. They had no one to administer the Sacraments. Many of the English clergy of the country had withdrawn or ceased to officiate on account of the war. At best there had been but few of them, and many Societies were far beyond the reach of their ministrations. In 1780 Wesley wrote to Dr. Lowth, Bishop of London. He had presented a petition to his Lordship for the ordination of some pious man who might minister to the needs of the people in America. His request was not granted. Dr. Lowth replied that there were "three ministers in that country already." Wesley answered that from sad experience he knew that the greater part of the missionaries in America were men who had neither the power nor the form of godliness, "men that lay no claim to piety, nor even decency." His whole letter shows how he mourned over the spiritual destitution of America.

Matters reached a crisis in 1784. During the previous ten years 12,915 new members had been added to the American Societies. They now numbered 14,988. Asbury pleaded urgently for help. He was in a difficult position. In 1779 the preachers in the south had arranged that three of the oldest men among them should ordain the rest. Asbury prevailed on them to give up the administration of the Sacraments till he could communicate with Wesley. His appeal stated that "a minister and such preachers" as Wesley could fully recommend would be very acceptable. Asbury's ardent desire was to see Wesley himself in America. That was clearly impossible; but at the Conference of 1784 Coke, Whatcoat, and Vasey were appointed. A month later Wesley, with the assistance of the Rev. James Creighton, a clergyman who had become one of his staff in London, solemnly set apart Dr. Coke as "Superintendent" over the American preachers and Societies. Asbury was to be his colleague, with equal powers. They were to ordain others to administer the Sacraments. After Dr. Coke had been set apart for his office, he assisted Wesley and Creighton to ordain Whatcoat and Vasey as elders, with power to administer the Sacraments in America.

Wesley had now taken a decisive step. He was fully convinced in his own mind that he was a Scriptural ἐπίσκοπος, but only the most pressing necessity drove him to exercise the power of ordination. All other plans for meeting the necessities and claims of his growing Societies in America had failed. He therefore was compelled to take this step. Next year, after careful deliberation, he yielded to the judgment of his friends, and set apart three of his well-tried preachers to administer the Sacraments in Scotland. "I trust," he says, "God will bless their ministrations, and show that He has sent them." In 1788 Alexander Mather was ordained "superintendent."

Charles Wesley was greatly disturbed by his brother's ordinations. He was not fully conversant with the necessities of the case, nor was he a practical man, like John

Wesley. He wrote an urgent letter begging him to stop and consider before he had quite broken down the bridge. Wesley had not acted under a sudden impulse. He had carefully weighed the matter and made good his position. He could not therefore yield to his brother's appeal. By-and-bye Charles Wesley's fears subsided. He saw that some of his apprehensions were groundless, and was able to leave the issues of the work to Him who had guided every step of its marvellous development.

Methodism only gained a legal constitution in 1784. For two years the Birstal Chapel case had awakened grave concern. A new preaching-place was required, and to give the trustees security for the money advanced for its erection, another deed was prepared. The trustees insisted that they and the leaders should have power to appoint preachers for their chapel after the death of the Wesleys. At one time it seemed as though Wesley would be compelled to leave these obstinate trustees with their chapel on their hands, and build another for his Society. He was determined to resist to the last any arrangement which would transfer the appointment of preachers to the trustees. His firmness, together with some timely concessions, brought the matter to a happy issue.

This struggle showed the necessity for some legal settlement to save Methodism from going to wreck after its founder's death. Before the matter was settled Wesley's life was in imminent danger. During the Bristol Conference he was seized with "a most impetuous flux," which was followed by violent and almost constant cramp. Three doses of opium stopped the cramp, but took away speech, hearing, and power to move, so that Wesley lay like a mere log. No one expected his recovery. Joseph Bradford, his old nurse, was with him. "I have been reflecting on my past life," the old man said to him;

"I have been wandering up and down between fifty and sixty years, endeavouring, in my poor way, to do a little good to my fellow-creatures; and now it is probable that there are but a few steps between me and death; and what have I to trust to for salvation? I can see nothing that I have done or suffered that will bear looking at. I have no other plea than this:

I the chief of sinners am,
But Jesus died for me."*

Wesley rallied from this severe attack, but the eighteen days of suspense had shown clearly that there was no time to be lost. Dr. Coke had read to the Bristol Conference the opinion of counsel, to the effect that the members of the Conference should be enrolled, and measures taken for the perpetuity of the body. On February 28th, 1784, Wesley, therefore, executed his Deed of Declaration. It was enrolled in Chancery a few days later. The deeds on which Methodist chapels had been settled for many years reserved to Wesley the power to appoint preachers; after his death his right was to pass to Charles Wesley; and if William Grimshaw survived both the brothers, he was to exercise it. After the death of the three clergymen, the power to appoint preachers passed to the yearly Conference. A legal constitution was now given to that body. The Deed of Declaration contained the names of one hundred preachers who were to form the Methodist Conference. They were to meet once a year, to fill up vacancies in their own number, appoint a president and secretary, station the preachers to various circuits, admit proper persons into the ministry, and have general control over all the Methodist Societies. The act of the majority was to bind all. Careful provision was made for various contingencies. There were one

* Moore, ii., 389.

hundred and seventy Methodist preachers at the time when this deed was executed. Some of those whose names did not appear in it were much hurt by the omission. Wesley himself chose the members of the Conference, and no man knew better than he who were most eligible. Considerable feeling was caused, however, by his selection, and five malcontents retired from the ranks. The following year Wesley published a defence of his conduct. To the argument that all the preachers should have been placed on the deed he justly objects that it would have doubled the expense of meeting and have left all the circuits without preachers during the Conference. He says that he had chosen the persons who seemed most suitable. "I did my best; if I did wrong, it was not the error of my will, but of my judgment."

Charles Wesley died on March 29th, 1788. His brother was in Staffordshire at the time. He was singing with his congregation Charles Wesley's hymn,

> Come, let us join our friends above,
> That have obtained the prize,

at the very hour when the poet of Methodism joined the company in heaven. By a mistake in the address of the letter, news of his brother's death did not reach Wesley till the day before the funeral. He was then at Macclesfield, so that he could not join the sorrowing company in the little graveyard of the old parish church at Marylebone, near Charles Wesley's residence. A fortnight later, when he attempted to give out his brother's hymn on "Wrestling Jacob" at Bolton, he broke down at those touching lines,

> My company before is gone,
> And I am left alone with Thee.

The patriarch burst into a flood of tears, sat down in the pulpit, and buried his face in his hands. The singing ceased, and all the congregation wept together. In a little while Wesley recovered himself, and was able to proceed with a service never to be forgotten by those who were present.

On his return from the north in the middle of July, Wesley spent an hour with his "widowed sister and her children." "They all seemed inclined," he said, "to make the right use of the late providential dispensation." He did everything in his power to supply his brother's place to his niece and his two nephews—the famous organists. When Sarah Wesley needed change of air, he begged her to consult Dr. Whitehead, his favourite physician, and promised her ten or twenty pounds if she went to Harrogate. No one could have been more tenderly careful of the widow and her children. It was a great grief to Wesley that the brother with whom he had been so intimately associated at the University and in Georgia, as well as throughout the course of the Great Revival, should have refused to be buried at City Road. That ground was unconsecrated. Charles Wesley was too stout a Churchman to consent to his burial there. He preferred to rest in the graveyard of the parish in which he resided. The brothers therefore lie apart. John Wesley sleeps under the shadow of the metropolitan church of Methodism; Charles rests with his wife and two sons behind the old parish church of Marylebone.

NOTE TO PAGE 300.

Coke wished every preacher in full connexion to be a member of the Conference. Fletcher had to mediate between Wesley and some of his sons at the Conference of 1784, in regard to their omission from that "wicked Deed."

CHAPTER XIX.

WESLEY'S CHURCHMANSHIP.

WESLEY'S Churchmanship has been much debated. At Oxford and in Georgia he was undoubtedly a stiff High Churchman. What he afterwards described as the "vehement prejudice of my education"* had sunk deep into his mind. No one was more scrupulously exact in his obedience to all the rubrics and customs of the Church of England. Both his father and his mother were converts to that Church from the ranks of the Nonconformists, and his elder brother Samuel was a strong Churchman. With such home influence and a long residence at Oxford, we are not surprised to find that both John and Charles Wesley brought trouble on themselves by their conduct in Georgia. Charles insisted on trine immersion as the only proper form of infant baptism. Parents were not quite willing to have their children thus plunged three times into the water. John Wesley pursued the same method. The second magistrate of Savannah had his child baptised by another clergyman because he would not allow Wesley to treat it in this fashion.

Dr. Rigg says,† "The resemblance of his practices to those of modern high Anglicans is, in most points, exceedingly striking. He had early and also forenoon service

---

* Works, ii., 6.

† "Churchmanship of John Wesley," pp. 28, 29.

every day; he divided the morning service, taking the Litany as a separate service; he inculcated fasting and confession and weekly communion; he refused the Lord's Supper to all who had not been baptised by a minister episcopally ordained; he insisted on baptism by immersion; he rebaptised the children of Dissenters; and he refused to bury all who had not received episcopal baptism. One thing only was wanting to make the parallel with our moderns complete: there is no evidence that he believed in the 'conversion of the elements' by consecration, or in their doctrine of the Real Presence."

In 1749 Wesley received a letter from John Martin Bolzius, which he inserted in his journal. Bolzius assures him that "the sincere love to his worthy person and faithful performance of his holy office which he had felt in Georgia was not abated, but increased." Wesley adds, "What a truly Christian piety and simplicity breathe in these lines! And yet this very man, when I was at Savannah, did I refuse to admit to the Lord's Table, because he was not baptised; that is, not baptised by a minister who had been episcopally ordained. Can any one carry High Church zeal higher than this? And how well have I been since beaten with my own staff!"*

Wesley's voyage home from Georgia in 1738 was a time of great heart-searching. "I, who went to America to convert others," he wrote, "was never myself converted to God." Peter Böhler, whom he met in London, led him into the way of faith. The great change which he then experienced in his temper and views almost justifies Miss Wedgwood's words, "Wesley's homeward voyage in 1738 marks the conclusion of his High Church period." This was certainly the beginning of a "new

* Works, ii., 160.

dispensation." The course of events still further modified Wesley's position. He and his friends found themselves shut out of the pulpits of the Church just when they were fully prepared to preach the Gospel. In his sermon preached on laying the foundation of City Road Chapel, Wesley states, that on his return from America he was in haste to retire to Oxford and bury himself in his beloved obscurity, but he was detained in London week after week by the trustees of the colony of Georgia. Meanwhile he was urged to preach in various churches, where "vast multitudes flocked" to hear him. After a time he was shut out of church after church. The reason given was usually, "Because you preach such doctrines." Wesley had therefore to choose between silence and irregularity. Hence arose the first field-preaching. Wesley could scarce reconcile himself to this strange method when he stood in Whitefield's congregation at Bristol, "having been all my life (till very lately) so tenacious of every point relating to decency and order, that I should have thought the saving of souls almost a sin if it had not been done in a church."* His feeling about lay-preaching and his hurried journey to London to stop Thomas Maxfield's sermons have been already referred to.

At the end of December, 1745, to his brother-in-law, Mr. Hall, who was urging the Wesleys to leave the Church of England, he wrote as follows: "We believe it would not be right for us to administer either Baptism or the Lord's Supper unless we had a commission so to do from those bishops whom we apprehend to be in a succession from the Apostles." He holds that field-preaching is contrary to no law, and though he is not clear about the

* Works, i., 185.

legality of lay-preaching, he maintains that, even if illegal, it is an exempt case in which he cannot obey with a good conscience. One point has special interest. Wesle expresses his belief that the threefold order of ministers—bishops, priests, and deacons—is not only authorised by its Apostolical institution, but also by the written Word. "Yet," he adds, "we are willing to hear and weigh whatever reasons induce you to believe to the contrary."*

Mr. Hall may have referred him to a book on the subject. At any rate, he writes three weeks later, "I set out for Bristol. On the road I read over Lord King's 'Account of the Primitive Church.' In spite of the vehement prejudice of my education, I was ready to believe that this was a fair and impartial draft; but if so, it would follow that bishops and presbyters are (essentially) of one order, and that originally every Christian congregation was a Church independent on all others!"† Lord King, the writer who thus influenced Wesley, died in 1734, having been Lord Chancellor for eighteen years. From the position then taken Wesley never withdrew.

In the year 1755 there was a crisis in Methodism. Some of the "preachers" were accustomed to absent themselves from the services of the Church, and went so far as to administer the Lord's Supper to those who held that close relationship with the Church of England could not be maintained or who felt unable to go to the Lord's Table at church with comfort or profit. The two sons of Mr. Perronet, Vicar of Shoreham (whom Charles Wesley used to call the Archbishop of Methodism), Joseph Cownley, a preacher of remarkable ability, and Thomas Walsh were at the head of this movement. The Wesleys

* Works, ii., 4—6. † *Ibid.*, ii., 6.

spent some time together at Birstal before the Leeds Conference of 1755 reading a Book on Dissent written by a Dissenter. Thus prepared, they went to its session. After three days' careful discussion, all fully agreed "that whether it was lawful or not to separate, it was no ways expedient."* Charles Wesley, full of painful forebodings, rode off to London the morning after the debate, and before the end of the month printed a poetical "epistle" to his brother on the subject which was uppermost in his mind and heart. He read it two nights in succession to large congregations in London.

Wesley did not share his brother's forebodings. He was perfectly satisfied with the concessions made by his preachers, and found wherever he went that the Societies were far more firmly and rationally attached to the Church than ever they were before. In 1758 he published his twelve "Reasons against a Separation from the Church of England." The conciliatory spirit which breathes in this pamphlet shows how careful he was to interfere with no man's liberty. "It would be well," he says, "for every Methodist preacher, *who has no scruple concerning it*, to attend the service of the Church as often as he conveniently can." Charles Wesley added a postscript, in which he expressed his approval, and declared his intention to live and die in communion with the Church of England. Two years later three preachers stationed in Norwich began to administer the Sacraments in that city. This step was taken entirely on their own responsibility. Charles Wesley was greatly excited. He sent a letter to his brother beginning with the ominous words, "We are come to the Rubicon." He also wrote to various preachers entreating them to discountenance and oppose the conduct

* Jackson's "Charles Wesley," ii., 78.

of their brethren at Norwich. John Wesley, who did not share these fears, went quietly on his way.*

The ordinations for America in 1784 roused all Charles Wesley's fears. Lord Mansfield told him that ordination was separation. Charles at first felt that the life-long partnership between himself and his brother was dissolved, and wrote several earnest letters of expostulation to Wesley. In his brother's reply occurs the famous sentence, "I firmly believe I am a Scriptural ἐπίσκοπος, as much as any man in England or in Europe; for the uninterrupted succession I know to be a fable, which no man ever did or can prove." Four years before he had expressed his conviction that he had as much right to ordain as to administer the Sacrament. Holding such views, Wesley took the step which his brother deplored, and ordained Dr. Coke as Superintendent of American Methodism. When Coke reached the States, he was instructed to ordain Asbury as his co-superintendent. We have seen that other ordinations to the ordinary work of the ministry in America, Scotland, and even in England † followed. In 1789 he requested his assistant, William Myles, an unordained preacher, to assist him in giving the cup to the communicants at Dublin. Such facts effectually disprove the statement that to the end of his life Wesley was a High Churchman in the modern sense of that term. Within seven years after his evangelical conversion the prejudices of his earlier life had begun to yield.

The step Wesley took in 1784 was the natural outgrowth of the conviction reached on reading Lord Chancellor King's book in 1746. He had carefully abstained for nearly forty years from taking action, but

* See pp. 297

† See Chapter XVIII.

the destitute condition of his American Societies at length drove him to make provision for the administration of the Sacraments. It is desirable to add that in a letter written to Lord North on behalf of the American colonists, Wesley describes himself as "a High Churchman, and the son of a High Churchman," but this refers to his political attitude as a clergyman, not to his doctrinal position.

Another question has great interest. Did Wesley intend his Societies to separate from the Church? He must have been strangely wanting in sagacity if he did not discern the drift of Methodist thought and feeling. The Wesleys had done all they could to bind their Societies to the Church. Their members at Bristol were at first constant communicants at St. James's Church, near the preaching-place in the Horse Fair. That was "our parish church" in Bristol. In London St. Luke's was the parish church for the Foundery Methodists. Even so late as December, 1789, eleven years after the opening of City Road Chapel, Wesley gives it this name. The connexion had been little more than a name, however, for many years. Wesley was at a very early date compelled to administer the Lord's Supper to his own people in London and Bristol. On Sunday, April 12th, 1741, after the "bands" of Kingswood had been denied the Sacrament at Temple Church, Bristol, Charles Wesley, who had himself been repelled, with many others, administered the Lord's Supper in Kingswood Schoolroom. "Had we wanted an house," he says, "I would justify doing it in the midst of the wood." When Wesley opened his West Street Chapel on May 29th, 1743, the Lord's Supper was regularly administered there every week to the London Methodists. In October, 1770, after Charles Wesley left Bristol, and there was some fear of an interruption of the arrangements which had been in force for many years, the brothers, at the request of their friends, arranged to administer the Lord's Supper at Bristol every other Sunday.*

Bristol and London were, however, favoured Societies. The country Methodists fared badly. Sometimes they were repelled from the Lord's Table; not seldom they were compelled to receive the Sacrament from a minister who either persecuted them or lived a life utterly unworthy of his profession. Wesley did his utmost to keep his members to the parish churches. He took care to attend himself, and earnestly exhorted the Societies to be regular in their attendance. But he found many difficulties. When he examined one Society in Cornwall, he discovered that out of ninety-eight persons all but three or four had forsaken the Lord's Table. "I told them my thoughts very plain; they seemed convinced, and promised no more to give place to the devil." †

Wesley's journals show what pains he took to promote good feeling between the clergy and the Methodists. He visited the clergy to clear up any misunderstandings, and rejoiced over every manifestation of friendliness on their part. Sometimes he refers to the devout and practical preaching he heard when he went to church with his people. In later years he was often asked to take the pulpit himself. After one such service in Wales he writes, "The bigots of all sides seemed ashamed before God, and, I trust, will not soon forget this day." ‡ Some of the sermons he heard at church grieved him deeply. A preacher at Birmingham in the Old Church, on July 14th, 1782, spoke with great vehemence against these "harebrained itinerant enthusiasts." "But," adds

* Wesley's Works, iii., 418. † *Ibid.*, iii., 16.
‡ Works, iii., 374.

Wesley, "he totally missed the mark, having not the least conception of the persons whom he undertook to describe." In one church he heard part of Bishop Lavington's "Papists and Methodists Compared" read for a sermon, but that did not lessen his own congregation in the afternoon.

During the last years of Wesley's life, the clergy generally learned to regard him as a friend. In January, 1783, after referring to two sermons preached in London, at St. Thomas's and St. Swithin's, he says, "The tide is now turned; so that I have more invitations to preach in churches than I can accept of." In December, 1789, he makes the same remark. His ordinations led some of his people to suppose that he was about to separate from the Church. Finding a report of this kind spread abroad in Bristol, in September, 1785, he openly declared on the Sunday evening that he had no more thought of separating from the Church than he had forty years ago.

Wesley's Deed of Declaration, his ordinations, and the licensing of his chapels and preachers under the provisions of the Toleration Act show, however, that he was more careful for the continuance of the work than for any formal connection with the Church of England. He did not allow that he separated from the Church, and told the Deptford Society, in January, 1787, that if they had their service in church hours, they should see his face no more. Next year, however, general liberty was given to hold services at such times wherever people did not object, except only on the Sacrament Sunday. Wesley took all possible care that Methodism should not perish with his death.* The principles which eventually led to separation were meanwhile extending and taking deeper root. The connection with the Church was becoming slighter. The

* See p. 299.

united Societies were gaining step by step a complete organisation of their own. Wesley's death removed the last barrier to complete independence. It was surely better, in the interests of religion, that Methodism should have the Sacraments duly administered by her own preachers than that the unsatisfactory arrangement existing at the close of Wesley's life should be maintained in order to avoid separation.

Wesley found many true helpers in the Church of England. The Rev. William Grimshaw, curate of Haworth, in Yorkshire, deserves the first place in the list of his clerical coadjutors. He became one of Wesley's assistants in 1745. Grimshaw took charge of two large Methodist circuits. In addition to his own parish duties, he met classes, conducted lovefeasts, and preached with awakening power, sometimes as many as thirty sermons a week. Wesley's itinerants always found his house their home. Sometimes he would give up his own bed and sleep in the barn because his Methodist friends had filled all his rooms. Grimshaw died in 1762, after sixteen years of unceasing devotion.

Wesley told Dr. Byrom in 1761 that he divided his assistants into regulars, half-regulars, and irregulars.* Madan and Romaine, he said, belonged to the second class. At that time Wesley was surrounded by a band of active workers among the clergy. In March, 1757, John Fletcher had sought holy orders, at Wesley's suggestion. After his ordination he became Vicar of Madeley, but to the end of his life he was the most valuable of all Wesley's helpers in the Church of England. He relieved him of the burden of the Calvinistic controversy in 1771 by his "Checks to Arminianism," travelled with

* "Journals," ii., 629.

him to encourage the Societies, and kindled anew the fire of devotion as often as he appeared among the preachers at their annual Conference. Wesley hoped that Fletcher would have in some measure filled his place after his death. But all such hopes were frustrated by the death of the Vicar of Madeley in 1785. Fletcher owed his conversion to Methodism. The service which he rendered to its Societies and preachers was invaluable. Wesley wrote his friend's life. "Within fourscore years," he says, "I have known many excellent men, holy in heart and life, but one equal to him I have not known, one so uniformly and deeply devoted to God. So unblamable a man in every respect I have not found either in Europe or America, nor do I expect to find another such on this side eternity." *

The year after Fletcher's ordination the Rev. John Berridge, Vicar of Everton, invited Wesley to visit him. He soon became an earnest ally. His church was crowded with people who came ten, twenty, or thirty miles to hear the awakened clergyman, and he laboured as an itinerant evangelist with great success. Sometimes he travelled a hundred miles, and preached ten or twelve sermons a week. Scenes like those which broke out under Wesley's preaching at Bristol and Newcastle became frequent under his ministry. Scores fell on the ground, and were carried to the Vicarage. Romaine, then lecturer at St. Dunstan's-in-the-West, was also a firm friend, and suffered much in consequence. He often had to address the crowds at St. Dunstan's Church with a lighted taper in his hand, because the churchwardens refused to light the building for the Methodist clergyman. Martin Madan, a witty young lawyer, went to hear Wesley that he might afterwards

* Works, xi., 365.

mimic him among his friends. When he returned to the coffee-house, they asked him if he had "taken off the old Methodist." "No, gentlemen," was the reply, "but he has taken me off." He became a popular evangelical clergyman, and travelled with Romaine, Wesley, Lady Huntingdon, and Henry Venn, then curate of Clapham, who afterwards became Vicar of Huddersfield, and laboured with great success in the surrounding district. Berridge and Madan took the Calvinistic side in the controversy of 1771. Berridge did himself little credit by his grotesque writing. Madan did not publish anything on that controversy, but revised Rowland Hill's writings and supported the Calvinistic party.

Vincent Perronet, the Vicar of Shoreham, who died in 1785, at the ripe age of ninety-two, was for thirty-nine years the intimate friend and adviser of the Wesleys. Two of his sons became Methodist preachers. Their father retained his parish, but made it a model Methodist circuit. The Wesleys and their itinerants often visited Shoreham, where they were greatly cheered by his unwavering faith and constant kindness. The great awakening spread rapidly among the clergy. When Romaine began to preach evangelical truth, he could only reckon up six or seven clergymen of evangelical views, but before his death in 1795 there were more than five hundred.*

The most notable figure in Wesley's staff of clerical helpers in the last years of his life was Dr. Coke. Expelled from his curacy because of his zeal and fervour, Coke boldly cast in his lot with Methodism in 1777. Wesley often said that Coke was a second Thomas Walsh to him.† The people flocked from all parts to hear the

* Life of Henry Venn, p. 14.

† Jackson's "Charles Wesley," ii., 381.

man whom persecution had driven into the Methodist ranks. He relieved Wesley of many burdens in his old age, and devoted himself with unwearying zeal to the united Societies. Coke is best known as the Missionary Bishop of Methodism. He made many voyages across the Atlantic, and died on May 2nd, 1814, on his way to Ceylon with a band of missionaries. His servant knocked at his cabin door at the usual hour, but there was no response. The lifeless form was found cold and stiff on the floor. Coke had illustrated the words which he is said to have used in the last sermon he preached in London. "Death! death! What is it to the Christian? Why, it is only stepping out of time into eternity!"*

* "Two West End Chapels," p. 155.

By the courtesy of the Rev. Charles H. Kelly, facsimiles are given of some of Wesley's Ordination Certificates. That of Coke as Superintendent of the Societies in America possesses unique interest.

CHAPTER XX.

PREACHER, WRITER, AND PHILANTHROPIST.

AS a preacher, Wesley was remarkable for simplicity of style and force of argument. Whitefield was an impassioned orator; Charles Wesley carried everything before him by his deep emotion and his forcible application; John Wesley appealed to the reason with irresistible power. "His attitude in the pulpit was graceful and easy; his action calm and natural, yet pleasing and expressive; his voice not loud, but clear and manly; his style neat, simple, perspicuous, and admirably adapted to the capacity of his hearers."* Henry Moore, his biographer and intimate friend, says that when he first heard Wesley preach he thought it strange that a man who spoke with such simplicity should have made so much noise in the world. He paid a great tribute to the sermon, however, for he said that he remembered more of it than of any he had ever heard.†

Wesley early learned this art of simplicity. As a young man, he once preached a highly finished sermon to a country congregation. The people listened with open mouths. He saw at once that they did not understand what he said. He struck out some of the hard expressions, and tried again. Their mouths were now only half open. Wesley, however, was resolved to carry them entirely

* Hampson, iii., 168.

† Mrs. R. Smith's Life of Henry Moore.

with him. He read the sermon to an intelligent servant, and got her to tell him whenever she did not understand. Betty's "Stop, sir," came so often that he grew impatient. But he persevered, wrote a plain word over every hard one, and had his reward in seeing that his congregation now clearly understood every word. Wesley's journals show what a lofty estimate he set on St. John's First Epistle. It was evidently his own model. He expounded it in his Societies, and advised every young preacher to form his style upon it. "Here," he says, "are sublimity and simplicity together, the strongest sense and the plainest language! How can any one that would 'speak as the oracles of God' use harder words than are found here?" *

His first extempore sermon was preached in All Hallows Church, Lombard Street, in 1735. He went there to hear Dr. Heylyn, but as he did not come, Wesley yielded to the request of the churchwardens and preached to the crowded congregation.† On the last Sunday of 1788, he preached again in that church. He told the attendant that as he was going up the pulpit stairs in 1735, he hesitated, and returned in much confusion to the vestry. A woman (the church-keeper) asked what was the matter, and when she found that Wesley had no sermon, she put her hand on his shoulder with the words, "Is that all? Cannot you trust God for a sermon?" Her question produced such an effect upon him that he preached with great freedom and acceptance, and never afterwards took a sermon into the pulpit.‡

* Works, iii., 146, 230, 483. † *Ibid.*, iv., 68.

‡ *Methodist Magazine*, 1825, p. 105. These facts were printed on a broad sheet by a Methodist churchwarden of All Hallows, and a copy, strongly framed, is hung up in the vestry of that church.

Wesley preached in gown and cassock even in the open air.* His clear voice was heard throughout Gwennap Amphitheatre. At Birstal in 1753 he was afraid that the people would not hear, but even those who sat in John Nelson's windows, a hundred yards off, distinctly caught every word.† On another occasion it was found by measurement that his voice could be clearly heard for a hundred and forty yards. Sometimes he took his stand on tables, sometimes on walls. At Haworth, where his friend Grimshaw was the minister, Wesley found a little platform erected outside one of the church windows. After prayers the people flocked into the churchyard. Wesley then stepped through the window, and addressed the multitude gathered from all parts.‡

The power of his preaching is evident from every page of the journals. There were cases of imposture and hysterical excitement, but allowing for these, no preaching of the Evangelical Revival produced such effect on the conscience as John Wesley's. John Nelson, who had long been seeking peace, felt his heart beat like the pendulum of a clock when he heard him at Moorfields, and thought the whole discourse was aimed at him. His words were often "as a hammer and a flame." § He tells us that when speaking on the righteousness of faith he was constrained to break off in the midst of his discourse. "Our hearts were so filled with a sense of the love of God, and our mouths with prayer and thanksgiving. When we were somewhat satisfied herewith, I went on to call sinners to the salvation ready to be revealed."|| At one place a number of people were seated on a long wall built of loose stones. In the

* Works, i., 430.
† *Ibid.*, ii., 291.
‡ *Ibid.*, iii., 67, 260.
§ Works, i., 343.
|| *Ibid.*, i., 380.

middle of Wesley's sermon this wall fell down all at once. None screamed; few altered their position. No one was hurt; they simply seemed to have dropped into a lower seat. During this strange incident there was no interruption of the sermon or of the marked attention of the congregation.*

The scenes in Epworth churchyard in 1742 bear witness to Wesley's power as a preacher. The gentleman drinking in every word, Wesley's personal appeal to him, and his touching answer, "Sinner indeed"—that incident forms one of the most impressive scenes of Wesley's ministry.† The conquest of the mob at Bolton‡ in 1749 is not less striking. At York in 1753 Wesley says, "I began preaching at seven, and God applied it to the hearts of the hearers. Tears and groans were on every side, among high and low. God, as it were, bowed the heavens and came down. The flame of love went before Him; the rocks were broken in pieces, and the mountains flowed down at His presence." Finding many fashionable people in his congregation at the Court House at Castlebar in 1771, he says, "I spoke with such closeness and pungency, as I cannot do but at some peculiar seasons. It is indeed the gift of God, and cannot be attained by all the efforts of nature and art united." His beautiful expressions, "God Himself made the application," § "Truly God preached to their hearts," || show how he recognised the Divine blessing.

The applications of Wesley's sermons were never slurred. The discourses in the Scotch kirks struck him as specially defective in this respect.¶ On one occasion

* Works, ii., 55.
† See p. 164.
‡ See p. 185.
§ Works, iv., 83, 277.
|| *Ibid.*, iv., 486; v., 293.
¶ *Ibid.*, iv., 155.

he speaks of the excellent truths he there listened to, but adds, "As there was no application, it is likely to do as much good as the singing of a lark."* His own experience in Scotland was not encouraging. Though he never met with people who loved preaching like his friends across the Tweed, he often felt helpless in the presence of those self-contained hearers. "Use the most cutting words, and apply them in the most pointed manner, still they *hear*, but *feel* no more than the seats they sit upon!"

Wesley was always careful in his choice of texts. A young gentleman at Armagh, in June, 1787, observed that he had quite mistaken his subject—his sermon was suitable for the vulgar, but not for gentlefolk.† He did not know Wesley's method, however. A friend once complained because he preached to a respectable congregation from the words, "Ye serpents, ye generation of vipers, how can ye escape the damnation of hell?" That text would have done for Billingsgate, but not for such hearers, was the criticism. Wesley replied that if he had been in Billingsgate, he should have preached from "Behold the Lamb of God, which taketh away the sin of the world." It was his rule to preach the Law to the careless.‡ To speak of justification by faith before people desired to find it was, he felt, only likely to do harm; when people were "ripe for the Gospel," then Wesley preached it with power. He availed himself of all circumstances that might render his message impressive. A passing bell was tolling out as he stood in Llanelly churchyard, and led him strongly to enforce the words, "It is appointed unto men once to die." § A lady of great ability, deep piety, and a fine person had died between two of his visits

* Works, iv., 272.
† *Ibid.*, iv., 384.
‡ Works, iv., 95, 460.
§ *Ibid.*, iv., 165.

to Castle Cary. Wesley therefore earnestly applied the words, "Whatsoever thy hand findeth to do, do it with thy might; for there is no work, nor device, nor knowledge, nor wisdom, in the grave." "All the people seemed to feel it."

Wesley was sometimes so drawn out, that he scarcely knew how to close his sermon. At Berwick in 1748 * the word of God was "as a fire and a hammer." He began again and again after he thought he had done, and his words grew more and more weighty. At Stanley, near Gloucester, in 1739,† he preached on a little green near the town. "I was strengthened," he says, "to speak as I never did before; and continued speaking near two hours, the darkness of the night and a little lightning not lessening the number, but increasing the seriousness, of the hearers." Twelve days later at Cardiff almost the whole town came together. Wesley spoke on the Beatitudes with such enlargement of heart, that he knew not how to give over, so that they "continued three hours." When expounding the ninth chapter of Romans at the Foundery during the Calvinistic debates of 1741, he was constrained to speak an hour longer than usual. At Birstal, in April, 1745, he writes, "I was constrained to continue my discourse there near an hour longer than usual; God pouring out such a blessing, that I knew not how to leave off." Three years before he had another long service there. "I began about seven, but could not conclude till half an hour past nine."‡ Twelve days later he was holding his farewell service in Epworth churchyard. A vast multitude had assembled from all parts, among whom Wesley continued nearly three hours. Even then he and his congregation scarcely knew how to part. In the last years of his life his sermons were generally short,

* Works, ii., 105. † *Ibid.*, i., 229. ‡ *Ibid.*, i., 375.

seldom more than half an hour in length.* In 1765 Wesley says that he preached eight hundred sermons a year.† During his half-century of itinerant life he travelled a quarter of a million miles, and delivered more than forty thousand sermons. Such a restless and far-reaching itinerancy exerted an enormous influence on behalf of evangelical religion throughout the United Kingdom.

Leslie Stephen‡ pays a high tribute to Wesley as a writer. "He shows remarkable literary power; but we feel that his writings are means to a direct practical end, rather than valuable in themselves, either in form or substance. It would be difficult to find any letters more direct, forcible, and pithy in expression. He goes straight to the mark, without one superfluous flourish. He writes as a man confined within the narrowest limits of time and space, whose thoughts are so well in hand, that he can say everything needful within these limits. The compression gives emphasis, and never causes confusion. The letters, in other words, are the work of one who for more than half a century was accustomed to turn to account every minute of his eighteen working hours."

Wesley's service to popular literature entitles him to a distinguished place among the benefactors of the eighteenth century. Most of his writings and his brother's hymns were published at prices that put them within the reach of all. Many were in the form of penny tracts, so that even the poorest could purchase them. In 1771 to 1774 he published an edition of his own works, in weekly numbers of seventy-two pages, stitched in blue paper, at sixpence each. They were afterwards issued in thirty-two small volumes. Particular attention was paid to the

* Whitehead, ii., 467. † Works, iii., 211.

‡ "History of English Thought in the Eighteenth Century," ii., 409.

quality of the paper, and new type was cast for this work. Whilst this edition was passing through the press, Wesley writes, "I have laboured as much as many writers; and all my labour has gained me, in seventy years, a debt of five or six hundred pounds."* In later years, however, he found, to his surprise, that his cheap publications had made him rich.† He created an appetite for reading among his people, and as the Societies grew, the demand for his books became enormous.

Wesley published little before his mission to Georgia. A collection of prayers for every day in the week, published in 1733, was the beginning of his strength. Next year he prepared an abridgment of Norris's "Treatise on Christian Perfection." His father's letter of advice to a young clergyman, a sermon of his own on "The Trouble and Rest of Good Men," and the "Imitation of Christ," in two editions, were printed in 1735. He also published a hymn-book at Charlestown, America, in 1737. This represents Wesley's literary activity before 1738. From that time to the end of his life he made as abundant use of the press as of the pulpit. His journals represent the history of the Evangelical Revival. The hymnology was mainly his brother's contribution to the great cause to which they were both devoted heart and soul. John Wesley took his share in this work, however. One original hymn of his, a paraphrase of the Lord's Prayer in three parts, will be found in the present Wesleyan Hymn Book.‡ There may be others, but as the early collections of poetry were published in the name of both brothers, we have sometimes no means of ascertaining what hymns John Wesley himself may have contributed. His translations from the

* Works, iii., 503. † *Ibid.*, vii., 9. ‡ Nos. 235, 236, 237.

German, however, bear witness to his power as a poet. There are twenty-one of these in the Wesleyan Hymn Book, with one from the French and one from the Spanish. They are not mere translations. Wesley enriches the thought, and adds greatly to the force of the original. In January, 1740, Molther, the Moravian minister at Fetter Lane, asked Wesley to supply him with a rendering of a German hymn. To this request Methodism owes one of its most treasured hymns:—

> Now I have found the ground wherein
>   Sure my soul's anchor may remain,
> The wounds of Jesus, for my sin
>   Before the world's foundation slain,
> Whose mercy shall unshaken stay
> When heaven and earth are fled away.*

One of his finest translations is from Scheffler. We can only quote one verse:—

> I thank Thee, uncreated Sun,
>   That Thy bright beams on me have shined;
> I thank Thee, who hast overthrown
>   My foes, and healed my wounded mind;
> I thank Thee, whose enlivening voice
> Bids my free heart in Thee rejoice.†

Tersteegen's hymn beginning

> Thou hidden love of God ‡

was translated by Wesley in Georgia in 1736.§

Wesley not only contributed to the preparation of the Methodist hymnology: he taught his people to sing. In 1742 he published "A Collection of Tunes as they are

---

* Wesleyan Hymn Book, No. 189.
† *Ibid.*, No. 210.
‡ *Ibid.*, No. 344.
§ "Christian Perfection."

commonly sung at the Foundery." Mr. Lampe, the theatrical composer, who was converted by reading Wesley's "Farther Appeal," rendered good service to Methodism by preparing a tune-book for the use of the united Societies. In sending Boyce's "Cathedral Music" to his brother as a present for his eldest boy, Wesley adds, "A little you can perhaps pick out for the use of our plain people." His preachers were expected to take special oversight of the singing. "Exhort every one in the congregation to sing," he says; "in every large Society let them learn to sing; recommend our tune-book everywhere."

Wesley's "Sermons" had an enormous circulation. They must not be taken altogether to represent his ordinary preaching. The substance of his discourses is doubtless to be found in them, but they were prepared for the press rather than for the pulpit. The first series, consisting of fifty-three sermons, was published in four small volumes between 1746 and 1760. These four volumes, with Wesley's "Notes on the New Testament," form the doctrinal standard of Methodism. Henry Moore says that after some years of labour in all parts of the country, Wesley felt the necessity of preparing some concise, clear, and full "body of divinity" to guide his preachers and people. After thinking much on this subject, he retired to the house of his friend Mr. Blackwell at Lewisham, where he composed at several visits the first four volumes of his sermons.* He simply took his Hebrew Bible and Greek Testament with him. His purpose was to furnish "plain truth for plain people." "My design," he says in his preface, "is, in some sense, to forget all that I have ever read in my life."

One paragraph of the preface is so striking a revelation

* Moore, ii., 403.

of his motives and methods, that we must not omit it. Wesley never wrote anything more lofty in its tone. "To candid reasonable men, I am not afraid to lay open what have been the inmost thoughts of my heart. I have thought, I am a creature of a day, passing through life as an arrow through the air. I am a spirit come from God, and returning to God, just hovering over the great gulf; till a few moments hence, I am no more seen; I drop into an unchangeable eternity! I want to know one thing, the way to heaven, how to land safe on that happy shore. God Himself has condescended to teach the way; for this very end He came down from heaven. He hath written it down in a book. Oh, give me that book! At any price, give me the book of God! I have it; here is knowledge enough for me. Let me be *homo unius libri.* Here then I am, far from the busy ways of men. I sit down alone; only God is here. In His presence I open, I read His book, for this end: to find the way to heaven. Is there a doubt concerning the meaning of what I read? Does anything appear dark or intricate? I lift up my heart to the Father of lights. 'Lord, is it not Thy word, If any man lack wisdom, let him ask it of God? Thou givest liberally, and upbraidest not. Thou hast said, if any man be willing to do Thy will, he shall know. I am willing to do; let me know Thy will.' I then search after and consider parallel passages of Scripture, comparing spiritual things with spiritual. I meditate thereon, with all the attention and earnestness of which my mind is capable. If any doubt still remains, I consult those who are experienced in the things of God, and then the writings whereby, being dead, they yet speak. And what I thus learn, that I teach."

The Second Series consists of sermons prepared for his Magazine, and published in four volumes in 1788. They are not so doctrinal, and have more variety and literary illustration. Other sermons were published afterwards. That on "Faith is the evidence of things not seen" was finished only six weeks before Wesley's death. His pen was busy to the last. In March, 1790, he wrote his sermon on the Wedding Garment. "My eyes," he says, "are now waxed dim; my natural force is abated. However, while I can, I would fain do a little for God before I drop into the dust." Wesley's "Notes on the New Testament" are singularly concise. His great aim was to make them as short as possible, that the comment might neither swallow up nor obscure the text. His revision of the text is admirable. Readers of the Notes were put into possession of some of the best results which the New Testament Company gave the public in 1881.

Wesley's Christian Library, in fifty volumes, was his boldest literary venture. He abridged the choicest works of practical divinity, beginning with the Apostolic Fathers. He wished to place the whole range of such literature within the reach both of his preachers and his people. This publication entailed a loss of two hundred pounds. It is remarkable that he did not lose more by so great an undertaking. Wesley's Magazine, of which the first number was published in January, 1778, laid a heavy literary burden upon him. His editor was not competent for the revision of the press, so that many errors crept into its pages, greatly to Wesley's distress. The *Arminian Magazine* gave Methodism an official organ, in which its distinctive teaching could be explained and defended. But its hold on the Societies was largely due to the fact that all phases of Methodist life were preserved in its pages. The biographies of preachers and Methodist people make its volumes a mine of history. For a Methodist a place in the Magazine was something like a niche in the Abbey for a statesman or a poet. The Magazine, which has been issued monthly ever since 1778, was never so attractive or popular as it is to-day.

Wesley's "Appeals," published in 1744 and 1745, did much to explain the true character of Methodism. They vindicate Wesley's position and work with a dignity and tenderness which must have been almost irresistible with reasonable men. His desire for the salvation of others breathes in every line of the "Earnest Appeal." He calmly weighs all objections, and proves that Methodism was faithful to the doctrines of Scripture and the Church of England. Doddridge wrote to him in 1746, "I have been reading (I will not pretend to tell you with what strong emotion) the fourth edition of your 'Farther Appeals,' concerning which I shall only say, that I have written upon the title-page, 'How forcible are right words!'"* Three months earlier, Wesley mentions † that two clergymen who had just read his "Farther Appeal" invited him to call on them. "I thought," he adds, "the publication ot this tract would have enraged the world above measure. And, on the contrary, it seems nothing ever was published which softened them so much!" On January 6th, 1748, Wesley was visited by "Counsellor G——, many years eminent for an utter disregard of all religion." A lady, whom he had attacked for her Methodism, said to him, "Sir, here is a fuller answer to your objections than I am able to give." She handed him a copy of the "Earnest Appeal." By this he was thoroughly convinced that there was something in religion. He told Wesley all that was in his heart, and was much affected at the watchnight service he attended.‡ The same

* Moore, ii., 101. † Works, ii., 6.

‡ Francis Gilbert, a member of Wesley's Society in England, sent some of his publications to Antigua, where his brother

"Appeal" led to the conversion of Mr. Lampe.* In September, 1748, Wesley breakfasted at Wadebridge with Dr. W——, for many years "a steady, rational infidel. But it pleased God to touch his heart in reading the 'Appeal'; and he is now labouring to be altogether a Christian." The prejudice which Mrs. Gwynne, of Garth, felt against the Wesleys, melted away when she read this "Appeal."

Controversial writing was always distasteful to Wesley. When he began to write his second letter to Bishop Lavington, who had compared the Methodists to the Papists, he describes his task with a sigh.† "Heavy work, such as I should never choose; but sometimes it must be done. Well might the ancient say, 'God made practical divinity necessary, the devil controversial. But it is necessary: we must "resist the devil," or he will not "flee from us."'" "Oh that I might dispute with no man!" he says on another occasion. "But if I must dispute, let it be with men of sense."‡ Wesley's controversial writings are brief and direct. The real issue is kept resolutely in view; all disguises are torn away; not a word is wasted. Wesley was attacked from every quarter by men of all shades of thought, but his skill in argument and the strength of his cause brought him off victorious in these encounters. When he discovered errors of scholarship, he did not mention them in his reply, but sent a private letter to the writer. For this he received the special thanks of some of his most distinguished opponents.

The controversy with Dr. Lavington, Bishop of Exeter, was one of the most painful Wesley ever had. Southey

---

Nathaniel was Speaker of the House of Assembly. Mr. Gilbert regarded Wesley as an enthusiast, but his sister read him the "Appeal," which opened his eyes (Tyerman, ii., 298). When he visited England he invited Wesley to his house, and afterwards introduced Methodism into the West Indies.

* Works, i., 532. † *Ibid.*, ii., 247.

‡ Moore, ii., 415; Southey, ii., 212.

considers that he did not treat the Bishop with the urbanity which he showed to all other opponents. The fact is that Lavington, who wrote anonymously, indulged a spirit sadly unbecoming such a subject and such a writer. Miss Wedgwood says,* He "deserves to be coupled with the men who flung dead cats and rotten eggs at the Methodists, not with those who assailed their tenets with arguments, or even serious rebuke." Wesley clearly pointed this out: "Any scribbler with a middling share of low wit, not encumbered with good-nature or modesty, may raise a laugh on those whom he cannot confute, and run them down whom he dares not look in the face. By this means, even a comparer of Methodists and Papists may blaspheme the great work of God, not only without blame, but with applause, at least from readers of his own stamp. But it is high time, sir, you should leave your skulking place. Come out, and let us look each other in the face." The controversy continued for two years. It is pleasant to add that in August, 1762, a fortnight before the Bishop's death, Wesley was at Exeter Cathedral. "I was well pleased," he says, "to partake of the Lord's Supper with my old opponent, Bishop Lavington. Oh, may we sit down together in the kingdom of our Father!" †

Wesley's masterly treatise on "Original Sin" was written in answer to Dr. Taylor, of Norwich, whom Fletcher calls "the wisest Arian, Pelagian, and Socinian of our age." In this work Wesley carefully observed his own rule laid down in a letter to Dr. Taylor himself, whom he greatly esteemed "as a person of uncommon sense and learning." "We may agree," he says, "to leave each other's person and character absolutely untouched, while

* "John Wesley," p. 313.

† See p. 338.

we sum up and answer the several arguments advanced as plainly and closely as we can." The treatise has therefore permanent value as a careful discussion of the important subject of which it treats.

Wesley's tracts are models of brevity and of searching appeal. "A Word to a Sabbath-breaker," "A Word to a Drunkard," "A Word to a Smuggler," "A Word to a Methodist," are the titles of some of these vigorous writings. They were composed in moments of quiet, snatched during the incessant labours of his itinerancy, and were spread broadcast through the country. Wesley was one of the pioneers of tract-writing and distribution. "Two-and-forty years ago," he writes, "having a desire to furnish poor people with cheaper, shorter, and plainer books than any I had seen, I wrote many small tracts, generally a penny apiece, and afterwards several larger. Some of these had such a sale as I never thought of; and by this means I unawares became rich." * One glimpse of Wesley's literary activity at the age of eighty-three is given in his journal for September, 1786: "I now applied myself in earnest to the writing of Mr. Fletcher's life, having procured the best materials I could. To this I dedicated all the time I could spare till November from five in the morning till eight at night. These are my studying hours. I cannot write longer without hurting my eyes." By such unwearied labour the press as well as the pulpit was made to serve the cause of the Revival.

Wesley's charity was only limited by his income. At Oxford he lived on twenty-eight pounds, and gave away the rest.† As his income increased, his charities extended. He thus distributed more than thirty thousand pounds during his lifetime.‡ He received an allowance of thirty

* Works, vii., 9. † See p. 65. ‡ Moore, ii., 434.

pounds a year from the London Society; the country Methodists very occasionally paid his travelling expenses. Wesley's private charities were drawn from the income of his Book Room. In 1782 he spent £5 19*s.* on his clothes, gave away £356 himself, and £237 13*s.* through his book steward. In 1783 the amount expended was £832 1*s.* 6*d.*; in 1784, £534 17*s.* 6*d.*; in 1785, £851 12*s.*; in 1786, £738 5*s.*; in 1787 (including travelling expenses), £961 4*s.*; in 1788, £738 4*s.*; in 1789, £766 and travelling expenses, £60. Even this statement does not fully represent the case. Samuel Bradburn said that between the Conference of 1780 and that of the following year Wesley distributed more than £1,400 in private charities.* He told Bradburn in 1787 that he never gave away less than £1,000 a year.

One or two instances will show how much Wesley did to relieve those in distress. At Bath he gave four guineas to save from jail some one who had already been arrested.† In London, in February, 1766, a gentleman who had been defrauded of a large fortune, and was now starving, called upon him. Wesley wished to help him, but he had run short of money. He therefore asked him to call again. Just before the time appointed some one put twenty guineas into Wesley's hands, so that he was able to clothe this man from head to foot and send him back to Dublin. Once, when his chaise stuck fast in an Irish slough, he walked forward, leaving his friends to get the carriage out. A poor man who had been turned out of doors because he could not pay twenty shillings due for rent overtook him in deep distress. When Wesley gave him a guinea, the man knelt down in the road to pray for his benefactor.‡

* Tyerman, iii., 616. † Dunn's Life of Adam Clarke, p. 73.
‡ Works, iv., 123.

Then he cried out in his joy, "Oh, I shall have a house! I shall have a house over my head!" Whenever poor people thanked him, Wesley used courteously to lift his hat.* His patience was sometimes sorely tried. A clamouring crowd of beggars once surrounded his carriage at Norwich. He turned round and asked somewhat sharply whether they thought he could support the poor everywhere. Entering his carriage, he slipped, and fell. "It is all right, Joseph," he said, "it is all right; it is only what I deserved, for if I had no *other* good to give, I ought at least to have given them good words." †

Wesley's personal charity was only a part of his service for the poor. For more than forty years all the class money given by the London Society, amounting to several hundred pounds a year, was distributed to those who were in distress.‡ He did not confine his care to his own Societies. At Bristol, in January, 1740, the severe frost threw many out of work. They had no assistance from the parish, and were in the last extremity. Wesley made three collections in one week, and was thus able to feed a hundred, sometimes a hundred and fifty, a day. The twelve or thirteen hundred French prisoners at Knowle, near Bristol, whom he visited in October, 1759, also found in him a zealous friend and helper. The evening after his visit he preached a special sermon, in which he pleaded for these strangers so earnestly, that the sum of twenty-four pounds was raised to provide them with warm clothing. Wesley also wrote a letter on their behalf to *Lloyd's Evening Post.* The distress they suffered from want of clothing was soon abundantly relieved.

* Tyerman, iii., 616.
† Everett's "Adam Clarke Portrayed."
‡ Moore, ii., 108.

Wesley was a father to the Methodist people. In November, 1740, he tells us that the clothes brought by friends who could spare them were distributed among the poor of the London Society. An arrangement was also made at the same time by which for four months the Society room at the Foundery was turned into a place for carding and spinning cotton.* Twelve of the poorest members were thus employed and maintained for very little more than the produce of their labour. Next May Wesley made another request for clothing and for contributions of a penny a week. He wished to employ all the women who were out of work in knitting, for which they were to be paid the ordinary price. Whatever they needed in addition to their earnings was to be added. Twelve persons were appointed to inspect the work, and visit all the sick in their district every other day. In 1743 London was mapped out into twenty-three divisions, for each of which two volunteer visitors were appointed.† Great spiritual and temporal good was the result. The sick and poor were both relieved and comforted by these timely ministries.

In 1744 Wesley raised fifty pounds by a collection for the deserving poor, which he began at once to lay out on clothes and shoes. Ten days later he made another collection; then he went through the classes begging for further help. The appeal to the classes and three collections yielded about two hundred pounds, with which three hundred and sixty or seventy poor people were provided with clothing.‡ Similar efforts were made in other places. At Newcastle he made a collection to relieve the poor, and at one place in Ireland the clergyman of the parish

* Works, i., 292.
† *Ibid.*, viii., 254.
‡ *Ibid.*, i., 451, 455, 458.

stood at the door after Wesley's sermon to receive the people's help for a family in trouble.* Sometimes Wesley was overwhelmed by the distress with which he had to cope. In November, 1750, he began to take an account of all his people who were in want, but the numbers increased so fast upon him, particularly about Moorfields, that he "saw no possibility of relieving them all, unless the Lord should, as it were, make windows in heaven." On the last day of 1772, the great embarrassment caused by the necessities of the poor drove him and his officers to special prayer.

At Bristol, in September, 1783, Wesley collected ninety pounds for his poor members. But the most touching and interesting glimpse of the aged philanthropist is in January, 1785, when he was in his eighty-second year. At the new year coals and bread were distributed among the poor of the Society. Wesley saw that they needed clothes also, and set out to beg the money. The streets were filled with melting snow, which lay ankle-deep on the ground, so that his feet were steeped in snow-water nearly from morning to evening.† Four days of such travelling all over London brought on a violent flux; but his friend Dr. Whitehead came to his relief. Two years later Wesley made another begging tour of the metropolis, which yielded two hundred pounds. Six or seven of his people gave ten pounds each, but Wesley was disappointed that he did not find forty or fifty to help in the same way. He was anxious to provide for two hundred cases of distress.

One of the most useful of Wesley's funds was a lending stock. It began in July, 1746, with a capital of about thirty pounds, out of which two hundred and fifty-five persons were relieved in eighteen months.‡ The capital

* Works, ii., 413, 443. † *Ibid.*, iv., 295. ‡ *Ibid.*, ii., 17, 81, 270.

was afterwards raised to fifty pounds, and more than twenty years later Wesley's "strong words" lifted it to one hundred and twenty pounds. The stewards attended every Tuesday morning to do business. Loans of twenty shillings and upwards were made, to be repaid weekly within three months.* Mr. Lackington, the bookseller who secured the shop in which he started business through the kindness of the Methodists, received a loan of five pounds from this fund in the year 1774 to increase his little stock of books. He prospered so greatly that the year after Wesley's death his profits for the twelve months were five thousand pounds.† For a long time he sold one hundred thousand volumes annually. Lackington says ‡ that he has known Wesley give ten or twenty pounds at once to tradesmen who were in need. He adds that "in going a few yards from his study to the pulpit, Wesley generally distributed a handful of half-crowns to poor old people of his Society." The charity schools at the Foundery and West Street also rendered great service.

Wesley's medical knowledge helped him to relieve much suffering. In 1746, the same year that the lending stock was started, he began to give medicines to the poor. Thirty came the first day.§ In six months six hundred cases had been treated; two hundred were sensibly better, fifty-one thoroughly cured. This was done at an expense of thirty pounds.‖ This success led Wesley to form a dispensary at Bristol, which soon had two hundred patients. Wesley's shrewd

* Works, viii., 257.

† Life of James Lackington, Letters 21, 40, 41; also Lackington's "Confessions."

‡ Life, Letter 29.

§ Works, ii., 39, 59, 81.

‖ *Ibid.*, xii., 83.

observations on medical works show how carefully he sought the best light of his time. Electricity greatly interested him. During the first year he supplied medicines to the poor he went, with some friends, to see the electrical experiments in London.* He carefully read Dr. Franklin's "Letters" and Dr. Priestley's "ingenious book."† We find him advising a woman, who was suffering from a stubborn paralytic disorder, to try the new remedy.‡ She was electrified, and found immediate relief. Wesley afterwards procured the proper apparatus, and ordered several persons to be electrified.§ From this time he fixed certain hours every week, then an hour every day, "wherein any that desired it might try the virtue of this surprising medicine." Patients became so numerous, that they had to be met at four different parts of London. Hundreds, perhaps thousands, Wesley says, received unspeakable good.|| He himself was no stranger to the benefits of electrical treatment. After his serious illness in Ireland his hand shook so that he could hardly write his name. A drive of four or five hours over very rough pavement electrified him so thoroughly, he tells us, that his hand was quite steady. In 1780 we find a medical man in attendance twice a week, for three hours each time, at the chapel-house in West Street, London. He prescribed and provided medicines for any who showed their tickets of membership or came with a note from Wesley or his preachers. If any were too ill to come, they were visited in their own homes.

Wherever Wesley went he made use of his medical skill. His favourite remedy for consumptive tendencies

* Works, ii., 73.
† *Ibid.*, iii., 280, 311.
‡ *Ibid.*, iii., 279.
§ Works, iii., 388.
|| *Ibid.*, iv., 50.

was a country journey, and several friends were invited to share his itinerancy with a view to the restoration of their health.* His "Primitive Physic," of which a twenty-third edition was published in the year of his death, grew out of his medical attention to the poor. For nearly thirty years before its publication he had made anatomy and physic the diversion of his leisure hours. He had studied them with special attention before he went to Georgia. His dispensary in 1747 was started with the assistance of an apothecary and an experienced surgeon. Wesley himself now studied medicine more carefully. He published his "Primitive Physic" in 1747 or 1748. Its quaint remedies often provoke a smile. Pounded garlic applied to the soles of the feet was a "never-failing" remedy for hoarseness and loss of voice. Boiled nettles and warm treacle were sovereign cures for colds and swellings.† An eminent medical man, however, some years ago pronounced the book incomparably superior to any non-professional work of the same date.‡

A writer in the *Gloucester Times* § states that a poor widow, who had several times heard Wesley when he was in that district, was in deep trouble about her only daughter, who was worn to a shadow with a distressing cough, and had severe pains in her side and back. Her skin was yellow, and her legs much swollen. Whilst sitting one day in great distress, a neighbour looked in and asked if she was not aware that her friend Mr. Wesley was preaching that night at Gloucester. The widow at once resolved to ask his advice for her child. Wesley listened to her

* Works, ii., 40; iv., 282.

† *Ibid.*, iv., 46, 192; ii., 132.

‡ Rev. Romilly Hall's Lecture on Wesley.

§ July, 1885.

sad account, and said that he would call next morning. "I am to preach at Tewkesbury at twelve o'clock, and shall pass your cottage." When he came, he told the girl, "I have thought over your state, and will give your mother a remedy which, with God's blessing, I trust will do you good; and if God spares my life, I will call upon you when I come this way again." The medicine led to the girl's complete restoration. In March, 1790, exactly a year after his first visit, Wesley came again. He said to the widow, "I see that you are blessed by God with faculties to use the medicines mercifully given by God for our use, so that I will instruct you in some further remedies that I have discovered lately, and as my body will soon be laid with the clods of the valley, waiting for the resurrection, I shall like to give you these remedies. Use them for God, and may He bless you, and be with you." Wesley left with her a small manuscript, in his own handwriting, containing instructions for the treatment of prevalent diseases. They won for the widow the name of "the village doctor." Her daughter's son, who became a skilful physician in the north of England, afterwards acknowledged that Wesley's remedies, handed down to him by his grandmother, had been the most successful he had prescribed during fifty years of professional life.

NOTE TO PAGE 329.

Archdeacon Hare says in his "Mission of the Comforter," p. 269: "One of our bishops wrote a book against enthusiasm, as a quality fit only for Papists and Methodists. It would have been difficult to pronounce a severer sentence against our Church." The book, he adds, shows no sympathy with the deep feelings and wants and consciousnesses which were venting themselves even in the most offensive absurdities of the Methodists.

CHAPTER XXI.

WESLEY'S LAST YEARS AND DEATH.

WESLEY made two pleasant excursions with some friends to Holland in the summers of 1783 and 1786. The notes of his tours show how thoroughly the old man enjoyed the change of scene. Nothing seemed to escape his attention. The cleanliness of the streets and houses was such that he could not find a speck of dirt. The women and children seemed the most beautiful he had ever seen. "They were surprisingly fair, and had an inexpressible air of innocence in their countenances." He had much pleasant intercourse with pious people, and returned to his work at home refreshed and cheered by his three weeks of holiday. In the summer of 1787 Wesley spent nearly four weeks in the Channel Islands. Methodism had already been introduced into those lovely islands. Wesley's visits greatly encouraged the workers there. He preached every day to large congregations, and was everywhere received with marked respect. The beauty and fruitfulness of the islands made a great impression on him, whilst the kindness of friends and the pleasant change of scene added to his preaching tour the charm of a summer holiday.

Wesley lived three years after his brother Charles. Those years were full of honour. The Methodist Societies felt that their founder could not long be with them, and hung eagerly upon his lips. His visits to all parts of the country were public holidays. Multitudes thronged to listen to the venerable preacher, who had endeared himself to all by his labour of love. Increasing infirmities did not check his restless itinerancy. On the first anniversary of his brother's death he landed at Dublin on his last visit. He remained in Ireland for three months and a half. Gravel Walk House, he says, was "filled as I never saw it before; and they all seemed to hear as for life." Another of his congregations was a brilliant assembly. Honourables and Right Honourables were present, and he felt that all were given into his hands. At Pallas, near Limerick, all the neighbouring gentry came to hear him. No place would hold the crowd, so that Wesley was obliged to stand outside. "The people, as it were, swallowed every word; and great was our rejoicing in the Lord."

Such scenes marked every step of Wesley's progress through Ireland. One instance may show how he was received in the homes of the people. When he was about to leave a house where he had stayed, "one and another fell on their knees all round me, and most of them burst out into tears and earnest cries, the like of which I have seldom heard; so that we scarce knew how to part." When Wesley embarked for England, on July 12th, 1789, multitudes followed him to his vessel. Before he went on board they sang a hymn together; then Wesley fell on his knees and implored God's blessing on their families, their Church, and their country. It was a bitter but a blessed hour. Not a few fell upon his neck and kissed him. The ship moved from the shore he was nevermore to see whilst the venerable patriarch stood on deck, with his hands lifted in prayer for Ireland.*

The vessel was the *Princess Royal*, of Parkgate, the

* Tyerman, iii., 578.

neatest and most elegant packet Wesley had ever seen. The company on board was exceedingly agreeable, and he slept as well as if he had been in his own bed. Next day he shut himself up in his chaise on deck and read the life of a man who claimed to be the premier nobleman of Ireland, one of the most cool, deliberate, and relentless murderers Wesley ever heard of. He felt such interest in this extraordinary story, that he had already devoted nearly two pages of his journal to an account of him. In the evening Wesley and his friends sang a hymn on deck, which soon drew the company around him. Without delay he began to preach on "It is appointed unto men once to die." All seemed affected by the solemn message. This was a fitting close to Wesley's visits to Ireland.

On his return to England, he suffered much from thirst and fever, but Dr. Easton, whom he consulted in Manchester, gave him medicine, which soon relieved him. A month after he landed from Ireland he paid his last visit to Cornwall. At Falmouth the change wrought by God's grace filled him with thankfulness. "The last time I was here," he writes, "above forty years ago, I was taken prisoner by an immense mob, gaping and roaring like lions. But how is the tide turned! High and low now lined the street, from one end of the town to the other, out of stark love and kindness, gaping and staring as if the King were going by. In the evening I preached on the smooth top of the hill, at a small distance from the sea, to the largest congregation I have ever seen in Cornwall, except in or near Redruth. And such a time I have not known before since I returned from Ireland. God moved wonderfully on the hearts of the people, who all seem to know the day of their visitation."

Wesley's reception at other places was equally enthusiastic. He had scarcely ever spent such a week in Cornwall before. More than twenty-five thousand assembled at Gwennap Amphitheatre, the scene of so many memorable Cornish services. When he made a passing call at Marazion, the preaching-place was filled in a few minutes, so that he could not refrain from giving them a short sermon. In the market-place at St. Ives, on August 25th, 1789, "well-nigh all the town attended, and with all possible seriousness." "Surely," he adds, "forty years' labour has not been in vain here." This was Wesley's last visit to Cornwall, the Methodist county.

Wesley's health was wonderful. He had suffered much on several occasions from the family gout,* of which his mother died, but abstemiousness and constant exercise had helped him to throw off this weakness. In 1782 he writes, "I entered into my eightieth year, but, blessed be God, my time is not 'labour and sorrow.' I find no more pain or bodily infirmities than at five-and-twenty. This I still impute (1) to the power of God, fitting me for what He calls me to; (2) to my still travelling four or five thousand miles a year; (3) to my sleeping, night or day, whenever I want it; (4) to my rising at a set hour; and (5) to my constant preaching, particularly in the morning."

On January 1st, 1790, he wrote, "I am now an old man, decayed from hand to foot. My eyes are dim; my right hand shakes much; my mouth is hot and dry every morning; I have a lingering fever almost every day; my motion is weak and slow. However, blessed be God, I do not slack my labour: I can preach and write still." Henry Moore, who lived with Wesley at this time, was surprised at this description. Wesley still rose at four, and went through the work of the day with much of his old vigour, and with astonishing resolution. His own state-

* Works, xiv., 266.

ment, therefore, sets Wesley's devotion to his work in a striking light. One of the most interesting services of the year was held in West London. "I preached a sermon to the children at West Street Chapel. They flocked together from every quarter; and truly God was in the midst of them, applying those words, 'Come, ye little children, hearken unto me; and I will teach you the fear of the Lord.'"

On the 1st of March, 1790, he issued a circular giving the dates for his visits to various towns in his northern journey. He still caught and treasured up those pleasant little facts which give such life to his journals. Wigan, for many years proverbially called "wicked Wigan," was not what it once had been. The people, he says, "in general had taken a softer mould." Other touches show that Wesley's interest in everything he saw was unabated. Crowds assembled to hear him. On Sunday, August 4th, he preached at the cross in Epworth market-place to such a congregation as was never seen in the town before. A correspondent of the *Methodist Recorder** mentions that he had conversed with an old Methodist in one of our villages who "stated that a large number of Wesley's admirers accompanied him on the way from one town or village to his next appointment, never leaving him till they were met by another company coming from an opposite direction, to whom they safely delivered their precious charge." The women walked on one side of the road, and the men on the other. Such scenes were frequent in these last days.

When he visited Colchester on October 11th, Wesley had a wonderful congregation. Rich and poor, clergy and laity, assembled to do honour to the old man and

* November 6th, 1885.

listen to his message. Henry Crabb Robinson heard him in the great round meeting-house. One of his preachers stood on each side of him in the wide pulpit, holding up the veteran. "His feeble voice was barely audible; but his reverend countenance, especially his long white locks, formed a picture never to be forgotten. There was a vast crowd of lovers and admirers. It was for the most part a pantomime, but the pantomime went to the heart. Of the kind, I never saw anything comparable to it in after-life." After the people had sung a verse, Wesley rose and said, "It gives me a great pleasure to find that you have not lost your singing, neither men nor women. You have not forgotten a single note. And I hope, by the assistance of God, which enables you to sing well, you may do all other things well." A universal "Amen" followed. A little ejaculation or prayer of three or four words followed each division of the sermon. After the last prayer, Wesley "rose up and addressed the people on liberality of sentiment, and spoke much against refusing to join with any congregation on account of difference in opinion." *

Crabbe, the poet, who heard him a few days later at Lowestoft, was much struck by Wesley's venerable appearance and the way in which he quoted Anacreon's lines with an application to himself:—

> Oft am I by woman told,
> "Poor Anacreon! thou grow'st old;
> See, thine hairs are falling off:
> Poor Anacreon! how they fall!"
> Whether I grow old or no,
> By these signs I do not know;
> But this I need not to be told,
> 'Tis time to *live*, if I grow old.

* "Diary, etc., of Henry Crabb Robinson," vol. i., p. 20.

At Lynn every clergyman in the town was in his congregation, except one who was lame. "They are all," he says in one of the last lines he wrote in his journal, "prejudiced in favour of the Methodists, as indeed are most of the townsmen, who give a fair proof by contributing so much to our Sunday-schools, that there is near twenty pounds in hand."

The rest of the year was devoted to short journeys in his "home circuit"—the counties lying around London. His last "field-preaching" was at Winchelsea on October 6th, 1790. Many a pilgrimage has been made to the large ash-tree under which Wesley took his stand. The tree was near a ruined church. Most of the inhabitants of the place listened while he spoke from those words, "The kingdom of heaven is at hand; repent, and believe the Gospel." "It seemed," Wesley wrote, "as if all that heard were, for the present, almost persuaded to be Christians." One who was with him bears witness that "the word was attended with mighty power, and the tears of the people flowed in torrents." The old field-preacher had not lost his power.

In these last days people gazed on Wesley with veneration as he passed through the streets. He returned their friendly greetings in the words of his favourite Apostle, "Little children, love one another." In 1790, the summer before his death, he ceased to keep any account of his personal expenditure. "I will not attempt it any longer," he writes, "being satisfied with the continual conviction that I save all I can and give all I can; that is, all I have." No entreaty could make the old man omit any duty. His constant prayer was, "Lord, let me not live to be useless!" At every place he visited he gave the Society his last advice "to love as brethren, fear God, and honour the king." He generally closed these touching services with the verse which he gave out so often in the family circle at the preachers' house in City Road:—

> Oh that, without a lingering groan,
> I may the welcome word receive,
> My body with my charge lay down,
> And cease at once to work and live!

Wesley fully intended to make his usual journey to the north in March, 1791. He sent his own carriage and horses to Bristol, and secured places for himself and friends in the Bath coach. That journey, however, was never taken. He preached at Lambeth on February 17th.* When he returned to City Road, he seemed unwell, and said he thought he had taken cold. Next day, however, he read and wrote as usual. In the evening he preached at Chelsea, but his cold compelled him to pause once or twice. On Saturday the fever and weakness increased, but he was able to read and write. The following day, February 20th, he rose early, but was so unfit for his Sunday's work,† that he lay down again for a few hours. When he awoke, he said, "I have not had such a comfortable sleep this fortnight past." In the afternoon he slept an hour or two, then two of his discourses on the "Sermon on the Mount" were read to him, and he came down to supper. On Monday he seemed better and dined at Twickenham. He preached for the last time in City Road Chapel on Tuesday evening. Next day he preached at Leatherhead, in a private house, on "Seek ye the Lord while He may be found; call ye upon Him while He is near." This was his last sermon.

* These were some of his appointments on the Plan for the Preachers in London (January to March, 1791). This Plan is printed in Stevenson's "History of City Road Chapel," p. 118.

† Spitalfields at ten; City Road at five.

His last letter was written on Thursday from Mr. Wolff's, at Balham, to William Wilberforce. It shows both the old man's sympathy with the wrongs of the slave and his warm interest in Wilberforce's great mission. Wesley had become familiar with the horrors of slavery during his residence in America, and Wilberforce was well known to his brother Charles and himself.

"LONDON, *February 24th*, 1791.

"MY DEAR SIR,—Unless the Divine Power has raised you up to be as Athanasius, *contra mundum*, I see not how you can go through your glorious enterprise in opposing that execrable villainy which is the scandal of religion, of England, and of human nature. Unless God has raised you up for this very thing, you will be worn out by the opposition of men and devils; but *if God be for you, who can be against you?* Are all of them together stronger than God? Oh, '*be not weary in well-doing.*' Go on, in the name of God and in the power of His might, till even American slavery, the vilest that ever saw the sun, shall vanish away before it.

"Reading this morning a tract, wrote by a poor African, I was particularly struck by that circumstance that a man who has a black skin, being wronged or outraged by a white man, can have no redress; it being a *law* in our colonies that the *oath* of a black against a white goes for nothing. What villainy is this!

"That He who has guided you from your youth up may continue to strengthen you in this and all things is the prayer of, dear sir, your affectionate servant,

"JOHN WESLEY."*

One could wish for no more beautiful close to Wesley's

* Moore, ii., 437.

correspondence than this trumpet-peal to the young soldier stepping out for his life-long struggle. The letter is a prophetic epitome of the history of emancipation.

About eleven o'clock on Friday morning Mrs. Wolff brought Wesley home to City Road to die. He sat down in his room, and desired to be left alone for half an hour. Some mulled wine was then given him, and he was helped to bed, where he lay with a quick pulse in a high fever. His friends sent for Dr. Whitehead. When he came, Wesley smiled and said, "Doctor, they are more afraid than hurt." On the Saturday he scarcely moved. If roused to answer a question or take a little refreshment, he soon dozed again. On Sunday morning, February 27th, he got up, took a cup of tea, and seemed much better. As he sat in his chair he looked quite cheerful, and repeated the lines,—

Till glad I lay this body down,
Thy servant, Lord, attend;
And, oh! my life of mercies crown
With a triumphant end!

The friends who were present talked too much, so that he was soon exhausted, and had to lie down. About half-past two he told those who were about him, "There is no need for more; when at Bristol, my words were,—

I the chief of sinners am,
But Jesus died for me."

His head was sometimes a little affected by the fever, which rose very high. In the evening, however, he got up again. Whilst he sat in his chair he said, "What are all the pretty things at Balham to a dying man?" Speaking of a lady whom he had only lately known, he said he believed "she had real religion. How necessary for every one to be on the right foundation!

I the chief of sinners am,
But Jesus died for me.

We must be justified by faith, and then go on to sanctification." Next day he slept much. Once, in a low, but very distinct, manner, he said, "There is no way into the holiest but by the blood of Jesus." After a very restless night he began to sing,—

All glory to God in the sky,
  And peace upon earth be restored!
O Jesus, exalted on high,
  Appear, our omnipotent Lord!
Who, meanly in Bethlehem born,
  Didst stoop to redeem a lost race,
Once more to Thy people return,
  And reign in Thy kingdom of grace.

Oh, wouldst Thou again be made known,
  Again in the Spirit descend;
And set up in each of Thy own
  A kingdom that never shall end!
Thou only art able to bless,
  And make the glad nations obey,
And bid the dire enmity cease,
  And bow the whole world to Thy sway.

He lay still a while, then asked for pen and ink. When they were brought, he was too weak to use them. Some time after he said, "I want to write." The pen was put into his hand, and the paper held before him. "I cannot," he said. Miss Ritchie, one of the company, answered, "Let me write for you, sir; tell me what you would say." "Nothing," he replied, "but that God is with us."

In the afternoon he wished to get up. While his clothes were being brought, he broke out singing with such vigour that all his friends were astonished,—

I'll praise my Maker while I've breath,
And when my voice is lost in death,
  Praise shall employ my nobler powers;
My days of praise shall ne'er be past,
While life, and thought, and being last,
  Or immortality endures.

Happy the man whose hopes rely
On Israel's God: He made the sky
And earth and seas, with all their train;
His truth for ever stands secure,
He saves the oppressed, He feeds the poor,
And none shall find His promise vain.

When helped into his chair, Wesley seemed to change for death. With a weak voice, he said, "Lord, Thou givest strength to those that can speak and to those that cannot. Speak, Lord, to all our hearts, and let them know that Thou loosest tongues." He then sang—

To Father, Son, and Holy Ghost,
Who sweetly all agree.

Here his voice failed, and he gasped for breath. His mind seemed to wander. "Now we have done," he said. "Let us all go." He was laid on the bed from which he rose no more, and after sleeping a little, begged those around him to pray and praise. When they got up from their knees he gave various directions, then begged them once more to pray and praise. The friends who were downstairs were called up. Wesley's fervour of spirit and his loud "Amen" to the petition that God would continue and increase His blessing upon His servants' work showed how fully he joined in these devotions. After they rose from prayer he took Mr. Broadbent's hand, drew him near, and with the utmost placidness saluted him, and said, "Farewell, farewell." He thus took leave of all who were in the room. When some one entered, he strove to speak. Finding that his friends could not understand what he said, he paused, and with all his remaining strength, cried out, "The best of all is, God is with us." "Then, lifting up his dying arm in token of victory, and raising his feeble voice with a holy triumph not to be expressed, he again repeated the heart-reviving words, 'The best of all is, God is with us.'"

When Mrs. Charles Wesley came to see him, he thanked her as she pressed his hand, and endeavoured to kiss her. His lips were moistened; then he broke out in the words of the grace he used after meals, "We thank Thee, O Lord, for these and all Thy mercies. Bless the Church and King, and grant us truth and peace, through Jesus Christ our Lord, for ever and ever." Other words fell from his lips; then he called those who were in his room to join in prayer. His fervour was remarkable, though his bodily strength was fast ebbing away. During the night he often attempted to repeat the forty-sixth Psalm, but he was too feeble. He was heard, however, to say, "I'll praise—I'll praise." A few minutes before ten o'clock the next morning, Wesley found the long-sought rest. Joseph Bradford was praying. His niece, Sarah Wesley, and a few friends, knelt around his bed. The last word they caught was "Farewell." Then, as Mr. Bradford was inwardly saying, "Lift up your heads, O ye gates; and be ye lift up, ye everlasting doors; and let this heir of glory come in," without a lingering groan, Wesley passed to the presence of his Lord. His friends, standing around the bed, sang together—

> Waiting to receive thy spirit,
>   Lo! the Saviour stands above,
> Shows the purchase of His merit,
>   Reaches out the crown of love.

Wesley died on Wednesday, March 2nd, 1791, in the eighty-eighth year of his age. The day before the funeral his body was laid in City Road Chapel, near the entrance. A heavenly smile lingered on his face. The crowd that came to take a last look upon the man to whom they owed so much was said to number ten thousand persons. It was therefore thought desirable to bury him between five and six in the morning. No notice was issued till a late hour the previous evening, but some hundreds of people were present. A biscuit was given to each in an envelope, on which was a portrait of Wesley in his canonicals, with a halo and a crown. According to directions in his will, the coffin was borne to the grave by six poor men, among whom six pounds was divided. "I particularly desire there may be no hearse, no coach, no escutcheon, no pomp, except the tears of them that loved me and are following me to Abraham's bosom." Those were his instructions, and they were faithfully observed.

The funeral service, on Wednesday, March 9th, was read by the Rev. John Richardson, who had been one of Wesley's clerical assistants for nearly thirty years. When he came to the words, "Forasmuch as it hath pleased Almighty God to take unto Himself the soul of our dear FATHER here departed," loud sobs took the place of silent tears. Wesley was laid in the vault which he had prepared for himself and the preachers who died in London. The inscription on his tomb says that "this great light arose (by the singular providence of God) to enlighten these nations." "Reader," it adds, "if thou art constrained to bless the instrument, give God the glory." At ten o'clock on the morning of his burial, a funeral sermon was preached in City Road Chapel by Dr. Whitehead, one of Wesley's preachers, who had retired from the itinerancy, and had long been his favourite physician. He was now one of the London local preachers. Black cloth draped the front of the gallery and the pulpit. Every corner of the building was crowded. Mrs. Gabriel, one of whose sons became Lord Mayor of London, was at this service, and often said that all the congregation was in mourning with the exception of one woman, who wore a piece of blue ribbon in her bonnet. When she noticed her singularity, she pulled out the ribbon and threw it under her feet.

Wesley's will provided that all profits arising from the sale of his books should be devoted to the support of Methodism. Eighty-five pounds a year was to be paid out of this amount to his brother's widow, according to the arrangement made at her marriage. Some other bequests were made to friends or to Methodist objects. Wesley's manuscripts were given to Dr. Coke, Dr. Whitehead, and Henry Moore, "to be burnt or published, as they see good."